CRIME AND PUNISHMENT
IN ANCIENT CHINA

Qu Jiang Wang, Judge of the 2nd Court of Hell, from one of a series of ten scroll paintings of hell; Chinese, late 19th century; private collection, Singapore. See text, p. 51, regarding the relevance of such paintings to an understanding of the physical environment of traditional Chinese tribunals.

CRIME AND PUNISHMENT IN ANCIENT CHINA

T'ang-Yin-Pi-Shih

（棠　陰　比　事）

R. H. van Gulik, LITTD.

（高　羅　佩）

Orchid Press

CRIME AND PUNISHMENT IN ANCIENT CHINA: *T'ang-Yin-Pi-Shih*
Translated with an introduction and notes by R. H. van Gulik

Second edition, 2007

Originally published as *T'ANG-YIN-PI-SHIH, "Parallel Cases from Under the Pear Tree": A 13th Century Manual of Jurisprudence and Detection*, E. J. Brill, Leiden 1956

ORCHID PRESS
P.O. Box 19,
Yuttitham Post Office,
Bangkok 10907 Thailand
www.orchidbooks.com

ISBN: 978-974-524-153-4

CONTENTS

ILLUSTRATIONS

PREFACE

The *T'ang-yin-pi-shih* is a collection of 144 selected criminal and civil cases, covering a period of about fourteen centuries, from ca. 300 B.C. till ca. 1100 A.D. The book was compiled in 1211 A.D. by Kuei Wan-jung, a scholar-official of the Southern Sung Dynasty.

This book is a representative example of the old-style Chinese case-book, a genre of legal literature that till recent times has enjoyed great popularity among Chinese scholar-officials.

In order to understand why this type of book was so popular, one must remember that according to the Confucianist tradition criminal and civil law and their enforcement constitute an inauspicious subject, because it owns its existence to flaws in a social order that should be flawless. The ideal State is that one where the Ruler rules by non-ruling; seated on his throne facing South, sunk in meditation, he is the link between Heaven and Earth and ensures peace and order "all under Heaven" solely by the aura of his virtue. Therefore they fondly believed that laws and the instruments of their enforcement were but deplorable phenomena of a decadent age — things reeking of vulgarity that should preferably be ignored by the scholar-official of refined taste. To him applies the often-quoted saying "One does not read the Code".

On the other hand, nearly all scholar-officials started their career as district magistrates, and the administration of justice formed an important part of their daily duties. The recruitment examinations —in Western literature not inappropriately referred to as "literary examinations"—ill prepared them for this work: the regular program centered round the Classics, law was a field of study entered upon only by a comparatively small number of specialists who after their graduation were as a rule appointed to one of the higher judicial organs of the central administration. The rank and file of provincial officials had but a superficial knowledge of the subject.

For those the case-books provided a welcome short-cut to a general acquaintance with the Penal Code and the methods of its enforcement, including also some elementary facts about jurisprudence and the detection of crime. Especially during the Ming and Ch'ing Dynasties when legal studies had become increasingly specialized, these case-books were a godsend for the young magistrate. Concisely written in good literary style they presented complicated legal problems in a palatable and easily digestible form, and the fact that the crimes described happened so long ago and were judged by such eminent persons of former ages tended to gloss over the vulgarity of the subject and lent it an elegant antique flavour. Thus the case-books provided the inexperienced scholar-official with reading-matter at once useful and agreeable, and in accordance with approved literary taste.

Especially in the later part of the Ch'ing Dynasty there were published comprehensive collections of contemporary ruling cases, such as the voluminous *Hsing-an-hui-lan* 刑 案 滙 覽 and the *Hsing-pu-pi-chao* 刑 部 比 照 . But these books were too technical and too recent to appeal to the ordinary country-magistrate, they could not compete in popularity with the old-style case-books, hallowed by age and the illustrious names of the ancient judges. Hence we find that as late as 1878 the 12th century case-book *Che-yü-kuei-chien* was reprinted for official use by the tribunal of Wu-ch'ang.

These old case-books are important also for the modern student of Chinese law. The Penal Code in its various redactions of succeeding centuries and the Judicial Sections occurring in the Dynastic Histories supply rich material for a study of the theory of Chinese law, the historical development of the legal system, and the application and interpretation of the law on a high governmental level. The case-books give valuable supplementary data. They tell us how the law was enforced in the lower strata of the administration, and how legal theory worked out in practice for the common people. They present a vivid and unvarnished picture of the routine duties of the country-magistrate, the kind of cases that were brought before his tribunal, and the manner in which he dealt with them. Thus the case books represent precious source-material for both judicial and sociological studies, all the more important since the compilers strove after authenticity: they selected only those cases of which it was reasonably certain that they had actually happened, and where the persons concerned are all mentioned by name. Therefore they did not include for instance any of the more or less theoretical cases related by the Han philosopher Tung Chung-shu (董 仲 舒 fl. ca.

150 B.C.), nor the legal examination-themes recorded by the T'ang writers Po Chü-i (白 居 易 772-846) and Yüan Chen (元 積 779-831), notwithstanding the fact that many of those might well be based on actual cases [1].

Moreover, the case-books played a role of their own in Chinese literary history, for they were eagerly studied by Chinese novelists and fiction-writers in general. Nearly all the plots found in Ming and later detective tales and crime novels are elaborations of themes occurring in the old case-books [2].

Finally, these books—and more especially the *T'ang-yin-pi-shih*— were used also in Korea, and enjoyed considerable popularity in Japan during the Tokugawa period. The *T'ang-yin-pi-shih* was re-printed in Korea, and early in the 17th century it was reprinted in Japan, and translated into Japanese.

The *T'ang-yin-pi-shih* is one of the three oldest case-books pre-served, the other two being the *I-yü-chi* 疑 獄 集 "Collection of Difficult Cases" compiled ca. 950 A.D., and the *Che-yü-kuei-chien* 折 獄 龜 鑑 "Magic Mirror for the Solving of Judicial Cases" of 1133 A.D.

In choosing the *T'ang-yin-pi-shih* for translation I was guided by three reasons. First and foremost, this text has been preserved better than the two others. The *I-yü-chi* and the *Che-yü-kuei-chien* were drastically revised during the Ming Dynasty; in the process the former was reduced to a bare skeleton of its original shape, while the latter was so burdened with additional material that it is difficult to discern the author's plan. The *T'ang-yin-pi-shih*, on the other hand, survives in two reprints of the original Sung editions, and one reprint of a Yüan edition of a manuscript antedating the Sung impressions. Second, since Kuei Wan-jung based his work on the unrevised versions of the two other texts, his collection embodies the essential features of both. Third, while the *I-yü-chi* arranges the cases in a rough chronological order without reference to their content, and while the *Che-yü-kuei-chien* divides them over twenty

---

[1] Seven cases recorded by Tung Chung-shu have been translated by Jean Escarra, in his book *Le Droit Chinois* (Peking 1936), page 279 sq. Translations of examination-themes by Po Chü-i and Yüan Chen will be found in R. des Rotours, *Traité des Examens* (Paris 1932), page 289 sq.

[2] Cf. for instance my notes to Case 16-B and 66-B.

rather vague legal categories, the *T'ang-yin-pi-shih* gives the cases in parallel pairs; the choice of these pairs in itself often supplies interesting data on the old Chinese conception of civil and criminal law.

The *T'ang-yin-pi-shih* contains a number of cases which throw revealing sidelights on legal problems; several quite good "detective tales", and scores of neat solutions of difficult cases. On the other hand there are given also many arguments that appear pointless caviling or even sheer sophistry, while a few of the cases deal with subjects of slight interest to the modern student. Doubtless a new selection from all the cases recorded in the *T'ang-yin-pi-shih*, *I-yü-chi* and *Che-yü-kuei-chien* would make much more profitable and interesting reading. However, I thought that as a first introduction to this particular genre of Chinese legal literature a complete and unmodified translation of one entire case-book was indicated. It is hoped that other workers in the field will treat the subject more systematically than the ancient compilers of the case-books. The first step would be to go through all the biographies of prominent judges of one single period, and to translate the more important cases solved by them. In such a work the historical and sociological background of each case, and its legal implications should be explained in detail.

Since the cases recorded in the *T'ang-yin-pi-shih* cover nearly fourteen centuries, in the present publication a detailed discussion of each separate case would lead us far beyond the scope of the text itself. The historical and legal background of the cases differ so widely that to go further into those aspects would come close to the proverbial carving of the chicken with a butcher's knife. Moreover, since the *T'ang-yin-pi-shih* is a 13th century text, when translating it as a whole rather than as a patchwork of quotations from older sources, one must interpret the text primarily from the viewpoint of the 13th century author. Now Kuei Wan-jung saw ancient ranks and institutions in very much the same light as those of his own time; it is highly doubtful whether he realized that the function of for instance the *yü-shih* of the Han period was greatly different from that of the *yü-shih* "Censor" of his own time. And the same applies to other administrative and geographical terms. I have tried therefore to express in my translation the contemporary connotations of such terms only there where necessary for a correct understanding of the point of a case. Since, however, in recent years Sinologues have generally accepted English renderings of certain Han terms—e.g. "commandery" for *chün*—I have adopted those when translating cases dating from that period.

In the notes added to each case I have confined myself to three points. First, verification of the source. It is curious that none of the later Chinese and Japanese editors of the *T'ang-yin-pi-shih* took the trouble of performing this task, although many of the sources quoted must have been readily accessible to them; in more than one instance reference to the source enabled me to restore corrupt passages and to fill in lacunae. Second, a few details about the main persons figuring in the case, mainly meant to establish the date of the occurrence. And third, a brief comment on the case itself there where such comment seemed necessary, and including also textual notes.

I also added to my translation an introduction in three sections where the history and background of this case book are sketched. The first section gives an account of the *T'ang-yin-pi-shih* and its author, the second describes the *I-yü-chi* and the *Che-yü-kuei-chien*, while the third presents an outline of old Chinese court procedure. A table where the 144 cases are classified chronologically is added in Appendix I.

The above may suffice to introduce the present publication to the reader. If he thinks many of the arguments quoted in this Chinese case book futile and the methods employed by the judges often crude or even arbitrary, he will do well to remember that case books like the *T'ang-yin-pi-shih* were during more than a thousand years the pillow-books of magistrates and influenced, for better or for worse, the fate of uncounted millions of people. For this reason alone already these books deserve our attention.

The Hague, spring 1955   R. H. VAN GULIK

LIST OF ABBREVIATIONS

A. WESTERN BOOKS

Balazs: Et. Balazs, *Le Traité Juridique du Souei-chou;* Bibliothèque de l'Institut des Hautes Études Chinoises, vol. IX, Leyde 1954.

BD: Herbert A. Giles, *A Chinese Biographical Dictionary,* London 1898; reprinted Peking 1939. This book is referred to where it gives an accurate sketch of a person's career; *Franke* is referred to for persons not listed in BD, or in cases where the item in the latter contains mistakes.

Bünger: Karl Bünger, *Quellen zur Rechtsgeschichte der T'ang Zeit;* Monumenta Serica, Monograph IX, Peking 1946.

EC: *Eminent Chinese of the Ch'ing Period,* edited by A. W. Hummel; Library of Congress, Washington 1943.

Franke: O. Franke, *Geschichte des Chinesischen Reiches;* 5 vls. Berlin 1930-1952.

Hulsewé: A. F. P. Hulsewé, *Remnants of Han Law,* Vol. I; Sinica Leidensia vol. IX, Leyden 1955.

des Rotours: Robert des Rotours, *Traité des Fonctionnaires et Traité de l'Armée,* traduits de la Nouvelle Histoire des T'ang; Bibliothèque de l'Institut des Hautes Études Chinoises, Vol. VI, Leyde 1947-1948.

A book there was no occasion for quoting but which proved of great use in preparing the translation was E. A. Kracke, *Civil Service in Early Sung China* (Harvard University Press, Cambridge 1953); in translating Sung ranks and titles I have generally followed Kracke's renderings.

B. CHINESE BOOKS

CYKC: *Che-yü-kuei-chien.* In the notes to the translation the edition in the *Ts'ung-shu-chi-ch'eng* (cf. page 33) has been referred to throughout, by both chapter and page number. Readers who have a blockprint of the *CYKC* may locate the case wanted by referring to the chapter number.

IYC: *I-yü-chi.* In the notes to the translation the blockprint of 1851 is refered to. Since there each chapter has its own pagination, I numbered the cases myself throughout the ten chapters of the book; thus each reference gives the number of the chapter, and the number of the case.

MHPT: *Meng-hsi-pi-t'an;* for this Sung source cf. the note to Case 6-A.

SF: *Shuo-fu;* the original Ming print is referred to.

SPTK: *Szu-pu-ts'ung-k'an,* the large collection of lithographed reprints published by the Commercial Press. Since this collection is available in most Western libraries, I referred wherever possible to books in this edition—although those are not necessarily the best texts available.

TYPS-I: *T'ang-yin-pi-shih,* the Sung impression of 1234 reprinted in 1849.

TYPS-II: *T'ang-yin-pi-shih,* Yamamoto Hoku-zan's edition of the Korean impression of the Yüan print of 1308.

TYPS-III: *T'ang-yin-pi-shih,* lithographed reproduction of the Chih-pu-tsu-chai manuscript, in *SPTK.* The present translation is based on this text.

YCTI: *Yin-chü-t'ung-i,* by the Yüan scholar Liu Hsün; cf. the discussion of cases from the CYKC quoted in this source, on page 38 sq.

YP: *T'ang-yin-pi-shih yüan-pien,* the abbreviated edition of TYPS published by Wu No; cf. page 22.

PART I
INTRODUCTION

INTRODUCTION

I. The t'ang-yin-pi-shih and its author

Kuei Wan-jung 桂萬榮, the author of the *T'ang-yin-pi-shih*, was styled Meng-hsieh 夢恊 and later in his life adopted the literary name Shih-p'o 石坡. He was a member of a prominent family of Tz'u-hsi 慈溪, a town in Chekiang Province, North of Ningpo, the famous old emporium of the Chinese trade with Korea and Japan. To the SW of Ningpo rises the Szu-ming 四明 mountain range, and Ningpo and surroundings is therefore often referred to as Szu-ming.

Kuei Wan-jung lived during the Southern Sung Dynasty (1127-1279 A.D.); he began his official career in the reign of the Emperor Ning (1195-1224 A.D.) and died at the end of the reign of his successor Li-tsung (1225-1264 A.D.). Throughout this time the Sung armies fought a losing battle against the Mongol invaders from the North. The statesman Han T'o-chou (韓佗胄, BD no. 628) who had placed Ning-tsung on the throne was defeated and executed in 1207, and neither did his successor as "statesman behind the throne" Shih Mi-yüan (史彌遠, died 1233; cf. Franke, vol. IV, page 299 sq.) have more success. However, daily life in the Southern Sung capital Lin-an (Hangchow) and in the Provinces outside the battle zone went on very much as usual, so that we need not wonder that Kuei Wan-jung's career was not affected by the critical times in which he lived. He had a moderately successful official career, beginning as Sheriff in a district and retiring as a Prefect. His interests lay in the practical problems of administration and in philosophy rather than in political intrigue and the jockeying for position that marked the higher government strata of that time.

His biography is not included in the Sung Dynastic History; the following details are based upon his biography in the Gazetteer of his native district Tz'u-hsi (*Tz'u-hsi-hsien-chih* 慈溪縣志),

and upon the data supplied by the prefaces and colophons attached to his *T'ang-yin-pi-shih* (hereafter referred to as *TYPS*).

As a youth Kuei Wan-jung studied in the prefectural school (*chün-hsiang* 郡庠) and proved a diligent young scholar. In 1196 A.D. he obtained the degree of *chin-shih* at the triennial examinations. This should have procured him immediately an official appointment; but for unknown reasons it was not until 1207 that he was given the modest office of Sheriff (*wei* 尉) of the Yü-kan 餘干 district in Jao 饒 Prefecture—the modern Po-yang 鄱陽 in Kiangsi Province. This prefecture is located on the SE corner of Lake Po-yang, and Yü-kan was a place directly to the South of the prefectural city. According to his preface to the first edition of the TYPS, it was in Yü-kan that he became interested in the administration of justice and the detection of crime. In 1208 he was nominated Police Inspector (*szu-li ts'an-chün* 司理參軍) of the prefectural administration of Chien-k'ang 建康, near the modern Nanking. This, however, was a provisional assignment (*tai-tz'u* 待次); it was at least three years before he was actually ordered to proceed to that post. Those years he spent in his native district.

He employed his leisure by studying two well known collections of judicial cases, viz. the *I-yü-chi* 疑獄集 composed in the 10th century by Ho Ning and his son Ho Meng, and the *Che-yü-kuei-chien* 折獄龜鑑 by Cheng K'o who flourished ca. 1130. While referring the reader for more details about these two books to Section II of this Introduction here it may be stated that since both the *I-yü-chi* and the *Che-yü-kuei-chien* were thoroughly revised during the Ming period, it is difficult to ascertain which of the two was Kuei Wan-jung's main source. In his preface he himself states that he relied chiefly on the *I-yü-chi*, and that he used the *Che-yü-kuei-chien* as a supplementary source. An examination of my notes added to the translation of the TYPS will show that 65 of the 144 cases recorded by Kuei Wan-jung are found in ch. 1-4 of the *I-yü-chi*—the part of that text (comprising 99 cases) which bears the names of Ho Ning and Ho Meng [1]; on the other hand all 144 cases of the TYPS are

---

[1] My references to the *other* chapters of the *I-yü-chi* (ch. 5-10) are added for the sake of completeness; cf. my remarks on p. 33.

found in the *Che-yü-kuei-chien*. The obvious conclusion is that in the course of the centuries the *Che-yü-kuei-chien* was greatly expanded, successive editors adding to it numerous judicial cases culled from other sources, including the TYPS.

Both the two Ho's and Cheng K'o endeavoured to incorporate in their books only those cases which were well authenticated. They based themselves on the same dependable sources as did the compilers of the Dynastic Histories, viz. tomb inscriptions composed [1] shortly after the person's death, local records and official documents. Ho Ning and Cheng K'o included only occasionally cases recorded in older literature, or communicated to them by reliable contemporaries.

Kuei Wan-jung followed this same principle while forming his own collection of judicial cases. One need not wonder, therefore, that many of the cases that occurred during the Northern Sung Dynasty recorded by him are found practically *verbatim* in the biographical section of the *Sung-shih*, which was compiled long after Kuei Wan-jung's demise; for both utilized the same sources. Most of these sources were as reliable as one can reasonably expect. This applies especially to the tomb inscriptions (*pei-chih* 碑志), the "Career Accounts" (*hsing-chuang* 行狀), and the "Records of Words and Works" (*yen-hsing-lu* 言行錄). These accounts were as a rule drawn up shortly after the death of the person concerned and by people who had an intimate knowledge of their affairs. When stripped of —easily recognizable—traditional phraseology (stereotyped statements such as "He was a brilliant student already in his early youth, memorizing a hundred pages per day" etc.), these records are accurate biographical accounts.

Kuei Wan-jung's editorial policy presents a combination of those followed by the two Ho's and Cheng K'o. The former headed each case by a title-phrase of four characters and arranged the cases in a loose chronological sequence, without regard to their content. Cheng K'o headed each case by the name of the main person figuring in it, and divided the cases over twenty categories according to their content: "Releasing the innocent", "Discerning false accusations", etc. The two Ho's apparently recorded the cases without further

---

[1] I purposely use the word "composed", because in many cases the inscription was written out for the engraver of the memorial tablet by another person, usually a well known calligrapher.

comment and without mentioning their source, but Cheng K'o
added to each case a commentary of his own, and a brief indication
of the source of each case.

Kuei Wan-jung adopted the four-character title-phrases of the *I-yü-
chi*, but arranged the 144 cases selected by him in 72 parallel pairs,
in such a way that the title-phrases rhyme alternately. This arrangement in pairs is an interesting novum. Cheng K'o (or a later
editor) added to most cases one or more duplicates differing only
in time, place and persons concerned. Kuei Wan-jung, on the other
hand, selected pairs of cases where the facts are quite different,
but which were solved by the same reasoning or by the application of
the same methods of detection. Some parallels are rather trite, but
the fact in itself that Kuei Wan-jung adopted this device proves
that he gave considerable thought to the subject.

Of the cases he chose from the *Che-yü-kuei-chien*, Kuei Wan-
jung took over in a few instances also Cheng K'o's commentary;
cf. Case 11-A, 21-B, 34-A, 41-A, 42-B, 48-B, 53-A, 58-A, 59-B, and
72-B. He refrained from adding any commentary of his own, but
briefly indicated the source of most cases, as was done by Cheng K'o.

Kuei Wan-jung completed this work in 1211 A.D. and gave it the
title *T'ang-yin-pi-shih* 棠陰比事, which I translated as "Parallel Cases from under the Pear Tree". A more prosaic but closer
rendering would be "Parallel Cases solved by Eminent Judges"; for
t'ang-yin "in the shadow of the pear three" is an old literary allusion
meaning a just and benevolent official (cf. page 46 below). He
wrote a preface where he stresses the importance of the judge's
office, and warns especially against hasty decisions —a warning
repeated throughout the TYPS. He added the remark that he planned
to publish the manuscript in print.

Although the TYPS is a compilation rather than an original
piece of creative writing, it does credit to Kuei Wan-jung's devotion to his work and his high conception of the duties of a judge,
both to the government and to the people entrusted to his care.

In the Sung Dynasty the art of block-printing had greatly developed,
but the publication of a book in print was still a costly undertaking;
hence for some years the TYPS circulated in manuscript copies only.

After the completion of his book, Kuei Wan-jung at last received
authorisation for proceeding to Chien-k'ang to take up his office of

Police Inspector there. The protracted period of waiting was a bitter disillusion, even for a philosophically-minded man like Kuei Wan-jung; all the more so since his degree of *chin-shih* should have ensured priority in promotion. This grievance rankled for many years, he even referred to it obliquely when in 1234 he was received in audience by the Emperor (see his postface added to the TYPS). Disappointed as he was, however, Kuei Wan-jung could not be induced to take a short-cut to high political office. During his period of waiting the powerful statesman Shih Mi-yüan (see above) invited him to become a member of his staff, but Kuei Wan-jung steadfastly refused. Acceptance would have meant becoming part of the political life in the capital, attractive only to those persons who did not mind becoming sycophants and plotters.

Before leaving Tz'u-hsi, Kuei Wan-jung had lent a copy of his manuscript of the TYPS to his brother-in-law Chang Fu, who at that time was stationed in Hsin-ch'ang (新昌 , SW of Ningpo) as local peace-preservation official (*an-fu-szu-shih* 安撫司事 , as he calls himself in his colophon to the TYPS; his biography in *Sung-shih* ch. 407 has *Che-tung-shuai shu-shuai-tu* 浙東帥屬帥督 "Assistant attached to the Commander of East Chekiang"), under the orders of the Commander in Shao-hsing. Chang Fu (張寔 styled Tzu-mi 子宓) was also a native of Tz'u-hsi, and had obtained the degree of *chin-shih* in the same year as Kuei Wan-jung; both were moreover disciples of the philosopher Yang Chien (see below). Chang Fu's marriage to Kuei Wan-jung's sister further strengthened what must have been a very close friendship. Although Chang Fu did not attain to high office he acquired the name of an able and just administrator and became known as a writer; his biography is included in ch. 407 of the *Sung-shih*. He left a book in 12 ch., entitled *Yüeh-ling-chieh* 月令解 "Commentary on the Rules for each Month" (ch. 4 of the *Li-chi* 禮記 "The Book of Rites"), which has been reprinted in the *Szu-ming-ts'ung-shu* (cf. page 26 below). When Kuei Wan-jung passed Shao-hsing (then called Yüeh-chou 越州) on his way to Nanking, Chang Fu returned the manuscript of the TYPS to him, together with a colophon he had written for it, "in lieu of a parting present". In this colophon, dated late in the year 1211, Chang Fu also refers to the long term of provisional nomination (Chang says it lasted *five* years) that Kuei Wan-jung then just had completed.

After his arrival in Chien-k'ang, Kuei Wan-jung lent his manuscript to Liu Li 劉隸, an otherwise unknown scholar from Fukien. Liu Li wrote a brief preface for the TYPS, dated 1213, where he says that he was going to have the book printed. However, something prevented the execution of this plan. Kuei Wan-jung kept Liu Li's preface, to be used later when the manuscript would eventually be printed. About Liu Li I could find no further details; the patronizing tone of his preface suggests that he was an elder scholar-official occupying a position of some consequence.

Kuei Wan-jung's term of office in Chien-k'ang lasted three years. In 1215 A.D. he was called to the capital and given a minor post in the Ministry of the Census, viz. that of Head of the Section of Records (*chu-kuan hu-pu chia-ko* 主管戶部架閣). It seems that the metropolitan officials recognized his abilities, for in 1216 he was promoted to Teacher in the National University, T'ai-hsüeh 太學. But life in the capital did not appeal to Kuei Wan-jung, and he asked insistently to be posted again in the provinces. Thereupon he was appointed Vice-Prefect of P'ing-chiang (*p'ing-chiang t'ung-pan* 平江通判), near Soochow, in Kiangsu Province. While serving there he showed himself a just and able administrator, and was promoted to Prefect of Nan-k'ang 南康. This was a Prefecture situated in the North of Kiangsi Province, South of Kiukiang and on the NW corner of Lake Po-yang; it is also called Hsing-tzu 星子.

In Nan-k'ang Kuei Wan-jung had at last the manuscript of the TYPS printed. This appears from his postface of 1234, where he states that it was first printed *hsing-chiang-mo-yüan-chih-chih* 星江莫遠之致; the Ch'ing scholar Chu Hsü-tseng (see page 23) points out that *hsing-chiang* refers to *Hsing-tzu*, the other name of Nan-k'ang. This reference also proves that it was Nan-k'ang in N. Kiangsi where Kuei Wan-jung served, and not in the place of the same name in the SW tip of that Province.

If we assume that Kuei Wan-jung stayed two years in the capital —from 1215 till 1217—and three years in P'ing-chiang, he would have arrived in Nan-k'ang ca. 1220. And if we assume that he served three years in Nan-k'ang—the average term of office in the provinces—this would mean that the first edition of the TYPS was published between 1220-1223.

As Prefect of Nan-k'ang Kuei Wan-jung curbed the arrogance of the local military authorities, put the finances on a sound basis, and saw to it that the taxes were paid on time. His successful administration had a result that can hardly have been welcome to him: he was again appointed in the capital, this time in the Imperial Archives (*pi-ko* 秘閣). According to the time-estimate given above, he would have returned to the capital ca. 1224.

During Kuei Wan-jung's second stay in the capital—which lasted about ten years—he reached the peak of his official career. First he was appointed Assistant Judge of the High Court (*ta-li-szu-cheng*), then promoted to Assistant Office Chief in the Office of Examination of Merits (*k'ao-kung yüan-wai-lang*). This information is not given in his biography in the *Tz'u-hsi-hsien-chih*, but the actual order relating to this promotion has been preserved in the *P'ing-chai-chi* 平齋集, the collected works of the scholar-official Hung Tzu-kuei (洪咨夔, died 1236 A.D.), who ca. 1230 was Minister of Justice; cf. the SPTK edition of the *P'ing-chai-chi*, vol. 7, ch. 18, page 15 b, the order *Ta-li-szu-cheng Kuei-wan-jung ch'u k'ao-kung-yüan-wai-lang* 大理寺丞桂萬榮除考功員外郎. Thereafter Kuei Wan-jung received the honorary rank of *ch'ao-san-ta-fu* 朝散大夫 (fourth class of the fifth degree), and he was promoted to Ministerial Secretary of the Right (*shang-shu-yu-lang* 尙書右郎). In 1234 he was appointed Academician of the Pao-chang Pavilion (*Pao-chang-ko* 寶章閣), one of the many official institutes of learning established by the Sung Emperors, similar to the Lung-t'u 龍圖, T'ien-chang 天章 and other better known Pavilions; according to *Sung-shih* ch. 162 the Pao-chang-ko was founded in 1226 A.D. by the Emperor Ning-tsung. We learn from his postface to the TYPS that in the seventh moon of the year 1234 he was received in audience by the Emperor Li-tsung, who praised the TYPS. The Imperial approval excited interest in the book in Court circles; since the first edition was apparently exhausted, Kuei Wan-jung thereupon republished the book, adding a postface wherein he sets forth the circumstances. This second edition begins with Liu Li's Preface, then Kuei Wan-jung's original preface of 1211, Chang Fu's colophon of the same year, and Kuei's postface of 1234.

In 1234 he also received the appointment of Prefect of Ch'ang-te 常德 in Hunan Province. He served there till he was retired on a pension (*jeng-tz'u* 奉祠).

If we assume that Kuei Wan-jung was 25 when in 1196 he obtained the *chin-shih* degree, and assume that he served three years as Prefect of Ch'ang-te, he would have been ca. 66 years old when he retired from official service. Then began what for him probably was the most satisfactory phase of his life.

He returned to his native district Tz'u-hsi and built a private academy on the slope of a mountain there, calling it *Shih-p'o-shu-yüan* 石坡書院 "Stone Hill Academy". There he devoted the remainder of his life to study and teaching. Since his biography states that he died at the age of 90 (other sources give even 96), his activities in the fields of philosophy and literary research covered a period of about twenty-five years.

Kuei Wan-jung was an ardent follower of the Neo-Confucianist philosopher Yang Chien, who was also a native of Tz'u-hsi [1]. Yang Chien was a disciple of the famous Sung philosopher Lu Chiu-yüan 陸九淵 1139-1193 A.D., better known by his literary name Hsiang-shan 象山 [2]. Lu Chiu-yüan was the founder of the Hsin-

---

[1] Yang Chien (楊簡 styled Ching-chung 敬仲, lit. name Tz'u-hu 慈湖, 1140-1225 A.D.) became *chin-shih* in 1169 A.D. When serving as Registrar in Fu-yang 富陽 he met Lu Chiu-yüan and became his disciple. Promoted to magistrate of Lo-p'ing 樂平 he distinguished himself by his just and benevolent administration. Ca. 1146 he was appointed Professor in the Directorate of Education (Kuo-tzu-chien 國子監) and in 1208 Librarian of the Imperial Library. Upon requesting an appointment in the provinces he was made Prefect of Wen-chou 溫州. Recalled to the capital he was appointed Academician of the Pao-mo Pavilion 寶謨閣 and received the honorary rank of *T'ai-chung-ta-fu* 太中大夫 (third class of the fourth degree). Cf. his biography in *Sung-shih* ch. 407.

[2] For Lu Chiu-yüan see Feng Yu-lan, *A History of Chinese Philosophy* (translated by Derk Bodde), vol. II (Leiden 1953), page 572 sq. Also the monograph

hsüeh 心 學 school of Confucianism, a rival of the Li-hsüeh 理 學 school founded by the celebrated Sung philosopher Chu Hsi. Kuei Wan-jung spent the remainder of his life in propagating the teachings of Lu Chiu-yüan and Yang Chien.

He assembled in the Shih-p'o-shu-yüan numerous students to whom he explained the idealist teachings of the Hsin-hsüeh school. At the same time he engaged in literary activities. His biography in the *Tz'u-hsi-hsien-chih* mentions three books written by him, viz. the *Shih-p'o-shu-i* 石 坡 書 義 (5 ch.), the *Lun-yü-ching-i* 論 語 精 義 (10 ch.), and the *Shih-p'o-tsou-i* 石 坡 奏 議 ; these books are not available. The first dealt apparently with the meaning of the Book of Documents, the second was a commentary on the Lun-yü, while the third was a collection of Kuei's memorials to the Throne.

The years of Kuei Wan-jung's birth and death are not known. According to the rough computation given above he would have been born ca. 1170 and died ca. 1260 A.D.

The influence of the Shih-p'o-shu-yüan lingered on for nearly five hundred years after Kuei Wan-jung's demise. This appears from an essay written by the great Ch'ing historian Ch'üan Tsu-wang (全 祖 望 1705-1755; cf. E.C. page 203), a native of Ningpo and hence specially interested in the prominent men produced by that region. This essay bears the title *Shih-p'o-shu-yüan-chi* 石 坡 書 院 記 and is found in Ch'üan Tsu-wang's *Chi-ch'i-t'ing-chi* 鮚 埼 亭 集 (cf. the SPTK edition, ch. 16 page 11b). There Ch'üan Tsu-wang states that at the end of the Ming Dynasty a descendant of Kuei Wan-jung continued the sacrifices to his ancestor. In 1736 the son of that descendant planned to rebuild the Shih-p'o-shu-yüan and it was for that occasion that Ch'üan Tsu-wang wrote this essay.

It seems that later the Kuei family or at least one of its branches moved to Lin-ju 臨 汝 in Honan Province. We learn from a preface added to the TYPS reprint in the *Szu-ming-ts'ung-shu* (see p. 26) of 1934, that in 1867 a Kuei Sung-ch'ing of Lin-ju had published an edition of the TYPS in movable type. I regret that the present difficulty in communicating with China prevented me from trying

Lu Hsiang-shan, a twelfth century Chinese idealist philosopher, by Miss Huang Siu-chi (American Oriental Society, New Haven 1944).

to contact members of that Kuei family of Lin-ju. Taking into consideration the remarkable tenacity of family-tradition in China, it is probable that they could have supplied additional data on Kuei Wan-jung's life and works.

As we saw in the above, Kuei Wan-jung himself published the TYPS twice, the first time ca. 1222, and the second in 1234 A.D. At the same time, however, copies of his original manuscript of 1211 remained in circulation.

One of these manuscript-copies was printed in the Yüan Dynasty, in 1308 A.D., about one hundred years after Kuei Wan-jung had completed his manuscript. This Yüan edition is apparently completely unknown in China. However, it found its way to Korea and was reprinted there; probably this occurred in the second half of the Ming Dynasty, when a great number of Chinese books were reprinted in Korea. This Korean reprint was imported into Japan.

These facts we learn from a manuscript copy of the Korean edition, now preserved in the *Naikaku-bunko* 內閣文庫 in Tokyo. It is listed under the title *Tōin-hiji-kashō* 棠陰比事加抄 "Augmented manuscript of the TYPS", and as copied out by the famous Japanese Sinologue Hayashi Dōshun (林道春, also called Razan 羅山, personal name Nobu-katsu, 信勝 1583-1659), the founder of the Shōhei Academy (*Shōheizaka-gakumon-jo* 昌平坂學問所) in Edo[1]. At the end of the manuscript Hayashi added the following note:

"This book, the TYPS in three chapters, was copied after a Korean printed edition. I read it aloud (in Japanese translation) on the request of Jūshō Gen-taku and ....[2], and had those in attendance add Japanese reading marks (i.e. *kaeri-ten* 返り點) in red ink. In our country the office of judicial investigator has much deteriorated since a long time. Now reading this book I could not but be moved

---

[1] For more details about Hayashi Dōshun and the Shōhei Academy, cf. my article *Kakka-ron, a Japanese echo of the Opium War*, in "Monumenta Serica", vol. IV (Peking 1940), page 481.

[2] Gen-taku indicates the well-known Sinologue and Court physician Noma Gen-taku (野間玄琢, professional name Jūshō-in 壽昌院, 1591-1646). The three other persons I could not identify.

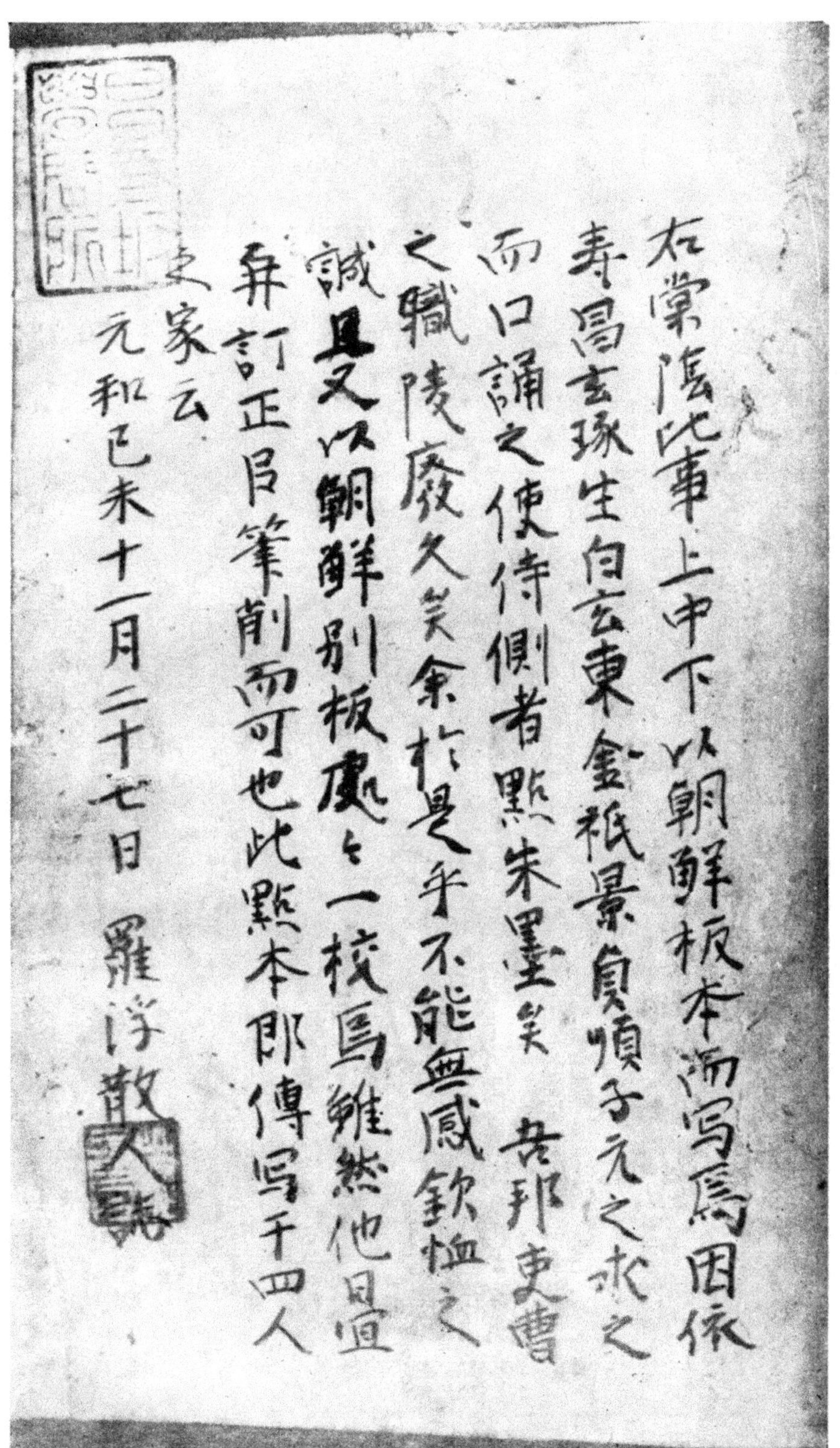

Hayashi Dōshun's colophon to the ms. copy of the TYPS

儻年不嗜酒臨而爲坐客二既希且其後屢數尚
多欲爲他日飜異逃死之計爾見范忠宣行録
鄭克曰凡善飜數奸者必善輭情也若不得
其情則後必飜異而姦人得計矣推覈之
際戒在疏略是故僕史稱嚴延年之治獄
也文案整盍不可得及雖酷吏無足道然
於此一節亦有取焉耳

唐中書舍人郭正一破平壤得一高麗婢名
玉素極姝好也豔令專知財物庫正一夜須
漿水粥非玉素復之不可玉素乃毒之良久

Hayashi Dōshun's copy of the TYPS, one page comprising the end of Case 8-A
and the beginning of Case 8-B.

by the sincere spirit of compassion that pervades it. Therefore I again collated the text throughout on the basis of another Korean printed copy; but on a later occasion it should again be corrected and collated a second time. The present copy provided with reading marks was written out in the houses of the four persons mentioned above.

"Written by Rafu-sannin [1] , on the 27th day of the 11th moon of the year 1619".

右棠陰比事上中下。以朝鮮板本而寫焉。
因依壽昌玄琢生白玄東金祇景貞順于元之
求之而口誦之。使侍側者點朱墨矣。吾邦吏
曹之職陵廢久矣。 余於是乎不能無感欽恤
之誠。且又以朝鮮別板。處處一校焉。雖然他
日宜再訂以筆削而可也。 此點本即傳寫于
四人之家云。
元和己未十一月二十七日羅浮散人誌

Because of the importance of this note for the history of the TYPS, it is reproduced on Plate I; the photograph was kindly sent to me by the Naikaku-bunko. The seal on top left is that of the Shōhei Academy.

As far as I could ascertain the Korean print used by Hayashi Dō-shun has at present become unavailable. However, it was still extant in the 19th century when it was reprinted by a Japanese Sinologue called Yamamoto Hoku-zan (山本北山, 1752-1812) [2].

Hoku-zan was a wealthy scholar and bibliophile of Edo who never

---

[1] One of the literary names of Hayashi Dōshun.

[2] The TYPS had always been most popular in Japan, while the *I-yü-chi* and the *Che-yü-kuei-chien* seem to have not been very wellknown in that country. Hayashi Dōshun's manuscript of 1619 was published in 1649 and soon thereafter there appeared a Japanese translation in *kana-zōshi* 假名草子 form. This Japanese version of the TYPS served as a source of inspiration for the famous Japanese judges and master-detectives Itakura Shigemune (板倉重宗 1587-1656) and Ō-oka Tadasuke (大岡忠相 1679-1751); the latter, affectionately referred to in Japanese literature as Ō-oka Hangan 大岡判官 "Judge Ō-oka", is for the Japanese what "Judge Pao" (see Case 23-B) is for the Chinese. Cf. W. J. S. Shand, "The Case of Ten-Ichi-Bo, a *cause célèbre* in Japanese history: a decision of Ooka" (Tokyo 1908). In

occupied any official position but devoted his entire life to literary pursuits. He studied Han and Sung philosophy under the Sinologue Inoue Kin-ga (井上金峨 1732-1784) and under his influence became an enthusiast advocate of the *Setchū-ha* 折衷派, a Japanese school of Confucianism that developed in the Tokugawa period; its adherents adopted towards the Chinese Classics an eclectic attitude, following a middle course between the views of Han and T'ang, and those of Ming and Ch'ing scholars. Hoku-zan was a man of catholic interests. Next to Chinese and Japanese classical literature he also studied astronomy, medicine, military science, divination and Chinese novels. He wrote nearly a hundred books in Chinese and Japanese, several of which appeared in print.

Hoku-zan published the reprint of the Korean edition of the Yüan impression of the TYPS on the request of the Seiri-kaku 靑藜閣, the well known printing house in the Asakusa quarter of Edo. This reprint, executed with movable type, is at present still fairly easily obtainable in the Japanese book trade.

From the typographical point of view this is a beautiful edition (cf. Figs. 1 and 2). The print page measures 178 by 232 mm., each page being divided into 10 columns, each having space for 18 characters. The outer margins have black *yü-wei* 魚尾 with a white flower-motif; this feature, together with the size of the book, give it a distinct Korean flavour. This edition is a close reproduction of the Korean

---

1831 the Yuzō-kan 有造館, the local school of the Tsu-clan 津藩 in Ise, published a new selection of famous Chinese judicial cases, compiled by a Confucianist official of the Shogunate (*jū-kan* 儒官), the Japanese Sinologue Tsuzaka Takayasu (津阪孝綽, better known by his literary name Tōyō 東陽, 1757-1825), under the title of *Chōshō i-an* 聽訟彙案. Tsuzaka says in his preface (dated 1806) that although he was a great admirer of the TYPS, he regretted that it showed some lacunae, and did not include cases from later dynasties; hence he chose 90 interesting cases from the Chinese Dynastic Histories and other literary sources. The *Chōshō i-an* is a carefully edited blockprint in three chapters (three volumes), where the Chinese text is punctuated and provided with Japanese reading marks throughout. Moreover title and chapter of the Chinese source are indicated in the upper margin of each case. The famous Sinologue Saitō Setsudō (齋藤拙堂 1797-1865), also a native of Ise, added a preface dated 1831, and Tsuzaka's pupil Kawamura Chiku-ha (川村竹坡, named Shōteki 尚迪, 1797-1875) added a colophon, dated 1831.

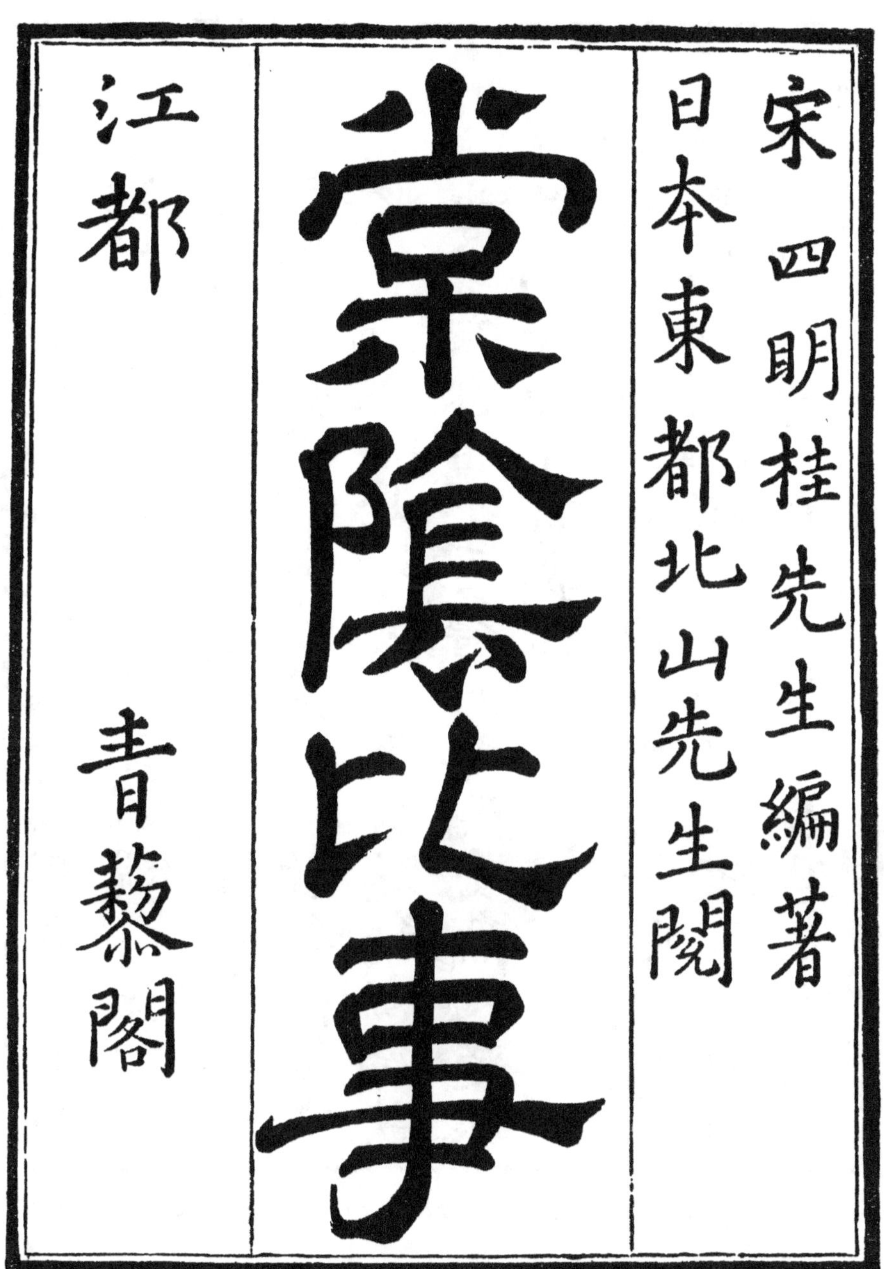

Fig. 1. The title page of Yamamoto Hokuzan's edition of the TYPS

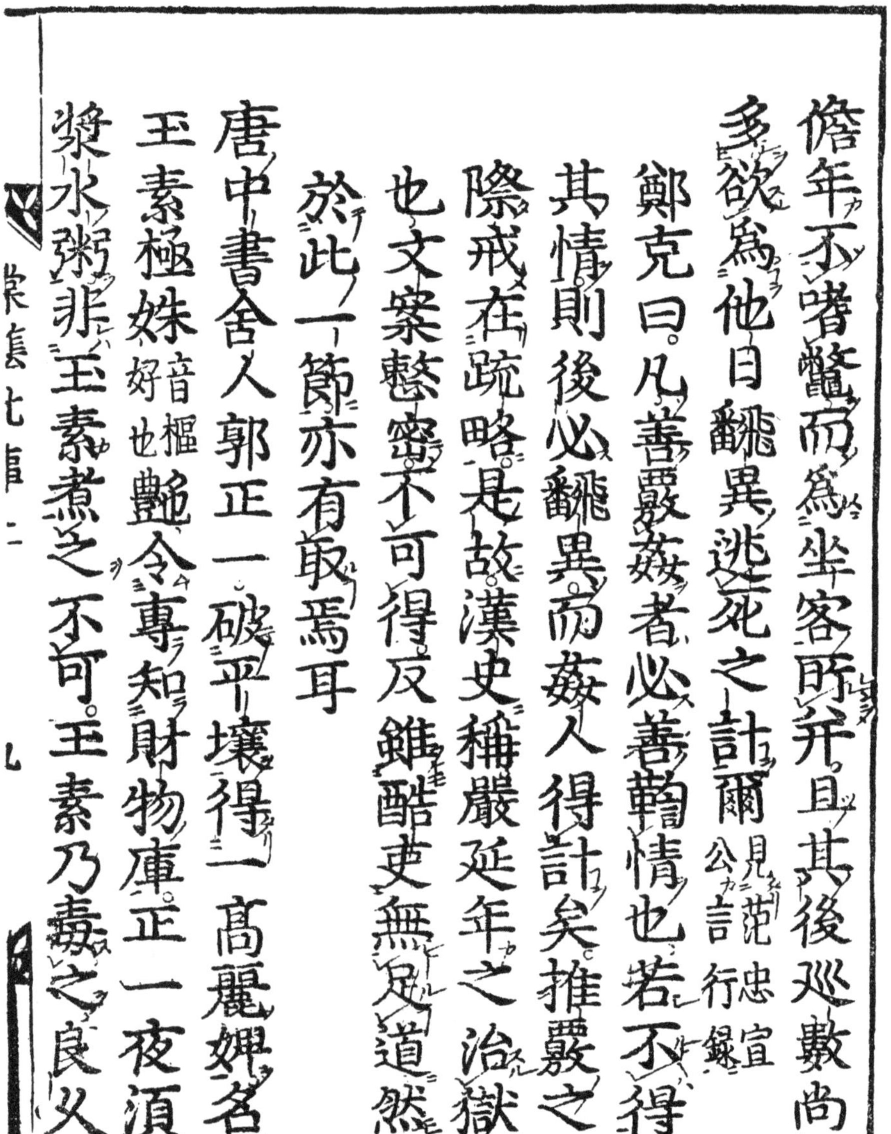

儋年不嗜鼈而為坐客所幷且其後巡數尚
多欲為他日醜異逃死之計爾 見范忠宣公言行錄
鄭克曰。凡善覆姦者必善鞫情也若不得
其情則後必醜異而姦人得計矣推覈之
際戒在疏略是故漢史稱嚴延年之治獄
也文案齊密不可得反雖酷吏無足道然
於此一節亦有取焉耳
唐中書舍人郭正一破平壤得一高麗婢名
玉素極姝（音樞好也）艷令專知財物庫正一夜須
漿水粥非玉素煮之不可。玉素乃毒之良久

Fig. 2. One page from Yamamoto's edition of the TYPS, same text as Plate II.

original; size and arrangement of the print-page correspond exactly with those of Hayashi Dōshun's traced copy preserved in the Naikaku-bunko; cf. Plate II and fig. 2. Perhaps the Korean edition was also printed with movable type—a technique which was highly developed in Korea.

The book is divided into three parts, each bound in one volume. Part I (*shang* 上) contains a preface by Hoku-zan, a preface by the Yüan editor, Kuei Wan-jung's preface of 1211, the table of contents, and Case I-A to 24-B. Part II (*chung* 中) contains Case 25-A till 48-B, Part III (*hsia* 下) Case 49-A till 72-B. There is no *okuzuke* (奥 附, publisher's note with date and place of publication); my copy has instead 7 (double) pages containing a descriptive list of other books published by the Seiri-kaku.

Hoku-zan's preface, composed in Sino-Japanese and written out by a certain Ba 馬 (Baba 馬場?) Nobusuke 信輔, is extremely meagre in factual information, it consists chiefly of a rambling discourse on the importance of judicial studies. Hoku-zan does not say anything about Hayashi Dōshun's edition, and nothing about the features of the Korean impression; he does not even say that it was a Korean print—for this information we are indebted to Dōshun's note at the end of his manuscript. Neither does Hoku-zan say whether he edited or revised the text; probably he confined himself to adding Japanese reading marks. Finally, Hoku-zan does not make it clear to whom the Korean print belonged—to himself, the Seiri-kaku or some third party.

However this may be, the data supplied by Dōshun's manuscript and Hoku-zan's reprint prove that there existed a Yüan print of the TYPS published in 1308 which next to the preface of the Yüan editor had only Kuei Wan-jung's preface of 1211 attached to it; there were no other prefaces, no postface and no colophon. Apparently the Korean editor of that Yüan print added no preface or colophon of his own.

Before going further into the contents of the Yüan edition, I first translate here the preface by the Yüan editor.

"Criminal cases are most important, but still more important are doubtful cases. How should those in charge of judicial affairs not devote all their mental capacities to those? In the glorious days of high antiquity laws and penalties were established but their categories were not yet differentiated. Later the 'five punishments' [1] were applied to three thousand kinds of offenses, and this was not felt as confusing. When the barbarians harassed China, Kao Yao when Minister (of the mythical Emperor Shun) combined the military and the judiciary in one office. In the Chou Dynasty the judicial officials dealt at most with sixty categories of criminal offenses. However, it was found that during the reigns of succeeding Emperors the ways of the people changed; their disposition became different from that of the ancients, and countless kinds of falsehood arose. In the Chou Dynasty the official called Hsiao-szu-k'ou when hearing the litigations of the ten-thousand people searched their feelings by listening to their speech [2]. In the chapter Lü-hsing (of the Book of Documents) this is called 'investigating cases on the basis of the features (of the persons concerned') [3]. But what is called there 'ascertaining and verifying guilt on the basis of the five pleadings' is necessarily followed by 'If the guilt is not ascertained the case should not be heard' (i.e. it should be dismissed). What the ancient literati meant by 'unascertained' is that the pleading could not be verified; in other words: a doubtful case. Few indeed are those who try not to err in cases where the features cannot be investigated and speech supplies no clues. Therefore in recent dynasties there were written the *I-yü-chi* of Mr. Ho, the *Che-yü-kuei-chien* of Mr. Cheng, and the *Hsi-yüan-lu* by the Judicial Intendant Sung (Tz'u) [4], now all available in print; the main point of these books is their aim to prevent judges to commit errors.

---

[1] I.e. to brand, to cut off the nose, castration, cutting off the feet, and the death-penalty.   [2] Cf. page 50 below.

[3] Cf. page 49, and my remark about *mao* on page 58.

[4] Sung Tz'u 宋慈, fl. ca. 1250 A.D.) served in the beginning of his career as Judicial Intendant (t'i-hsing 提刑) in Hsiang-yang 襄陽 (Hupeh Province). His *Hsi-yüan-lu* "Records of the Redressing of Wrongs" is a famous Chinese handbook for coroners containing rich material on forensic medicine. At an early date it attracted the attention of Western scholars. In 1780 there appeared an abbreviated French version (in *Mémoires concernant l'histoire, les sciences, les arts etc. des Chinois*, vol. IV pp. 421-440), and in 1863 the Netherlands Sinologue C. F. M. de Grijs published an excellent complete translation in Dutch (*Geregtelijke Geneeskunde, uit het Chinees vertaald*). There also appeared an English translation by H. A. Giles under the title "Instructions to Coroners", in the *China Review* vol. III (1874), and later in *Proceedings of the Royal Society of Medicine*, vol. XVII, London 1924. The *Hsi-yüan-lu* contains many interesting criminal cases and their solution.

"In the year 1303, when I had been ordered to serve as judge in Li-chou, I obtained the *T'ang-yin-pi-shih* by Mr. Kuei from Szu-ming. Contemplating its knowledge of redressing wrongs, discerning falsehood, discovering evil, disclosing what is hidden, and also of searching and probing concealed wickedness and its methods for tracing criminals and for enticing criminals, it seemed to me like a good physician who diagnoses life and death by the condition of the pulse, or like a brilliant mirror that shows the difference between beauty and ugliness by its reflected images, so that everything becomes clear at a glance. In hours of leisure left over from official duties I took the critical comments (added to the cases recorded) in the book of Mr. Cheng from K'ai-feng, and added those at the end of each pertaining case (in the TYPS); I marked the salient features of each case; I explained the pronunciation and meaning (of difficult characters) and added notes in the upper margin. Thereupon I ordered an artisan to engrave the text elegantly on the printing blocks, so as to broaden the book's circulation and to enable all judicial officers and all criminal investigators to obtain this book. If they study it thoroughly they will find that not only it suffices to broaden their insight in human nature, but also perhaps contributes to making injustice disappear in our Empire. If there are no innocently persecuted persons, then the atmosphere will be harmonious, appearances will be harmonious, speech will be harmonious, and Heaven and Earth will be in harmony in response. How then could this book be dismissed as but a small contribution to the minute examination [1] of punishments as practised by the (ancient) eminent judges?

"Respectfully written on a lucky day of the 10th moon of the first year of the Chih-ta era (i.e. 1308 A.D.) by the Assistant Secretary T'ien Tse from Chü-yen, Judge attached to the office of the Commander-in-chief of Li-chou-lu".

[1] *Chia-shih hsiang-hsing* is quoted from the last phrase of the chapter Lü-hsing 呂 刑 in the Book of Documents. *Hsiang-hsing* 祥 刑 means literally "felicitous punishments"; but other old sources write this compound 詳 刑 "minutely examined punishments", which is doubtless the original meaning. That later authors still preferred to write 祥 is partly because of deference to the authority of the Book of Documents, partly because it suggested the pleasing thought that every punishment, if correctly applied, ultimately leads to a felicitous result.

刑獄事之至重。而疑獄爲尤重。任事者詎容不重用其心哉。古昔盛時。象以典刑。未始詳於條目。及後世五刑之屬。至于三千。而不以爲繁。蠻夷寇賊。皋陶作士。兵與刑合爲一官。而周官司刑之屬。其多至於六十。蓋嘗考之帝降而王。世變風移。人心不古。情僞萬端。成周小司寇聽萬民之獄訟。以五聲求民情。在呂刑則謂之惟貌有稽。然所謂五辭簡孚。必繼之曰無簡不聽。先儒謂無簡云者獄辭之無可核實。是爲疑獄。既非貌之可稽。聲之可聽。其欲勿誤也鮮矣。此近代所以有和氏疑獄集。鄭氏折獄龜鑑。宋提刑洗冤錄。已行於世。其要皆期於勿誤云爾。

大德癸卯。澤被命推刑蘭澧。得四明桂氏所編棠陰比事。觀其釋冤辨誣摘姦發伏。以至察慝鈎慝之智。迹賊譎賊之術。如良醫眡脈候之生死。明鑑別物象之奸娸。一見瞭然在目。輒因公退之暇。取開封鄭氏評語。列之各條之下。且復揭其綱要。疏其音義。而標題於上。命工繡梓。用廣其傳。俾凡爲士師之官。掌刑之吏。得是書而熟閱之。不惟足以資夫人之多識。亦庶幾乎天下無冤民。無冤民則氣和形和聲和。而天地之和應矣。其於嘉師祥刑。豈曰小補云。

時至大元年孟冬吉日。承事郎澧州路總管府推官居延田澤謹序。

About T'ien Tse I could find no further details. According to his signature he was a native of Chü-yen, a place in Kansu Province on the Mongolian border. Li-chou is a Prefecture in Wu-ling-tao 武

陵 道 in Hunan Province, which during the Yüan period was called Li-chou-lu. It is also called Li-yang 澧 陽 , but I could not identify the name Lan-li 蘭 澧 given in the text of the Preface.

According to his own words, T'ien Tse confined his editing of the TYPS to four points. First, he added to each case the commentary by Cheng K'o as found in the CYKC; as we have seen above, Kuei Wan-jung himself added Cheng K'o's commentary is only nine cases. Second, T'ien Tse "marked the salient features of each case". As long as we have not seen the Yüan impression it is difficult to know what T'ien Tse means by this statement; perhaps he marked the most important passages by adding a circle on the right side of each character. Third, T'ien Tse added glosses explaining the meaning and pronunciation of difficult characters; in Hoku-zan's reprint these glosses are printed as interlineary commentary in two columns of smaller characters. Fourth, he added comments in the upper margin; these do not appear in Hoku-zan's reprint.

It is important to note that T'ien Tse does not say that he *re-printed* the TYPS, as is usual in the case of an editor re-publishing a book that had been printed before. I add in passing that the term *hsiu-tz'u* 繡 梓 , here translated "to print in an elegant manner", often refers to an illustrated edition; thus T'ien Tse added perhaps pictures to the text, but this point cannot be verified till the original Yüan print becomes available.

If one compares T'ien Tse's text with the Sung print of 1234, one will notice important differences. The Yüan text gives a great number of cases in a much more elaborate version, that is close to the CYKC text, and to the original versions in the Dynastic Histories available in Kuei Wan-jung's time. Throughout the Sung print one notices a tendency to abbreviate the text as much as possible; not a few cases are even abbreviated to such a degree that the point of the argument is either obscured or completely lost. I refer, for instance, to the Cases 6-A, 9-A, 32-B, 46-A and 60-B, where I had to disregard the Sung version and base my translation on the Yüan text or on the original version of the source.

If it had been T'ien Tse who restored the abbreviated cases to their more elaborate form—which would have involved the rewriting of practically the entire book—he would certainly have recorded this fact in his preface. One has to conclude, therefore, that Kuei

Wan-jung himself first wrote the TYPS in a more elaborate form, and that he abbreviated his manuscript when it was about to be printed. As was remarked already above, book printing was a costly undertaking, so that it was probably reasons of economy that motivated Kuei Wan-jung to curtail his original manuscript. Thus T'ien Tse apparently did not know the two Sung impressions, and based his edition on an early manuscript copy of the TYPS which was still circulating in his time, with attached to it only Kuei Wan-jung's preface of 1211—in which he stated that he *intended* (*ni* 擬) to have this manuscript published. This explains the absence of Liu Li's preface, Chang Fu's colophon and Kuei Wan-jung's postface of 1234.

The fact that T'ien Tse's edition is based on a copy of Kuei Wan-jung's original manuscript that antedates the two Sung impressions makes his edition all the more precious. One can only hope that some day the original Yüan print will come to light. In the mean time we must be grateful to the unknown Korean editor and to Hayashi Dōshun and Yamamoto Hoku-zan for having preserved this version.

Manuscript copies of the TYPS, and the two Sung impressions, had become unobtainable in China in the second half of the Ming Dynasty. Till the 19th century the only text generally available was a Ming edition drastically revised by Wu No. This was the edition entered into the Imperial Catalogue (*Szu-k'u-ch'üan-shu-tsung-mu* 四庫全書總目) which was completed in 1782.

Wu No (吳訥 styled Min-te 敏德, lit. name Szu-an 思菴) became known at Court in the Yung-lo era (1403-1424) as a physician, and in 1425 A.D. was appointed Investigating Censor; his biography is found in *Ming-shih* ch. 158. He made a study of the TYPS, and thought that the title-phrases rhymed faultily, and that the cases were not arranged in a logical order. He therefore edited the text anew reducing its contents to 80 selected cases, arranged in the order of the seriousness of the crimes treated. He left out Cheng K'o's commentary there were the TYPS had inserted it, but added to a few cases a commentary of his own—largely digressive and not contributing much to our understanding of the text. He added Kuei Wan-jung's original preface and his postscript, but omitted Liu Li's preface and Chang Fu's colophon. This text Wu No published under the title

T'ang-yin-pi-shih-yüan-pien 棠陰比事原編; he added a sequel (*hsü-pien* 編續) consisting of 23 cases selected by him, and a supplement (*pu-pien* 補編) dated 1442 containing 27 additional cases, and incorporated the book in his large work *Hsiang-hsing-yao-lan* 祥刑要覽 reprinted in 1834 and 1894. When Ts'ao Jung (曹溶 1613-1685; cf. E.C. page 740) compiled his *ts'ung-shu Hsüeh-hai-lei-pien* 學海類編, he included there Wu No's curtailed version. For text-critical purposes this edition is of slight value; for the sake of completeness, however, I added to the present Introduction a concordance of the 80 cases selected by Wu No and the cases of the complete text (Appendix II).

The complete text of the TYPS was found in 1808 A.D. Then the famous bibliophile Huang P'ei-lieh (黃丕烈 1763-1825; cf. E.C. page 340) found in the library of his friend Ku Shan (顧珊, lit. Name Ting-yü 聽玉) the original Sung impression of 1234, that emanated from the Ch'uan-shih-lou 傳是樓, the library of the well known scholar and book-collector Hsü Ch'ien-hsüeh (徐乾學 1631-1694; cf. E.C. page 310). Huang P'ei-lieh purchased this book from the Ku family, and added a colophon on the last page, from which the above details are borrowed. At the end of this colophon he expresses the hope that the eminent scholar Sun Hsing-yen (孫星衍 1753-1818; cf. E.C. page 675) who was then engaged in reprinting other old books on legal studies, would also undertake the publication of the Sung impression of the TYPS.

This hope was not realized. But in the summer of 1849 the Sung impression in Huang P'ei-lieh's collection was purchased by the scholar-official Chu Hsü-tseng 朱緒曾 who was then serving as magistrate of Chia-hsing 嘉興 in Chekiang Province. Chu Hsü-tseng, styled Shu-chih 述之, was a native of Shang-yüan 上元, in Kiangsu. He was an ardent bibliophile who maintained close relations with the other great book-collectors of that time (cf. his biography in the *Pei-chuan-chi-pu* 碑傳集補, publ. by the Yenching University in 1931, ch. 49 page 8 *b*; the years of his birth and death are not recorded there). In the winter of that same year

Chu Hsü-tseng published a beautiful facsimile edition (*ying-k'o* 影 刻) of the Sung print. The famous calligrapher Ho Shao-chi (何 紹 基 1799-1873; cf. E.C. page 287) wrote the title page for it (Fig. 3).

This edition opens with a preface by Chu Hsü-tseng, dated the 10th moon of the winter of 1849. Then follows Kuei Wan-jung's preface of 1211, Chang Fu's colophon, and Kuei Wan-jung's postface of 1234. Thereafter comes an additional note by Chu Hsü-tseng in which he explains that when he wrote the preface he had not yet consulted Kuei Wan-jung's biography in local gazetteers; in the note he supplies additional data on Kuei Wan-jung's career, and on his descendants. Then follows the text of the TYPS itself: 5 single pages with the table of contents, 104 single pages (52 double pages) with the 144 cases, not divided into chapters. The book ends with Huang P'ei-lieh's colophon, and a final note by Chu Hsü-tseng where he identifies the Mr. Chiang of Case 31-A, and gives some data on Cheng K'o, the compiler of the CYKC. That Liu Li's preface is missing must be due to the fact that that first page had become detached from Huang P'ei-lieh's Sung print.

Each print page of the text measures 173 by 227 mm. and contains 10 columns with space for 18 characters. The outer margins have one black *yü-wei* 魚 尾 on top, the title of the book, the page number and the names of the persons who collated the text (cf. Fig. 4). Although the Ch'ing copyist who traced the Sung impression for Chu Hsü-tseng (Shen Hsi-t'ang 沈 錫 堂 from Chao-hsi 苕 溪) and the artisan who engraved that traced copy of the blocks (Wang Shih-kuei 王 世 貴 from Wu-lin 武 林) did not entirely succeed in reproducing the elegance of the Sung printed characters, the reprint is a nicely executed piece of work; all Sung taboos are carefully reproduced (cf. on Fig. 4 the character 賔 printed with one stroke missing) and there is no reason for doubting that it is a fair facsimile of the Sung impression. The two additional notes added by Chu Hsü-tseng as an afterthought betray the haste in which he published the book. But we learn from his biography in the *Pei-chuan-chi-pu* that in that same year 1849 he was actively engaged in organizing relief during the disastrous floods that occurred in that area; that despite onerous official duties he yet found time to publish this reprint is eloquent proof of his devotion to literary studies.

Fig. 3. The title page of Chu Hsü-tseng's reprint of the TYPS

Unfortunately Chu Hsü-tseng's reprint is now extremely scarce, as pointed out by Chang Yüan-chi in his colophon to an edition of the TYPS in the *Szu-pu-ts'ung-k'an* (see p. 28), and by Chang Shou-yung, the editor of the *Szu-ming-ts'ung-shu* (see below). I myself had considerable difficulty in locating a copy on the book market in Peking. The reason of this scarcity of a comparatively recent print is explained in the preface of a reprint published in 1867 by a descendant of Kuei Wan-jung, a Mr. Kuei Sung-ch'ing 桂嵩慶 of Lin-ju 臨汝. This edition, entitled *Chü-chen T'ang-yin-pi-shih* 聚珍棠陰比事 "The T'ang-yin-pi-shih, reprinted with copper movable type", I have not seen myself: but it was used by Chang Shou yung when he prepared his version of the TYPS for inclusion in his *Szu-ming-ts'ung-shu* (see below). Chang Shou-yung reprinted there Kuei Sung-ch'ing's preface from which I translate the following passage: "Mr. Chu (Hsü-tseng) reprinted it facsimile and thereby made this book generally known. He made again evident what had become obscured, and completed again what had been defective. But the printing blocks were burned in Nanking during the military troubles, so that I feared that in the end the book would disappear. Hence I printed several hundred copies of it with movable type, in order to make it widely circulate" 朱氏爲之影刻流布。乃使晦者復顯。闕者復全。而版在金陵燬於兵燹。嵩慶懼其卒就湮沒也。爰以活字集印數百本。俾廣其傳。

Thus the printing blocks were destroyed in Nanking at the end of the T'ai-p'ing rebellion (1851-1865), when in 1865 that stronghold of the T'ai-p'ing leaders was retaken by the government armies.

It was this reprint of Chu Hsü-tseng's edition that was used in 1934 by Chang Shou-yung 張壽鏞 when he prepared a version of the TYPS for inclusion in his *Szu-ming-ts'ung-shu* 四明叢書. This *ts'ung-shu* is a collection of reprints of writings left by prominent people of the Szu-ming region; Chang Shou-yung took a special interest in the history of that area because he himself was a native of Ningpo. Chang Shou-yung was unable to obtain a copy of Chu Hsü-tseng's edition, and therefore used Kuei Sung-ch'ing's reprint of it. Earlier in 1934 the Commercial Press

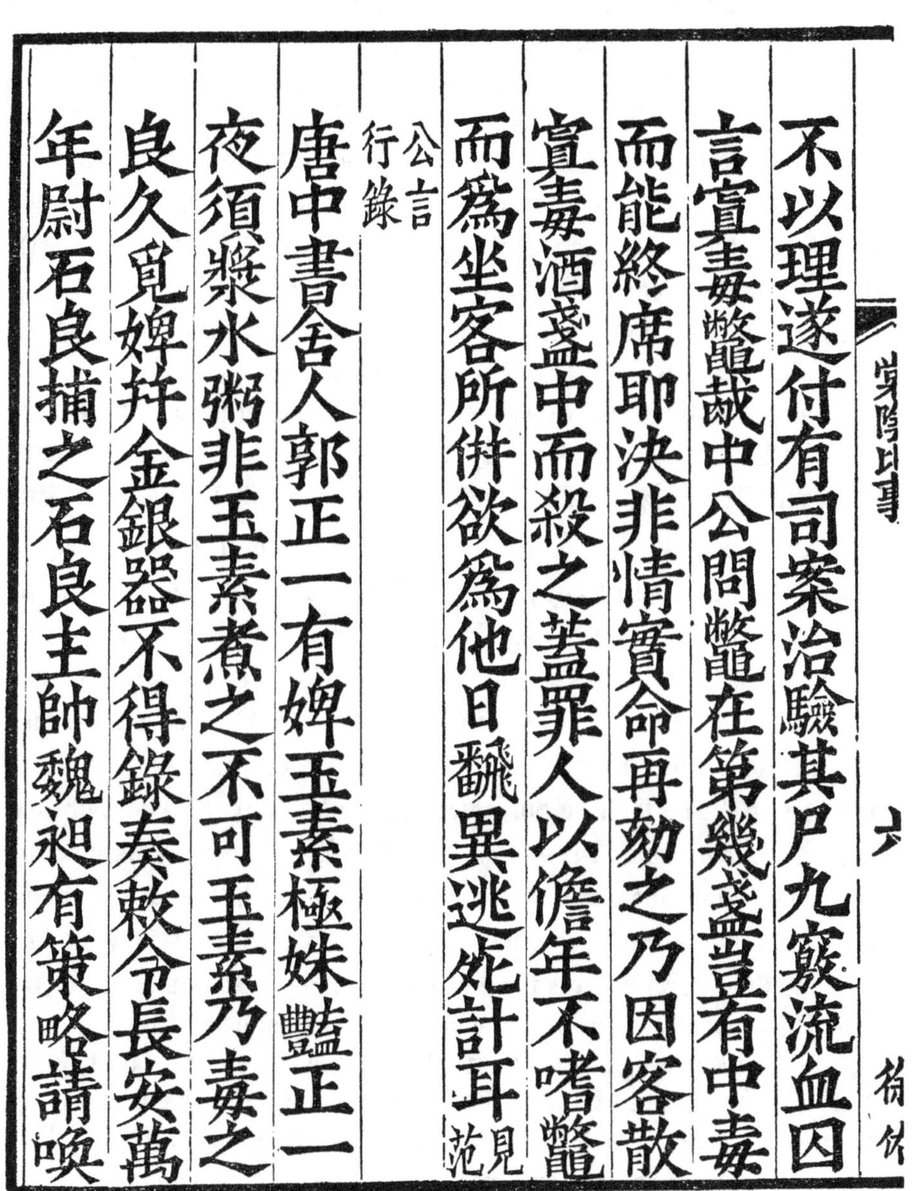

不以理遂付有司案治驗其尸九竅流血因
言宣毒鷩戠中公問鷩在第幾盞豈有中毒
而能終席耶決非情實命再効之乃因客散
宣毒酒盞中而殺之蓋罪人以儋年不嗜鷩
而為坐客所併欲為他日飜異逃死計耳

公言
行錄

唐中書舍人郭正一有婢玉素極姝豔正一
夜須凝水粥非玉素煮之不可玉素乃毒之
良久覓婢并金銀器不得錄奏敕令長安萬
年尉石良捕之石良主帥魏昶有策略請喚

Fig. 4. One page from Chu Hsü-tseng's reprint, containing end of Case 8-A and beginning of 8-B.

had published a lithographed reprint of a manuscript of the TYPS, and Chang Shou-yung collated the text on the basis of this edition and that of Kuei Sung-ch'ing. However, this work was not very carefully done although Chang says in his colophon that he spent ten entire days on it. He eliminated easily recognizable Sung taboos (such as the character *chen* 眞 printed with the right bottom stroke missing), but he left less obvious taboo characters in proper names unchanged (cf. for instance *shang* 商 for *yin* 殷 in Case 42-A). He also failed to correct some misprints (cf. my note to Case 52-A). Therefore in the textual notes to my translation I have not taken into consideration Chang Shou-yung's edition.

Finally we have to describe here the lithographed reprint of the TYPS published in 1934 by the Commercial Press. Mr. Chang Yüan-chi 張 元 濟 , the editor of the huge collection of reprints *Szu-pu-ts'ung-k'an* 四 部 叢 刊 , chose for inclusion in the first sequel (*hsü* 續) a manuscript copy of the TYPS, made by the well known bibliophile Pao T'ing-po (鮑 廷 博 1728-1814; cf. EC page 612), the owner of the famous Chih-pu-tsu Library 知 不 足 齋 in Hang-chow. According to a brief note written by Pao T'ing-po on the last page of the manuscript, he made this copy on the basis of a Sung impression of 1234 which he borrowed from a Mr. Wu 吳 whose library was called *Nan-ch'üan-ts'ao-t'ang* 南 泉 草 堂 . Pao's manuscript copy was later obtained by the modern bibliophile and expert on Sung impressions Fu Tseng-hsiang (傅 增 湘 1872-1945), who lent it to the Commercial Press for reproduction in the *Szu-pu-ts'ung-k'an*.

In this text the contents are arranged as follows: Liu Li's preface, Kuei Wan-jung's preface of 1211, Table of contents, text, Kuei Wan-jung's postface of 1234, Chang Fu's colophon. The editor Chang Yüan-chi added a brief colophon set in ordinary type. The text of the cases is divided into two parts. The first, *shang-chuan* 上 卷 , pp. 1-28 (double pages) contains Case 1-A to 36-B, the second, *hsia-chuan* 下 卷 pp. 1-31, Case 37-A to 72-B.

Pao T'ing-po states in his note at the end of the manuscript that he wrote it out in 1812, when he was already 84 years old. This fact explains the unequal quality of the manuscript. On the one hand

there are a number of good emendations, but on the other there occur
a large number of *lapsus calami*; cf., for instance, my notes to Case 29-
A, 43-A, 45-A, 53-B, 55-B etc. This manuscript is certainly a *ming-chi*
名 蹟 "a famous document"—as Chang Yüan-chi calls it in his colophon—but chiefly as a proof of the remarkable zeal of that indefati-
gable scholar. From a textual point of view it is certainly neither the
best nor the most interesting version. Chang Yüan-chi had been better
advised if he had chosen for reproduction in the *Szu-pu-ts'ung-k'an*
Chu Hsü-tseng's reprint, or, better still, Hayashi Dōshun's or Yamamoto Hoku-zan's version of Kuei Wan-jung's original manuscript.
As is well known the editors of the *Szu-pu-ts'ung-k'an* often drew from
Japanese sources, and many items in that work are reproductions of
Chinese books and manuscripts preserved in Japanese private and
public collections.

That notwithstanding its many shortcomings I yet chose the text
as published in the *Szu-pu-ts'ung-k'an* as basis of the present translation was solely because it is the only edition of the TYPS that
is easily accessible to Sinologues in the West. It seemed futile to
refer to texts which are rare in China and Japan and practically
unobtainable in Western countries. I may add that I had originally
planned to reprint here the text of Yamamoto Hoku-zan's edition,
but had to abandon this project because of the prohibitive cost.

II. THE I-YÜ-CHI AND THE CHE-YÜ-KUEI-CHIEN

The *I-yü-chi* (hereunder referred to as IYC) was written by the
10th century scholar Ho Ning and his son Ho Meng. Ho Ning (和
凝 , styled Ch'eng-chi 成 績 , 898-955 A.D.) was a noted scholar-
official who served under no less than five different dynasties. In
the Later Liang Dynasty (907-923 A.D.) he served on the staff of a
Regional Commander, in the Later T'ang Dynasty (923-936) he became a member of the Han-lin Academy, under the Later Chin
Dynasty (936-946) he was appointed Ministerial Right Executive, and
under the Later Han Dynasty (947-950) he was Preceptor of the Heir-
Apparent being also ennobled as Duke of Lu 魯 國 公 . Finally he
served under the Later Chou Dynasty (915-960). Ho Ning acquired
fame as a composer of "chanted verse", *tz'u* 詞 and *ch'ü* 曲 , of
which he left a voluminous collection.

30 INTRODUCTION

His son Ho Meng (和嶸, styled Hsien-jen 顯仁, 951-995) was also well known as a poet; he edited and supplemented the ICY written by his father.

The Bibliographical Section of the *Sung-shih* mentions an *I-yü-chi* by Ho Ning in 3 ch.; but the Imperial Catalogue lists the IYC as counting 4 ch., the former two ch. written by Ho Ning, and the latter two by Ho Meng; this Catalogue adds that there is appended a sequel in 6 ch. by the Ming writer Chang Ching 張景, so that the book counts a total of 10 ch.

The Bibliographical Section of the *Sung-shih* mentions under the heading *Hsing-fa-lei* 刑法類 also an *I-yü-chi* in 3 ch. by Chao T'ung 趙仝, and a *Hsü-i-yü-chi* 續疑獄集 in 4 ch. by Wang Hao 王皞. Since these two books are lost it is not possible to ascertain whether they had any connection with the IYC of Ho Ning and his son.

My edition of the IYC is a blockprint published in 1851 by the Ch'ing scholar Chin Feng-ch'ing 金鳳淸, in 2 vls. containing 10 ch. and one Appendix (*fu-lu* 附錄). This is a well printed edition; the print page measures 132 by 224 mm., each page containing 9 columns of 19 characters. The title page is written in beautiful chancery script. Notwithstanding its fairly recent date this book is scarce. As far as I know, however, it is the only printed edition of the IYC available.

Chin Feng-ch'ing states in his preface that this blockprint is a reprint of a miniature edition (*hsiu-chen-pen* 袖珍本) published by the well known printing-house Sao-yeh-shan-fang 掃葉山房 which he found in the collection of his father, a prominent judge. Since that print contained many mistakes, Chin Feng-ch'-ing published a corrected text as a tribute to his father's memory.

The Sao-yeh-shan-fang edition was apparently based on a Ming print, for Chin Feng-ch'ing's preface is followed by one signed by the Ming scholar Li Sung-hsiang 李松祥, dated 1535. He says that Chang Ching 張景, then a Court Censor, enjoyed reading the IYC, and augmented its contents with 6 ch. of cases culled by him from older literature. Li Sung-hsiang adds that Hsü Chieh (徐

階 1494-1574), then Superintendent of Education of Chekiang Province, published the work in this expanded form of 10 ch., and had copies distributed among all the judicial officials in Chekiang Province (凡吏浙者人授一帙). Hsü Chieh was one of the great statesmen of the second half of the Ming period; cf. BD no. 761 (where the wrong dates are given), and his detailed biography in *Ming-shih*, ch. 213.

Li Sung-hsiang's preface is followed by one written by the Yüan scholar Tu Chen 杜震, dated 1295 A.D., where he states i.a. that he wrote the preface on the request of his friend Ch'iao Hsiang 譙祥, for the latter's reprint of the book.

Finally there is an undated preface by Ho Meng. He there says that his father had assembled a number of *causes célèbres*, and that he made bold to continue his father's work by adding a series of other cases, bringing the total to one hundred articles (*t'iao* 條). At the end he says: "This text I wrote out in four rolls; the first part comprising two rolls (chapters) were completed by the Minister my late father, the second part comprising two rolls (chapters) by me his unworthy son Meng, as a sequel" 勒成四軸。上二卷先相國編纂。下二卷小子矇附續。

Thereafter follows a table of contents listing the title phrases of the cases, and the first two chapters bearing Ho Ning's name, and collated by Chin Feng-ch'ing, 47 cases in all. Then the two chapters written by Ho Meng, again collated by Chin Feng-ch'ing, containing 52 cases. Thus these four chapters contain together a total of 99 cases. In the text each case is headed by the same four-character title-phrase as listed in the table of contents.

These 99 cases give but a very general idea of the text as printed in 1295 by Ch'iao Hsiang. The Yüan catalogue *Chih-chai-shu-lu-chieh-t'i* (see page 36 below) states that the IYC consisted of 3 ch., viz. 2 by Ho Ning and 1 containing the sequel by Ho Meng; that the text was divided over 67 articles (*t'iao* 條); and that the cases were arranged under 20 categories (*men* 門). Also the Bibliographical Section of the *Sung-shih* states that the book counted 3 ch. Now this difference in the number of chapters need not unduly worry us. In my opinion Chinese bibliographers attach too much importance to the number of chapters in deciding the state and authenticity of a text. Especially in those cases where the subject-matter itself does not suggest a definite division into chapters, and in those times when manuscript rolls were still more common than printed books, the division into chapters was not seldom arbitrarily changed to suit the convenience of the copyist. The TYPS provides a case in point; as we have seen in the above, some editors published that text in 1 ch., others in 2, others again in 3, without interfering with the text itself. Serious, however, is the evident difference in the arrangement of the text. The present version gives each case as a separate unit, there are no examples of two or more cases being combined into one article (*t'iao*); neither is there the division into 20 categories (*men*). Since Ho Meng states in his preface that the book contained 100 articles, it must have contained many more cases than the 99 it has now. Moreover, the Ming editors did not only revise the text of individual cases, they also changed the sequence, and inserted not a few cases borrowed from other sources; how arbitrarily those cases were chosen is proved by the fact that for instance ch. 4, although it bears the name of Ho Meng who died in 995 A.D., contains many cases solved by his younger contemporaries, and even one (no. 73) ascribed to Szu-ma Kuang who lived 1019-1086. The conclusion is that the present version of the work by Ho Ning and his son represents a series of fragments placed in a new frame, and thus gives but a very general idea of plan and contents of the original work.

The remaining 6 ch. of the present blockprint were added by the Ming scholar Chang Ching, as a sequel (*hsü-pien* 續編), again collated by Chin Feng-ch'ing. This sequel consists of 128 cases, mostly borrowed from the CYKC and the TYPS, and betraying a distressing preference for cases with an erotic slant. The four chapters by Ho Ning and his son, together with Chang Ching's sequel in 6 ch., represent the text as it was reprinted in 1535 by Hsü Chieh, and which was listed in the Imperial Catalogue. Pelliot mentions in his *Notes de Bibliographie Chinoise*, II ("Bulletin de l'École Française de l'Extrême Orient", vol. IX page 128) that this edition was again reprinted in 1564 or 1565, but this I have not seen.

Finally, the blockprint of 1851 has an Appendix of 30 cases selected by the editor Chin Feng-ch'ing.

Needless to say that only ch. 1-4 of the IYC as we have it before us now have any value for text-critical research, and only if we keep in mind that later editors revised and partially re-wrote the text, omitted some cases and added others, and changed their sequence. As regards ch. 5-10, these are of interest only in so far that they show how those editors revised the cases they borrowed from the TYPS and CYKC.

In my notes to the translation of the TYPS the IYC is referred to throughout, but the reader will have to pay attention to the numbers of the chapters indicated. References to ch. 1-4 of the IYC mean that the pertaining cases in the TYPS were probably borrowed from the IYC, while those to ch. 5-10 mean on the contrary that the editors of the IYC borrowed those cases from the TYPS.

The *Che-yü-kuei-chien* was compiled by the Northern Sung scholar-official Cheng K'o 鄭 克. His biography is not included in the *Sung-shih*, and his own preface to the CYKC became lost at an early date; the meagre information given here was collected by Chu Hsü-tseng and recorded in the final note which he added to his reprint of the TYPS. Cheng K'o's style was K'o-ming 克 明, and he was a native of K'ai-feng. He started his career as Sheriff (*wei* 尉) of Shang-yüan 上 元 in Kiangsu Province. Ca. 1133 A.D. he served as Judicial Intendant (*t'i-hsing* 提 刑) in Hunan Province, and at that time compiled the CYKC, as an enlarged version of the IYC.

At present the CYKC survives only in one, revised version. We do not have any early prints of this book nor varying later editions, as in the case of the TYPS. The most accessible edition is the text re-printed in 1937 by the Commercial Press at Shanghai, as no. 0783 of the *Ts'ung-shu-chi-ch'eng* 叢 書 集 成. This is a reprint from the *Mo-hai-chin-hu* 墨 海 金 壺, a *ts'ung-shu* compiled by the Ch'ing bibliophile Chang Hai-p'eng (張 海 鵬 1755-1816; E.C. page 36), and issued in 1817 A.D. Hereunder follows a description of this text.

The book begins with a preface by a Yüan scholar Yü Ying-lung 虞 應 龍 dated 1282 A.D. This preface states that a group of scholars undertook to reprint a number of Sung dynasty works, the blocks of which were preserved in the Prefectural Library [1] (*chün-*

---

[1] Scholar-officials often kept their private libraries, and the printing blocks they had carved on government orders or as a private undertaking, in the official residences occupied by them when serving as Prefect in the provinces. Thus

chai 郡 齋) in I-ch'un 宜 春, in the NW part of Kiangsi Province. Among those the CYKC is mentioned.

Then follows the text itself, consisting of 395 cases arranged under 276 articles (*t'iao* 條), and divided into 20 categories (*men* 門); these twenty *men* are distributed over 8 chapters. In the text each article is headed by the name of the person who dealt with the first case of the article. But the text is preceded by a table of contents, where the main point of each case at the head of the articles is summed up in one longer phrase.

Each article contains, next to the main case, an indication of its source, and critical notes by an unknown later editor, in smaller characters printed in two columns. Then one or more similar cases, mostly differing only in time, place, and the persons concerned, together with comments by Cheng K'o, beginning with the word *an* 按 "I find that ...".

The following table shows how the twenty categories are divided over the 8 chapters.

Ch. 1-2	I. *Shih-yüan*	釋 冤	Redressing wrongs
Ch. 3	II. *Pien-wu*	辨 誣	Discerning false accusations
	III. *Chü-ching*	鞫 情	Searching the feelings
Ch. 4	IV. *I-tsui*	議 罪	Discussing guilt
	V. *Yu-kuo*	宥 過	Leniency
Ch. 5	VI. *Ch'eng-wo*	懲 惡	Punishing evil
	VII. *Ch'a-chien*	察 姦	Investigating depravity

Ch'ao Kung-wu (晁 公 武, 12th century) gave his descriptive catalogue (see page 23 below) the title *Chün-chai-tu-shu-chih* "Account of books read in the Prefectural Library", because he had stored his collection of books in the office of Jung-chou 榮 州 Prefecture in Szuchuan when he served there as Prefect. As regards printing blocks, in the case of official editions they remained permanently in the government office where they were carved and, since those blocks were cumbersome to take along, also private owners frequently left the blocks behind when they were transferred to another post. Thus it would often happen that at a later date an official serving in such a place had the blocks he found there struck off again, adding only a new preface of his own. Cf. K. T. Wu's instructive article "Ming Printing and Printers", in: *Harvard Journal of Asiatic Studies*, vol. 7 no. 3 (1943), page 247.

Ch. 6	VIII.	*Ho-chien*	覈姦	Thoroughly examining depravity
	IX.	*T'i-chien*	摘姦	Exposing depravity
	X.	*Ch'a-t'e*	察慝	Investigating hidden evil
	XI.	*Cheng-t'e*	證慝	Proving hidden evil
Ch. 7	XII.	*Kou-t'e*	鉤慝	Searching out hidden evil
	XIII.	*Ch'a-tao*	察盜	Investigating thieves
	XIV.	*I-tao*	迹盜	Tracing thieves
	XV.	*Chüeh-tao*	譎盜	Enticing thieves
	XVI.	*Ch'a-tsei*	察賊	Investigating armed robbers
	XVII.	*I-tsei*	迹賊	Tracing armed robbers
	XVIII.	*Chüeh-tsei*	譎賊	Enticing armed robbers
Ch. 8	XIX.	*Yen-ming*	嚴明	Severity
	XX.	*Ching-chin*	矜謹	Compassion

The text ends with a colophon by the Yüan scholar Chao Shih-t'o
趙時彙, dated 1261 A.D., in which he describes how he edited the
Chün-chai text by collating it with a copy in his own collection.

This is the text as we have it now. There are no varying versions
with which it could be compared, all later editors reprinted it in
substantially the same form; they only added prefaces of their own
which do not supply new facts relating to the history of the text.

For forming an opinion on the question in how far the present
version corresponds to Cheng K'o's original text, we must first examine the descriptions of this book given in two old catalogues.

The *Chün-chai-tu-shu-chih* 郡齋讀書志 [1]. of 1151 A.D. says
in ch. 8:

"*Chüeh-yü-kuei-chien*, in 20 ch. This book was compiled by Cheng
K'o of our present dynasty. During the period of the Five Dynasties Ho Ning wrote the *I-yü-chi*, and in recent years Chao T'ung
wrote the *I-yü-shih-lei* [2]; but neither of these books is really ex-

---

[1] For further details about this catalogue cf. Teng and Biggerstaff, "An
Annotated Bibliography of Selected Chinese Reference works" (Harvard University Press 1950), page 19.

[2] As remarked on page 30 above, the *Sung-shih* gives the title of Chao T'ung's
book as *I-yü-chi*.

haustive. Therefore Cheng K'o enlarged these collections. Following the example of Liu Hsiang when editing the *Yen-tzu-ch'un-ch'iu* [1], he added a table of contents which sums up the main features (of each case), and he divided the contents into twenty categories (*men*), altogether 395 cases (*shih*)".

決獄龜鑑二十卷。右皇朝鄭克編次。五代
和凝有疑獄集。近時趙仝有疑獄事類。皆未
祥盡。克因增廣之。依劉向晏子春秋舉其綱
要。爲之目錄。分二十門計三百九十五事。

The *Chih-chai-shu-lu-chieh-t'i* [2] 直齋書錄解題 of ca. 1250 A.D. says in ch. 7:

"*Che-yü-kuei-chien*, in 3 ch. (I find that the *Wen-hsien-t'ung-k'ao* writes *Chüeh-yü-kuei-chien*, and says that the book consists of 20 ch.). Compiled by the Cheng-chih-lang [3] Cheng K'o, son of Cheng Wu [4] from K'ai-feng. Ho Ning, Prime Minister of the Period of the Five Dynasties first wrote the *I-yü-chi*, and his son, the Secretary of the Bureau of Water-works Ho Meng [5] added a sequel, making a total of 3 ch. containing 67 articles (*t'iao*). Cheng K'o retained the division into twenty categories (*men*) of the book by the two Ho, but

---

[1] The *Yen-tzu-ch'un-ch'iu* is a philosophical text represented as the dicta of the Chou statesman Yen Ying (晏嬰, styled P'ing-chung 平仲, died 493 B.C.), traditionally considered as belonging to the school of Mo Ti; cf., however, Pelliot's observations in *T'oung Pao*, vol. XXII, pp. 354-355. The text consists of three parts, counting respectively 30, 30 and 18 sections. The famous Han scholar Liu Hsiang (劉向 77-6 B.C.) added to each section a longer title phrase summing up its contents; cf. the modern edition *Yen-tzu-ch'un-ch'iu-hsiao-chu* 晏子春秋校注, critically edited by Chang Ch'un-i 張純一 (Shih-chieh-shu-chü 世界書局, Shanghai 1935), where Liu Hsiang's preface is found on pp. 1-3.

[2] This catalogue is described on page 21 of the work referred to in note on p. 33.

[3] *Cheng-chih-lang* was one of the 29 honorary Court ranks bestowed on civilian officials; cf. *Sung-shih*, ch. 169, under the heading *Wen-san-kuan* 文散官.

[4] Later writers take Wu-tzu 武子 to be Cheng K'o's style; but since a Sung source (see page 39 below) states that his *tzu* was K'o-ming, *Wu* must have been his father's name.

[5] *Meng* is here wrongly written with the "water" radical, instead of "mountain".

he expanded the contents to 276 articles (*t'iao*), totalling 395 cases (*shih*), beginning with the case of Cheng Tzu-ch'an (cf. TYPS Case 16-A), and ending with cases of the present dynasty"

折獄龜鑑三卷。案文獻通考作決獄龜鑑
二十卷。承直郎開封鄭克武子撰。初五代宰
相和凝有疑獄集。其子水部郎和濛續爲三
卷六十七條。克因和氏之書。分爲二十門。
推廣之凡二百七十六條。三百九十五事。起
鄭子產迄於本朝。

As regards the title of the book, the reading *chüeh* 決 instead of *che* 折 is not important, since *chüeh-yü* is a synonym of *che-yü*. Neither should one attach value to the number of chapters being differently given as 3 and 20; evidently one editor made each category (*men*) into one ch., while another divided the contents into three parts, probably to suit the binder's convenience. Important is that both sources agree that the total number of cases was 395, and that the second source states that these cases were distributed over 276 articles (*t'iao*).

Since the present version does indeed contain 395 cases distributed over 276 separate articles and divided into twenty categories, one is inclined at first sight to assume that the text was transmitted practically intact. But a further examination of the meagre information available regarding its history proves that there is ground for considerable doubt.

The preface and the colophon added by the Yüan editors show that the text had become impaired already in their time. Chao Shih-t'o says in his colophon of 1261:

"In the Prefectural Library at I-ch'un were preserved of old the printing blocks of the *Che-yü-kuei-chien;* but in the course of the years these had become worn down so that the copies struck off showed characters difficult to decipher, which irked the readers. A few months after I had taken up the office of Prefect, I found that law-suits (in my territory) were simple. Thus in leisure hours left over from official duties I took a copy of the CYKC from my book-cases and edited it critically; having chosen an engraver I had the book re-published"

宜春郡齋。舊有折獄龜鑑。歲久字畫漫漶。
覽者病之。余叨守旣數月。獄訟簡淸。公暇出
篋中所藏一編參訂。遴匠重刊。

Twenty years later Yü Ying-lung said about the I-ch'un blocks in
general:

"Formerly there were in I-ch'un printing blocks engraved in the
Prefectural Library. At the time of the invasion of the Chin Tartars,
what had been assembled became dispersed, and there were no
previous prints to complete what had been lost" 宜春舊有書
板。鋟於郡齋。其在金日。蒐放失。補殘斷莫
先焉。

If one combines these two remarks one obtains a fairly dark picture:
part of the printing blocks had become lost, and those that remained
were badly worn down. We do not know how good the old print was
that Chao Shih-t'o produced from his book-cases, nor do we know to
what extent he revised the text. Neither do we know how Yü Ying-
lung and his friends handled the texts they re-published, since that
collection of reprints has not been preserved.

In the five centuries that followed even these Yüan editions
became impaired. In 1773-1782 the compilers of the Imperial
Collection could only find incomplete copies which contained 5 of the
20 categories. They discovered, however, in the great Ming encyclopedia *Yung-lo-ta-tien* 永樂大典 a better text. They vouchsafe
no details about its date or its state, merely saying that they combined
the defective text comprising 5 categories with that of the *Yung-lo-
ta-tien;* they add that since the original division into 20 ch. could
not any more be established, they divided the text into 8 chapters
(cf. *Imperial Catalogue* ch. 101). Since also the division into categories
(*men*) bears a provisional character (as indicated in brief editorial
notes added to their headings), the *Yung-lo-ta-tien* text cannot have
been a true copy of Cheng K'o's original edition.

As far as I could ascertain there are but two sources by which the
contents of the present version of the CYKC can be checked, dating
respectively from the middle and the end of the Yüan period.

The first source is the *Yin-chü-t'ung-i* 隱居通議, a collection
of miscellaneous notes in 31 ch., compiled by the Yüan scholar Liu

Hsün (劉壎 1240-1319), known as an able writer. This book was reprinted in 1799 by Ku Hsiu 顧修 in his *Tu-hua-chai-ts'ung-shu* 讀畫齋叢書. Ch. 31 contains 17 cases selected by Liu Hsün from the CYKC. He prefaces these cases by the following note:

"The Emperor Kao-tsung issued in 1133 an edict urging lenient punishments, as a warning to metropolitan and provincial officials so that they would cultivate compassion. At that time the Cheng-chih-lang Cheng (styled) K'o-ming served as Judicial Intendant in Hunan. (Encouraged by the Imperial edict) he read the *I-yü-chi* by Ho Ning and admired its thoroughness. He divided the cases into similar groups, from 'Redressing wrongs' and 'Discerning false accusations' till 'Examples of Severity and Compassion', altogether twelve categories (*men*). He changed the original name into *Che-yü-kuei-chien*. The cases recorded are all authentic, but many are irrelevant and could well be omitted. However, there are several that contribute to our knowledge and understanding. Those I selected and record here"

高宗紹興三年降詔恤刑。戒飭中外。俾務
哀矜。　時有承直郎鄭克明爲湖南提刑司幹
官。因閱和凝疑獄集。嘉其用心。乃分類其
事。自釋冤辨誣至嚴明矜謹。凡十二門。易舊
名曰折獄龜鑑。所載皆古事。亦多有不切可
删者。然有數事增人智識。爰摘錄之。

The first half of this note might well be based upon Cheng K'o's own preface to the CYKC that was lost at an early date. The number "twelve" instead of "twenty" is doubtless due to the mistake of a copyist.

Liu Hsün quotes at the beginning of each of the 17 cases the category (*men*) under which Cheng K'o classified it. He gives the text of the case only, without Cheng K'o's commentary. Although neither the *Chün-chai-tu-shu-chih* nor the *Chih-chai-shu-lu-chieh-t'i* mention the commentary, the preface which the Yüan writer T'ien Tse added to his edition of the TYPS (see page 19 above) proves that the commentary *did* form part of Cheng K'o's original text.

Although each of the 17 cases quoted by Liu Hsün does occur in the

present version of the CYKC[1], their text shows considerable differences, and also the classification under the twenty *men* does not tally.
These facts may be shown by the following table. The first column
states the category indicated by Liu Hsün, the second gives the name
of the person who dealt with the case (I give the Chinese characters
only of those names that do not occur in the TYPS), the third the
place where the case is found in the present version of the CYKC (as
reprinted in the *Ts'ung-shu-chi-ch'eng*), and the fourth (between
brackets) the number in my translation of the TYPS of those cases
which occur in that book too. Finally a brief indication of where Liu
Hsün's text differs from that of the present version of the CYKC.

(1) *Shih-yüan*	Yüan Tz'u	ch. 1, page 10	(Case 35-A) en-larged text
(2) *Pien-wu*	A Censor	ch. 3, page 30	(Case 49-A) an additional pas-sage about Li Ching's pardon, and the rest mo-re elaborate
(3) *Pien-wu*	Li Te-yü	ch. 3, page 32	(Case 57-B) slightly more elaborate and different phras-ing
(4) *I-tsui*	Wu-ti	ch. 4, page 45	(Case 61-B) iden-tical
(5) ..	Huang Pa	ch. 4, page 46	(Case 25-B) iden-tical
(6) ..	Wang Tsun	ch. 4, page 46	some small alte-rations

[1] Pelliot observes in his "Notes de bibliographie chinoise" (Bulletin de
l'École Française de l'Extrême Orient, vol. IX page 441) that the famous bibliophile Lu Hsin-yüan (陸心源, 1834-1894; cf. E. C. page 545) states in
ch. 39 of his *Ch'ün-shu-chiao-pu* 群書校補 that Liu Hsün's *Yin-chü-
t'ung-i* contains a number of cases which do *not* occur in the present version of the
CYKC; since Lu Hsin-yüan's work is not at my disposal here I am unable to
check this statement.

(7)	..	Hsü Yu-kung	ch. 4, page 49	(Case 62-B) a few alternate characters
(8)	..	Tu Hao	ch. 4, page 51	(Case 25-A) enlarged text
(9)	..	An official	ch. 4, page 54	(Case 59-A) id.
(10)	*Ch'eng-wo*	Sun Mien 孫泗	ch. 5, page 67	enlarged text
(11)	*Chai-chien*	Li Ch'ung	ch. 6, page 90	(Case 4-A) identical
(12)	*Kou-t'e*	Chang Yün-chi	ch. 7, page 101	(Case 20-A) much more elaborate version
(13)	..	P'ei Tzu-yün	ch. 7, page 103	(Case 20-B) two new phrases added at the beginning
(14)	..	Chao Ho	ch. 7, page 102	(Case 67-B) practically identical
(15)	..	Chang Chü	ch. 6, page 94	(Case 18-B) first phrase entirely different (see page 103 below)
(16)	..	Li Nan-kung	ch. 6, page 89	(Case 39-A) Entirely different; Li Nan-kung is not mentioned
(17)	..	Hou Lin 侯臨	ch. 7, page 102	different phrasing

Thus we see that the text of the 17 cases was changed by later editors, sometimes in a rather drastic manner. They also changed the sequence of the cases, after what is called "Chapter 6" in the present version; the sequence of nos. 1-14 corresponds, but that of nos. 15-17 does not tally.

The second Yüan source which provides a general check on the present version of the CYKC is the *Shuo-fu* 說郛, the huge collection of old works assembled towards the end of the Yüan Dynasty by

T'ao Tsung-i 陶宗儀 ; his exact dates are not known, but he was still active in the beginning of the Ming Dynasty [1].

Ch. 20 gives under the title *Hsi-yü-kuei-chien* 晰獄龜鑑 "Magic Mirror for clearing up Judicial Cases" fourteen cases; the category is not indicated, and Cheng K'o's commentary is omitted. The sequence of these cases accords with that of the present version of the CYKC, but the text differs, although not as much as in the case of Liu Hsün's versions.

The following table gives in the first column the name of the person who dealt with the case, in the second the place where the case is found in the present version of the CYKC, in the third—between brackets— the number of the case in the TYPS, while the fourth column indicates briefly where the *Shuo-fu* text differs from the present version.

(1) Hsiang Min-chung	ch. 2, page 16	(Case 1-A)	identical
(2) Ch'ien Chih 錢冶	ch. 2, page 21		alternate readings
(3) Ts'ai Kao	ch. 2, page 23	(Case 52-B)	some different characters
(4) Ch'ien Wei-chi	ch. 3, page 35	(Case 5-B)	practically identical
(5) Su Huan 蘇渙	ch. 3, page 37		one extra phrase at the end
(6) Ma Liang 馬諒	ch. 4, page 59		identical
(7) Hsüeh Yen 薛顏	ch. 5, page 66		identical
(8) Fan Ch'un-jen	ch. 6, page 85	(Case 8-A)	different version
(9) Ch'eng Hao	ch. 6, page 98	(Case 36-A)	practically identical
(10) Chang Yung	ch. 7, page 116	(Case 64-B)	practically identical

[1] The dates and content of the various editions of the *Shuo-fu* are discussed in detail by Ching P'ei-yüan in his excellent article "Étude comparative des diverses éditions du Chouo-fou", in *Scripta Sinica,* Bulletin Bibliographique, Centre Franco-Chinois d'Études Sinologiques, Peking 1946.

(11) Yen Su 燕肅   ch. 8, page 127   identical

(12) Ko Yüan 葛源   ch. 8, page 128   one phrase ad-
                                                            ded at the end

(13) Chou Hang 周沆   ch. 8, page 130   identical

(14) Wang Yen-hsi   ch. 8, page 140   identical
王延禧

Thus we arrive at the conclusion that although the present version of the CYKC reproduces generally the contents of Cheng K'o's original and the main features of the text, the cases were revised—some very drastically—and their sequence changed. As regards Cheng K'o's commentary, this can be checked to a limited extent by comparing the fragmentary passages inserted by the Yüan editor T'ien Tse in his edition of the TYPS, with the commentary as it appears in the present version of the CYKC; such a comparison shows that also the text of the commentary differs considerably. Whether these differences are caused by T'ien Tse re-writing the Yüan text, or by the later editors of the CYKC modifying and expanding the defective Yüan text they had at their disposal, is a problem that must remain undecided until more data will have become available. However this may be, if one remembers in addition that every single case of the TYPS is found in the present version of the CYKC, although Kuei Wan-jung states specifically that he based his work on the *I-yü-chi*, using the CYKC as a supplementary source, one must assume that the later editors of the defective text of the CYKC supplemented lacunae by inserting cases from the TYPS and perhaps also other sources, in order to restore the total of 395 cases mentioned in the descriptions of the CYKC in the two old catalogues mentioned above.

Finally I may add some details about later blockprints of the CYKC in the modern version.

In the first place, the *Mo-hai-chin-hu* version was reprinted ca. 1844 in the *Shou-shan-ko-ts'ung-shu* 守山閣叢書, utilizing the blocks of the former collection; cf. E.C. page 36.

Further, in the 19th century there also appeared several separate blockprints of this same version of the CYKC. The two that I have seen are both based upon a text edited by Hsü Lien in 1835. Hsü Lien 許槤 was an official of the Ministry of Justice, chiefly known as the

compiler of a standard work on jurisprudence, the *Hsing-pu-pi-chao*
刑 部 比 照 . According to his preface he obtained this text in the
same manner as the officials in charge of the Imperial Library; he
says:

"Since the Ming impressions (of the CYKC) lacked half of the contents, I searched for a complete text but could not obtain it until
I located one in the house of Mr. Li (Chang-yü 璋 煜 , styled)
Fang-ch'ih, of Chu-ch'eng (Ch'ing-chou 青 州 , in Shantung),
but the table of contents was missing. I find that Ch'ao Kung-wu's
(*Chün-chai-*) *tu-shu-chih* praises the precise character of this table
of contents; therefore I incessantly searched for it. I found this
table in the *Yung-lo-ta-tien*, then only was my text complete. Now
the biographical section of the *Sung-shih* states that the book counted
20 ch., while both Mr. Li's copy and the *Yung-lo-ta-tien* divide the
text into 8. The twenty chapters of the original text must each have
been devoted to one category (*men*), I do not know at what date some
of these *men* were combined (so as to make 8 ch. in all). If one observes
the (number of) columns (*hang*) and the style of the characters (*k'uan*),
one perceives that (Mr. Li's text) must be a traced copy of a Sung
print; thus this version dates from far back"

顧 明 刻 本 已 佚 其 半 。覓 全 書 不 得 。既 乃 得
之 諸 城 李 君 方 赤 所 。而 無 目 錄 。考 晁 公 武 讀
書 志 。稱 其 目 錄 體 例 并 然 。乃 輾 轉 訪 求 。復 於
永 樂 大 典 中 得 之 。始 成 完 本 。宋 惟 志 作 二 十
卷 。今 方 赤 本 與 大 典 本 並 八 卷 。蓋 原 本 分 二
十 門 。門 各 一 卷 。不 知 何 時 合 并 。觀 二 本 行
款 。知 就 宋 本 繕 錄 。則 由 來 已 久 。

Further on Hsü Lien states:

"At the beginning of the book there ought to be Cheng K'o's
own preface, but this has now been lost. Both versions (i.e. Mr. Li's
and that of the *Yung-lo-ta-tien*) have a preface by a Yüan writer
(i.e. Yü Ying-lung), but that describes the origin of a miscellaneous collection of reprints, it does not belong especially to this book;
therefore I did not arbitrarily include that preface here"

卷首當有克自敍。今未見。各本有元人敍。
乃當時雜刻諸書總敍緣起。不專系是書。故
不屬入。

. As we have seen above, Yü Ying-lung's preface does indeed not belong exclusively to the CYKC; but his remarks apply as well to the CYKC as to the other books he mentions, and they tally with the content of Chao Shih-t'o's colophon—which does belong exclusively to the CYKC. Hsü Lien is probably right in assuming that originally there was a preface by Cheng K'o. But one finds it difficult to agree with his opinion that a traced manuscript supplies sufficient data for deciding that the original was a Sung impression; as is well known, many small details of the calligraphic style of a print are lost in the tracing process.

The Sinological Institute in Leiden has a badly printed popular blockprint of Hsü Lien's edition, published in 1876 by the *Shuang-feng-shu-wu* 雙峰書屋 in Fu-chou 撫州 (Kiangsi Province). The text page measures 104 by 142 mm., and is divided into 11 columns of 20 characters. It begins with a preface dated 1876, written by a minor official called Lü Shih-t'ien 呂世田. He says that he served in the Ministry of Justice together with Jao Yü-ch'eng (饒 玉成, styled Hsin-ch'üan 新泉, mentioned E.C. page 282), who possessed a copy of Hsü Lien's version of the CYKC, which Jao had collated himself, and that they decided to reprint this version. The book consists of four volumes. The first three contain the CYKC with Hsü Lien's preface and Chao Shih-t'o's colophon, collated by Jao Yü-ch'eng. The fourth volume contains a coroner's manual entitled *Hsi-yüan-lu-chieh* 洗冤錄解, written by the Ch'ing scholar Yao Te-yü 姚德豫, and collated by Hsü Lien's friend Li Chang-yü. Finally a small work entitled *Pao-chien-pien* 寶鑑編, containing rhymed extracts from the *Hsi-yüan-lu*, by the Ch'ing scholar Fang Ju-ch'ien 方汝謙.

My own copy is a better block print, published in 1878 for official use by a group of officials of the tribunal of Wu-ch'ang 武昌, in Hopei Province. Fang Ta-shih 方大湜, then Prefect of Wu-ch'ang wrote the title page and added a preface. Then follows Hsü Lien's preface of 1835, and his version of the book itself. The print page measures 123 by 195 mm., and each page counts 9 columns of 24 characters. The book was published in four volumes, and has no other works appended to it; it ends with Chao Shih-t'o's colophon.

III. COURT PROCEDURE IN ANCIENT CHINA

T'ang-yin in the title of our text means literally "in the shadow of the *t'ang* tree". This term is an allusion to the Duke of Shao, Shao-kung 召公, a relative of Wu-wang, the King who ca. 1100 B.C founded the Chou Dynasty. Shao-kung was accustomed to deal with official affairs while sitting under a *kan-t'ang* 甘棠 or wild pear tree. When he had died the people would not have this tree cut down because they wished to preserve it as a relic of this just and benevolent official. Thus the term *t'ang-yin* came to stand for an able and wise official; hence "Parallel Cases solved by Eminent Judges" is a closer rendering of the title *T'ang-yin-pi-shih*.

The image of the judge holding court under a tree harks back to China's remote antiquity. Chou and Han sources state that the Minister of Justice used to hear cases under a *chi* 棘 jujube- or *huai* 槐 accacia-tree [1]. These two trees must have had magic associations that were forgotten at the time when ancient customs and institutions were placed on record, remoulded after Confucianist doctrine and adapted to the organized Chinese state. Han Dynasty commentators state that since the inside (*hsin* 心) of the *chi* wood is red (*ch'ih* 赤), it points to *ch'ih-hsin*, "completely honest heart", that should be displayed by all persons appearing before the judge [2]. And as regards the *huai* tree, they connect *huai* with the homonym *kuei* 歸 "to return", and explain it as referring to the fact that before the judge everything is reduced (*kuei*) to the simple truth [3].

---

[1] *Ch'un-ch'iu-yüan-ming-pao* 春秋元命苞 (a work of the Han Dynasty that survives only in fragments): 樹棘槐而聽訟其下. Cf. further *Chou-li*, under the heading *Ch'ao-shih* 朝士, and *Li-chi*, ch. *Wang-chih* 王制, section 4.

[2] Cf. the commentary by Cheng Hsüan (鄭玄 127-200 A.D.) on the *Li-chi* passage referred to in note 1.

[3] *Ch'un-ch'iu-yüan-ming-pao:* 槐之言歸也。情見歸實也。

These, however, are evidently secondary explanations. The *I-ching*, the ancient Book of Divination, uses under the hexagram *k'an* 坎 the term *ts'ung-chi* 叢棘 "jujube brush" in the sense of "prison", and *chi-szu* 棘寺, *chi-szu* 棘司 and *chi-yüan* 棘院, all of which mean literally "jujube office" have remained common terms referring to a court of justice—in later times more especially the High Court in the capital. Further, the places where the literary examinations were held were surrounded by a hedge of *chi* trees, *chi-chiang* 棘牆 of *chi-wei* 棘圍. All these terms have survived to the present day. From these data one would conclude that in archaic times the *chi* tree was credited with magic properties that made it especially suited for marking off a taboo area, the Greek τεμενος. The same would apply to the *huai* tree. The formation of the character itself—being composed of *mu* 木 "tree" and *kuei* 鬼 "ghost"—points to magic properties; *kuei* would hardly have been chosen for its phonetic value only.

Other important accessories of the place where justice was dispensed in high antiquity were two stones, called *fei-shih* 肺石 "lung stone" and *chia-shih* 嘉石 "beautiful stone". The *Chou-li* says under the heading Ta-szu-k'ou that the *fei-shih* was a stone slab on which persons who denounced their superiors had to sit in order to show their sincerity. The commentary explains this by the fact that in the ancient system of cosmic correspondences of the human body, the lungs stand for "south" and "fire"; since fire is red (*ch'ih* 赤), the term *fei-shih* is taken to refer to *ch'ih-hsin* "the completely honest heart" [1]. As regards the *chia-shih*, mentioned under the same heading in the *Chou-li*, the commentary observes "(A stone) with a beautiful grain is called *chia*, hence we know that the *chia-shih* was a beautifully grained stone. The intention was to make depraved persons reflect on its beautiful grain and thereby repent and mend

---

[1] 周禮疏：肺屬南方火。火色赤。肺亦赤。故知名肺石是赤石也。必使之坐赤石者。使之赤心不妄告也。

their ways" [1]. It goes without saying that these also are secondary explanations. The two stones must have been connected with ancient trials by ordeal, such as for instance the walking over red-hot stones and other physical tests resembling those found in old Teutonic law. This seems all the more probable since in ancient China the decision of difficult judicial cases was often left to divine judgement. It is related about Kao Yao 皐陶, the Minister of Justice of the mythical Emperor Shun, that he employed a one-horned ram which indicated the guilty party by butting it while leaving the innocent in peace (see below, p. 53 note 1).

Be this as it may, the archaic terms mentioned above passed into the literary language as elegant expressions referring to court procedure. I mention the oft-quoted couplet from an essay by Wang Yung (王融 467-493 A.D.) which says:

"On the *lung-stone* there are few who are not suffering under a wrong;

"Under the *jujube-tree* there are many ghosts wailing in the night" [2]

This couplet is i.a. referred to by Kuei Wan-jung in his preface to the TYPS (see page 73 below).

As to the actual conduct of cases in ancient times, some data may be derived from the chapter *Lü-hsing* 呂刑 in the *Shu-ching*, the "Book of Documents". Here we find, for instance, the term *yü* 獄, which has remained till the present day the most common literary expression for "court case". This character is composed of the element *yen* 言 "speech" between two *ch'uan* 犬 "dogs". Since these elements appear in the oldest forms of this character that are known, it must be assumed that it represented the two contesting parties in a law case as a pair of dogs angrily barking at each other. It should be noted that all old documents refer to cases brought before the judge by two contesting parties, and belonging to a fairly high social level [3]; one does not find data relating to the clan or the state pro-

---

[1] 有文乃稱嘉。故知文石也。欲使罷民思其文理以改悔自修。

[2] 肺石少不冤之人。棘林多夜哭之鬼。

[3] This appears clearly from H. Maspéro's excellent study "Le serment dans la procedure judiciaire de la Chine antique" (Mélanges chinois et bouddhiques,

ceeding against an offender. Presumably such cases were dealt with in a very summary manner. *Yü* 獄 also means "prison", which justifies the conclusion that in archaic times, exactly as later, the court and the prison were located in one and the same place.

This brief introductory note may be concluded with a few passages from the *Lü-hsing* and the *Chou-li* which have become *loci classici* in Chinese legal literature, and which are quoted in the prefaces to the TYPS.

The *Lü-hsing* tersely describes the conduct of a case as follows:

"When both (parties) have appeared fully prepared (sc. with testimonies), the court assessors (listen to =) deal with the five (kinds of) pleading. When by the five (kinds of) pleading one has ascertained and verified (the guilt), one attributes (the case) to (one of) the five punishments; if the five punishments are not ascertained =) found adequate, one attributes it to one of the five redemption fines; if the five redemption fines are not applicable, one attributes it to the five cases of errors" [1]

兩 造 具 備。師 聽 五 辭。五 辭 簡 孚。正 于 五 刑。
五 刑 不 簡。正 于 五 罰。五 罰 不 服。正 于 五 過。

And further:

"In doubtful cases of the five punishments there is condoning; in doubtful cases of the five redemption fines there is condoning. May you investigate it. You should ascertain and verify and (have the multitude =) act in concert with public opinion; you should (hair-finely =) minutely make investigation. If (the guilt) is not ascertained, you should not (listen to =) deal with (the case). You should all stand in awe of Heaven's majesty" [2].

五 刑 之 疑 有 赦。五 罰 之 疑 有 赦.其 審 克 之。
簡 孚 有 眾。惟 貌 有 稽。無 簡 不 聽。具 嚴 天 威。

Another much-quoted passage occurs in the *Chou-li*, under the

publ. by "Institut Belge des Hautes Études Chinoises", vol. III (1934-35), Brussels 1935, where i.a. the high deposits are mentioned which the contestants had to make.

[1] Translation of B. Karlgren, "The Book of Documents", in Bulletin of the Museum of Far Eastern Antiquities 22, Stockholm 1950.

[2] Same remark as in preceding note.

heading Hsiao-szu-k'ou, describing how a judge should probe the real sentiments of the persons appearing before him:

"The judge examines (lit.: listens to) criminal cases by the five expressions (lit.: the five sounds), and so obtains the real sentiments of the people (appearing before him). The five expressions are: first, examining their speech; second, examining their facial expression; third, examining their breathing (i.e. whether it gives clues to their emotion); fourth, examining their ears (i.e. their reactions to what they hear from the judge), and fifth: examining their eyes" [1].

以 五 聲 聽 獄 訟 . 求 民 情 。一 曰 辭 聽 。二 曰 色 聽 。三 曰 氣 聽 。四 曰 耳 聽 。五 曰 目 聽 。

Although the implications of the terms and phrases employed in these texts are far from clear, they have been quoted throughout the centuries by almost every author who wrote on court procedure. Ill-defined as they are, the ancient terms, hallowed by age, have thus become part and parcel of Chinese legal language. But through the mass of later explanations and interpretations we can still perceive, however dimly, some distinctive features of the administration of justice in archaic times. Although in the *Lü-hsing* and the *Chou-li* the judicial authority of the sovereign is delegated to officials specially charged with the administration of justice, and although the paraphernalia of the archaic court, such as the jujube- and accacia-tree and the two stones, are forcibly transferred from the seat of tribal justice in the open to the royal palace and allocated a place in the later highly-developed state-ritual, the spirit that pervades these texts is still that of the Priest-King of hoary antiquity, holding court in the open, in the shade of a tree.

As regards the provincial court room and court procedure from ca. 200 B.C. till the 12th century A.D.—the period covered by the cases recorded in the TYPS—we have but scant material at our disposal. Chinese writers of those periods concentrated their attention on the higher organs of justice in the capital, where the aura emanating from the Throne and the glamour of high office tended to gloss over the in-auspicious nature of the business conducted there. But they studious-

---

[1] Cf. E. Biot, *Le Tcheou-li ou Rites des Tcheou* (Paris 1851, reprinted Peking 1939), vol. II, page 319-320.

ly ignored the district tribunals in the provinces which showed crime and punishment in their stark reality. Yet it was those tribunals that brought the common people into direct contact with the Imperial laws and their enforcement, and which as such played an important role in the daily life of the Chinese people.

Next to the items of information scattered over the old case books, practically the only other source of reliable information are the pictures of the "Judges of Hell" which occupied a prominent place in Buddhist and Taoist iconography; for the artists who painted those modeled their pictures of the tribunal of the Nether World after the courtrooms of their own time [1].

Detailed descriptions of the district tribunal and its paraphernalia are found only in later literary sources, especially in crime novels and theatre pieces of the Ming and Ch'ing periods, where the subject matter made regular reference to court procedure unavoidable [2]. The accounts in Ming sources can be verified and amplified by the testimony of those Western writers who visited China in that period and who had the misfortune to come into personal contact with Chinese tribunals [3], while for the Ch'ing period we have many descriptions left by 19th century Western observers [4].

---

[1] Cf., for instance, the pictures of the *Fo-shuo-shih-wang-ching* 佛說十王經 ; a picture from a T'ang manuscript of this source is reproduced in my book "Dee Goong An, Three Murder Cases solved by Judge Dee" (Tokyo 1949), opposite page XX of the Introduction.

[2] Cf. my book "Dee Goong An" mentioned in the preceding note. This is a translation of the 18th century crime novel *Wu-tse-t'ien-szu-ta-ch'i-an* 武則天四大奇案 ; the scene of this story is laid in the T'ang Dynasty, but the judicial system described is that of the Ming period.

[3] Cf. C. R. Boxer, "South China in the Sixteenth Century, being the narratives of Galeote Pereira, Fr. Gaspar da Cruz O.P., Fr. Martin de Rada O.E.S.A. (1550-1575)", Hakluyt Society, London 1953, pp. 17-25, 163-185, 199-203, and 297-304. Also "Verhaal van het vergaan van het jacht De Sperwer (1656-1663)" by Hendrik Hamel (Linschoten Vereeniging, vol. XVIII, The Hague 1920), pp. 16-17 which give a graphic account of the experiences of Dutch sailors in a local Korean tribunal—which was modelled on those in Ming China.

[4] Cf. i.a. the Rev. Justus Doolittle, "Social Life of the Chinese", 2 vls. New York 1865, vol. II pp. 335-352. There, however, the shortcomings of the system are grossly exaggerated; it must be remembered that most books published by missionaries of that time stressed the shadow side of Chinese affairs. Moreover the pictures of Chinese punishments imported from Canton and published i.a. by G. H. Mason in his "The punishments of China" (London, William Miller 1804) enjoyed great popularity in Europe and further spread the ideas about excessive

A comparison of those data of the Ming and Ch'ing periods with those of the preceding dynasties proves that the ancient courtroom and its paraphernalia were, *mutatis mutandis*, essentially not much different. The general description which follows hereunder is based on a combination of old and later data, with special stress on those features which occur in the cases recorded in the TYPS.

In the local tribunals, court room and court procedure were primarily intended to impress everyone with the majesty of the law, and with the dreadful consequences of becoming involved with it. The presiding magistrate combined in his person all administrative, executive and judicial power in the district. Since he had practically full authority over all phases of the life of the people entrusted to his care, he is often referred to as *mu* 牧, the "pastor" of the people, or *fu-mu-kuan* 父母官 "father-and-mother official". When the court was in session the magistrate, decked out with the full regalia of his office, sat behind a high bench covered with red cloth and standing on an elevated dais; he was a forbidding figure, throning high above all that happened in the court below.

On the bench stood the objects regularly used by the magistrate and symbolizing his authority. In the first place the large square seal of the tribunal, wrapped up in brocade; no official was deemed to have executive powers before he had solemnly taken over this seal from his predecessor. When not in use this seal was kept in a special small shrine. Further the judge had before him a stave of hardwood of about one foot long which served as gavel; in later literature this gavel is significantly referred to as *ching-t'ang-mu* 驚堂木 "Wood that startles the hall". There were also two writing

Chinese cruelty; but these pictures, and also those published by Doolittle, are reproductions of Chinese "rice-paper pictures", made in Canton especially for the foreign market and catering to the public demand for sensation. Hamel's account mentioned in the preceding note failed to become popular in Europe because it did not contain enough horrors; (cf. P. A. Tiele, "Mémoire bibliographique sur les journaux des navigateurs néerlandais", Amsterdam 1867, page 275: "Les meurtres & autres excès sont bien plus rares dans ce récit que dans celui du voyage de Pelsaert. Aussi est-il devenu beaucoup moins populaire"). A much more balanced account of the Chinese administration of justice in the later part of the Ch'ing Dynasty is found in E. Alabaster "Notes and Commentaries on Chinese Criminal Law", 1 vol., London 1899. In recent years there appeared a number of sound Chinese, Japanese and Western studies on the subject; these are described in the bibliographical notes in Escarra's "Le Droit Chinois", and Hulsewé, op.cit.

brushes, resting on a stand shaped like a diminutive mountain with three peaks; one brush was for writing notes in black ink, the other for making notes in red ink. Further a double ink slab for preparing the black and red ink. These are the regular paraphernalia which appear on the bench, clearly discernible on pictures of as early as the T'ang dynasty. Copies of the Code and other books of legal reference are conspicuous by their absence.

In later times there was a canopy over the dais, called *nuan-ko* 煖閣 ; but this does not appear in older pictures.

The high bench was flanked on either side by a lower table behind which sat two or more scribes, or, in the case of larger tribunals, lower officials of the district administration.

Behind the judge stood a large screen, and smaller ones behind the tables of his assistants. Formerly those side screens were called *tung-ch'iang* 東 牆 "Eastern wall" and *hsi-chi'ang* 西 牆 "Western wall"; since the magistrate as a rule sat facing South, the former was at his right hand, the latter at his left. These three screens appear on pictures of the T'ang, Sung and Ming periods. As to the older times we know that in the Han Dynasty the courtroom was decorated with a painted picture of the *hsieh-chai* 獬 豸, the one-horned ram of Kao Yao that could distinguish between good and evil [1]; probably this picture was painted on the large screen behind the judge [2].

---

[1] The philosopher Wang Ch'ung (王 充 27 — ca. 97 A.D.) says in his *Lun-heng* 論 衡 , ch. 17 section 2: "At present the *hsieh-chai* of Kao Yao is depicted in court rooms. The literati say that this animal is a one-horned ram that naturally recognizes guilty persons. If Kao Yao when hearing a case had doubts about who was the guilty party, he let that ram butt them; it would butt the guilty, but not the innocent" 今 府 廷 畫 皐 陶 觟 𧣴 也 。 儒 者 說 云 觟 𧣴 者 一 角 之 羊 也 . 性 知 有 罪 。 皐 陶 治 獄 其 罪 疑 者 。 令 羊 觸 之 。有 罪 則 觸 。無 罪 則 不 觸 。

[2] In the Ming Dynasty one finds on the screen behind the judge a picture of the jade mountain rising from the waves, one of the twelve traditional symbols of Imperial authority; but in the Ch'ing Dynasty this was replaced by the old image of the one-horned ram, disguised as the *ch'i-lin* 麒 麟 , the unicorn symbolizing universal benevolence. Throughout the Ming and Ch'ing dynasties the *hsieh-chai* appeared on the square "mandarin badges" on the robes of judicial

In that same period judicial officials wore special caps called *hsieh-chai-kuan* 獬豸冠 which were modeled after the head of the one-horned ram [1].

The tribunal was open for law cases from autumn till spring, but it dealt with administrative affairs of the district throughout the year. All sessions were open for the general public, and all the business conducted *coram populo*.

As a rule the court formed part of the compound that housed the offices of the district administration, the private residence of the magistrate, and also the prison; ordinarily the prison adjoined the courtroom. These prisons were dismal places, the inmates were kept in chains all the time, and for their food had to depend largely on what was sent them by relatives and friends outside; as a consequence the rate of mortality among the prisoners was high. The doors of the prison bore the pictures of a pair of fierce mythical animals called *p'i-han* 狴犴 [2]; hence their name has become a common

officials; cf. Schuyler Cammann, "Chinese Mandarin Squares", in: University Museum Bulletin (Philadelphia, June 1953) vol. 17, no. 3, page 22, and figure 21.

[1] Cf. *Hou-han-shu* 後漢書, the section "Carriages and apparel" 輿服志, where it is said: "Judicial officials wear a Judge's Cap, also called *hsieh-chai* cap; the *hsieh-chai* is a divine ram that can distinguish between right and wrong" 法冠執法者服之。或謂之獬豸冠。獬豸神羊。能別曲直。The philosopher Huai-nan-tzu (准南子 died 122 B.C.) calls this cap *hsieh-kuan* 獬冠; the commentator Kao Yu 高誘 fl. ca. 200 A.D.) observes: "The *hsieh-chai* cap resembles the cap worn at present by Censors" 獬豸之冠如今御史冠. Cf. also A. & W. Eberhard, "Die Mode der Han- und Chin-Zeit" (Antwerp 1946), page 54.

[2] Although *p'i-han* as a term for "prison" occurs already in sources of the Han period, I could find no contemporary descriptions of these animals. In the Ming Dynasty *p'i-han* carved in stone or wood were placed at the entrance of the prison. The prolific Ming writer Yang Shen (楊慎 1488-1559) says in his *Sheng-an-wai-chi* 升菴外集: "The dragon has nine sons, the fourth of these is called *p'i-han*. In shape it resembles a tiger, it is impressive and forceful, therefore its image is set up at prison gates" 龍生九子。四曰狴犴。形似虎.有威力。故立於獄門. According to another Ming writer, the great poet Li Tung-yang (李東陽 1447-1516), the *p'i-han*

term for "prison" and "prison official". When the magistrate wished to hear a prisoner he would issue a wooden tally marked with the man's name to the keeper of the jail who then went and brought the prisoner before the bench.

While the magistrate was supported by all the pomp and circumstance of his office, court procedure placed everyone who appeared before him in a most disadvantageous and humiliating position. The accused had to kneel on the bare floor, far below the judge, and remain thus throughout the proceedings. Close by his side stood the *li* 吏, the constables, carrying their awe-inspiring paraphernalia, traditionally called *san-mu* 三木, the "three wooden instruments"; these were the cangue (*chia* 枷), manacles (*ch'ou* 杻) and fetters (*lao* 橑). The constables also carried flat bamboo staves used for meting out the punishment of bambooing (*chang* 杖) and whips of leather thongs (*pien* 鞭) or rattan (*ch'ih* 笞). Bamboo and whips were also used freely during the interrogation in order to urge an accused to confess, and further any time the accused, accuser or one of the witnesses said or did something that displeased the judge. The constables were both feared and despised by the people in general. Few decent persons would take this office, the constables were mostly rogues ready to abuse their power and to extort money from everyone who came to the tribunal. The magistrate had to supervise them strictly and often had them flogged themselves for breaches of discipline and other offenses. Boxer quotes a Portuguese observer of the 16th century who states that most constables were covered with scars from bamboo and whip and that they were proud of these, considering them as a kind of indispensable badge of their trade (op. cit. page 168). The famous Sung judge Pao Ch'eng was especially known for his severity towards the constables—who yet succeeded in deceiving him, as is related in Case 46-A. Being treated harshly themselves, they were completely merciless towards the prisoners and all other persons appearing before the bench.

only survived in the lion-heads depicted or placed on prison gates; he says in his *Huai-lu-t'ang-chi* 懷麓堂集 : "The *p'i-han* by nature love law-suits, the lion-heads one sees at present on prison gates are remnants of their full shape" 狴犴平生好訟。今獄門上獅子頭。是其遺象.

The guiding principle of the judge in dealing with a case was to assume every accused guilty as long as he had not proved himself innocent. As far as I know this principle is not laid down in so many words in Chinese legal literature, but it becomes distressingly clear from the case books. This principle is not based so much on harshness as on the idea that no really good citizen will ever become involved with the law; even a completely innocent person being falsely accused is guilty already in so far that he is a party to a disturbance of the peace in the district—which is an affront to the magistrate's administration. Moreover, it is held against him that his conduct was apparently not so blameless that wicked persons could not get a hold on him, or at any rate that he did not choose his acquaintances and associates with due discretion. If the official attitude to innocent persons was already so harsh it can be imagined how real criminals were treated. One need not wonder, therefore, that everyone brought before the tribunal is referred to as *ch'iu* 囚 "the prisoner", even before his case has been heard.

The principle of assuming *a priori* the guilt of an accused is one of the factors that brought into being the fixed custom of beating an accused—and often beating him cruelly—as soon as he denies his guilt. This custom, observed throughout the centuries, appears to Western students one of the most reprehensible aspects of Chinese court procedure. Another fact that gave occasion to beatings and other tortures in court was the old-established rule that no criminal could be convicted unless he had admitted his guilt; this necessitated the application of torture if a hardened criminal refused to confess even when confronted with irrefutable evidence. Wanton or lazy magistrates were all the more tempted to indulge in excessive beatings because whereas the law required them to report all cases involving one of the heavier punishments to the higher authorities, it allowed them to sentence a person to an unlimited number of strokes with bamboo or whip and to have that punishment executed, entirely on their own authority. Thus they might try to obtain a quick confession by torture, or they might even have a person purposely beaten to death if a case became too complicated or disclosed facts which the magistrate preferred to conceal from the higher authorities; such a death could be explained as having resulted from illness.

Even when conducted by conscientious judges the interrogation with legal severities often led to serious miscarriage of justice. This fact becomes abundantly clear from the case books. Phrases such as "he wrongly confessed because he could not stand the questioning under torture" 不勝楚掠乃自誣服 occur there with disconcerting frequency; cf. TYPS Case 1-A, 2-A, 7-A, 27-A, 30-A, 30-B, 33-A, 33-B, 34-B, 44-A, and 64-A. Especially the beatings with the heavy bamboo were very severe. Gaspar da Cruz is quoted by Boxer as saying: "They give the stripes on the hams of the man's legs, being laid on his breast, and his legs laid along, and his hands tied behind. These stripes are very cruel, for the first stripe at once draws blood. One stripe is two blows by the two beadles placed one on each side, each whipping one leg. After two stripes a man can not go on foot, and they pick him up by the arms and legs. And many die after receiving fifty of sixty stripes, for they destroy all the giblets of the hams" (op. cit. page 178). Da Cruz says further that many preferred to kill themselves in prison prior to being interrogated in court; for older times this is attested by Case 30-B of the TYPS.

Buddhist and Taoist monks found themselves before the tribunal in a position still more unfavourable than that of other accused persons. Since most of the magistrates and judges were confirmed Confucianists, they had little sympathy for Buddhism and Taoism, and were more than ever inclined to assume their guilt *a priori*. Also the compilers of the case books took the Confucianist view, and hence we find Buddhist monks and Taoist adepts depicted there in the darkest colours; in all cases dealing with Buddhist affairs (cf. Case 24-A, 24-B, 29-B, 38-A, 57-B, 58-B) the monks are the villains, and Taoist adepts and their disciplines do not fare much better (Case 6-B, 14-A, 53-A). This attitude is reflected also in later Chinese crime stories and detective novels, where especially Buddhist monks are as a rule depicted as profligate and lecherous rascals, and their temples the seats of secret iniquities.

Finally, while all persons appearing in Court were held to tell the truth and nothing but the truth, the magistrate had full freedom to act on hearsay evidence, and to deceive, intimidate and insult everyone connected with a case. The accused could not choose his own witnesses, and legal counsel did not exist. Shouted at and reviled by the magistrate, growled at and beaten by the constables, the position of the accused was a most unfavourable one indeed. Small wonder that having to appear in court was considered by the people at large as a terrible misfortune, an experience to be avoided if at all possible. Although it must be admitted that this fear of the tribunal acted as a deterrent to prospective criminals, it also estranged the people from the local authorities. In general people tried to settle their differences as much as possible out of court, by effecting a compromise or by referring the case to one of the age-old organs of private justice, for example the council of the family- or clan-elders, or the leaders of a guild.

Since the formalities of court procedure—arrest, submission of proof, indictment, various punishments etc. —have been described already in detail by Hulsewé, op cit. pp. 71 sq., here we need not go further into those. Here I add only a few details about some practical aspects of court procedure, referred to in cases in the TYPS.

While the court procedure in many ways encouraged abuses by cruel or inefficient judges, it also impeded the task of conscientious magistrates. Seated behind his high bench, the judge could not see or hear clearly the persons kneeling on the floor below. This was no mean handicap since the judge in order to form an opinion on a person's character relied to a large degree on his facial expression and his voice. Physiognomy, in China called *hsiang-fa* 相 法 is a very old and highly developed science in China, and throughout the centuries judges have set great store by it as a means for detecting falsehood, as attested by the passage from the *Chou-li* quoted on page 50 above. They also found support for the validity of this means of detection in the phrase *wei-mao-yu-chi* 惟 貌 有 稽 occurring in the *Lü-hsing* (cf. page 49 above). In this phrase *mao* is doubtless a phonetic loan for *mao* 緢 "hair", hence Karlgren's translation "You should (hair-finely=) minutely make investigation". But the traditional interpretation takes *mao* in its literal sense of "appearance" and reads: "The appearance of the accused must be investigated". As late as the 18th century the author of a famous handbook for magistrates calls examination of a person's features the first step in deciding a case [1]. As regards

---

[1] Cf. the *Hsüeh-chih-i-shuo* 學 治 臆 說 by Wang Hui-tsu (汪 輝 祖 1731-1807), the section entitled "In hearing a case investigation of the features (of the accused) comes first" 治 獄 以 色 聽 爲 先 . Wang's biography is given in E.C., page 824; there his *Hsüeh-chih-i-shuo* and another book of similar

the importance attached to the voice of suspected persons, this is again attested by the passage from the *Chou-li* mentioned above, and further illustrated by Case 16-A of the TYPS.

Further, the old-established rule—existing already in the Han Dynasty—that no magistrate could be appointed in his own native district must often have impeded the hearing of a case. The rule was well-meant: it aimed at preventing a magistrate from being influenced by local connections. However, his unfamiliarity with the local situation, and more especially with the local dialect, would often compel him to rely during the hearing of a case on the advice and intermediary of the lower court personnel—who were locally recruited and hence not free from bias. The dialect situation in old China is a problem as yet insufficiently explored, but it may be assumed that e.g. in the Han Dynasty there did already occur cases where a magistrate could not understand the speech of the persons brought before him, especially if they belonged to the lower social strata. At any rate the custom of voluntarily submitting written statements when appearing before the judge must have in part originated from the difficulty in making oneself clearly heard, and in the necessity of eliminating the difficulties caused by differences in dialect.

The case books relate how diligent magistrates tried to eliminate these handicaps. In order to obtain a clear view of a person's features they would lean over the bench and make the man look up at them (Case 64-B). And if they could not hear what the accused said or suspected secret interference from the lower court personnel, the magistrate would descend from his high seat and question the accused face to face, as described in Case 69-B. Moreover, it is told of nearly every famous judge of former times that he often went out in disguise in order to verify personally the facts of a case.

It must be added that conscientious judges in order to arrive at the truth relied on their native wit, their shrewd reasoning and—above all—on their profound knowledge of human nature, rather than on the means of coercion which the law placed at their disposal. The case books give many instances also of this lighter side of the picture. The TYPS records many cases which were cleverly solved without the application of torture or other forms of pressure; cf. for example

character written by him are called "two celebrated works on government which, until the establishment of the Republic (1912) were regarded as indispensable guides to local administrative officers".

Case 9-A, 10-B, 16-B, 26-A, 26-B, 33-A, 33-B, 35-A, 35-B, 40-B, 43-B, 45-A, 46-B, 49-B, 52-A, 52-B, 55-B, 57-A, 57-B, and 60-A; also the Solomon's judgements related in Case 4-B and 14-B.

In this connection I may mention also that although the old Chinese judges lacked as a matter of course the technical aids for crime-detection developed in modern Western criminology, they derived considerable assistance from the traditional Chinese sciences. Every scholar-official had a nodding acquaintance with medicine and pharmacology and hence knew some elementary medical facts (cf. Case 5-B, 6-A, 18-B) and the drugs and poisons available to the average criminal (cf. Case 39-A and B). As regards the more specialized aspects of forensic medicine, the magistrate could rely on the advice of the *wu-tso* 仵 作 or "coroner", a locally recruited officer who usually combined his position in the tribunal with the private enterprise of funeral undertaker. These coroners had a wide and varied experience and often achieved remarkable results by very primitive means [1].

In order to complete the lighter side of the picture drawn here of old Chinese court procedure, a few words must be said on the controlling factors that checked abuses of judicial authority.

In the first place, public opinion was a factor all magistrates had to reckon with. All cases except those of high treason were tried in public, from the preliminary hearings till the pronouncement of the sentence. Literary sources occasionally refer to secret interrogations inside the prison, but those are always branded as an evil practice of depraved

---

[1] Some striking examples will be found in the *Hsi-yüan-lu*, the 13th century coroner's manual described on page 18 above, note 4.

As regards Chinese methods of detection, it is a puzzling point that the old Chinese never utilized the finger print as a means for identifying a criminal, although they had ample occasion for making this discovery. Since the seal impression played a paramount role in authenticating documents, the detection of false seals had at an early date already developed into a highly specialized technique, every minute detail of the lines of the impression being scrutinized with meticulous care. Now the thumb print was used in the same manner as a seal, because the Chinese were perfectly aware that the finger print of each person has its own individual design that is apparent even to the naked eye. Thus it required but one step to realize that a murderer who leaves a bloody finger print on for example the wooden hilt of a knife, the plaster wall, or some other surface where the print can be analysed without technical aids, thereby as it were signs his name to the crime; an unknown criminal could of course not be tracked by such a print, but it could at least be compared with the finger prints of one or more suspects. But as yet I have found no indication that in the olden days Chinese judges ever used this simple means of identification.

magistrates and condemned in the strongest terms. It is eloquent proof of the democratic spirit of the Chinese that public opinion constituted one of the main checks on judicial abuses; the *Lü-hsing* already states that "judges should act in concert with public opinion" (cf. page 49 above), and the case books often record with satisfaction at the end of a case that "the people approved of this verdict". If a magistrate was manifestly unjust or unnecessarily cruel, the people of his district would by passive resistance sabotage the administration, which was an effective means for attracting the attention of the higher authorities to the situation.

A second check was that all proceedings relating to more serious cases had to be recorded in detail and forwarded to the higher authorities. Statements by accused and witnesses and the decisions of the judge were written down *in extenso* by the court clerks. The lack of stenography presented no difficulties, for the Chinese literary language is in itself a kind of shorthand; several long sentences in the colloquial can be accurately summed up in the literary idiom in one phrase of four characters, and these four characters can moreover be written in an abbreviated cursive style. Experienced court clerks could therefore keep notes of everything said. The rule that all court proceedings had to be recorded obtained already in the Han Dynasty, a time when wooden tablets were still the common material for writing. Hulsewé quotes a source of ca. 100 B.C. where it is stated that an official who had opposed the verdict left the court with an armful of inscribed wooden tablets relating to the case (op. cit. page 73). These case records were carefully studied by the various higher government agencies which they had to pass on their way upwards to the metropolitan judicial and administrative centers. If the officials concerned did not do so out of a sense of duty, then at least because the discovery of a mistake by a lower judicial official would be entered to the credit of the man who found it and improve his chances for promotion.

The case books show clearly how thoroughly the higher authorities investigated the case records passed on to them. A substantial number of the cases assembled in the TYPS consists of re-trials, instituted because the official who studied the records of such cases "conceived doubts". If they found a mistake, disciplinary action was taken against the responsible magistrate and, in the case of serious miscarriage of justice, the offending official was heavily punished according to the principle of *fan-tso* 反 坐 . This implies that the man who wrongly accused a person shall suffer the same punishment as the wronged person would have received if the accusation had been true. In this connection it should be noted that the magistrate's position of wellnigh absolute power and complete superiority over all persons brought before his bench was but borrowed glory, based not on his personal rank but solely derived from the prestige of the system he was temporarily appointed to represent. The law was inviolable, but not the judge who enacted it. All judicial officials enjoyed their special position only as long as the government allowed; they could claim for themselves no immunity or any special privileges on the basis of their office. As soon as a higher authority found fault with a judge, he was summarily divested of all his power and authority, and immediately reduced to the sorry state of "prisoner" before a tribunal, kneeling on the bare floor and beaten and insulted by the constables—until he had justified his conduct.

One need not wonder, therefore, that the officials of district and prefecture when confronted with a difficult case often preferred to refer it to a higher authority so as not to burn their fingers. Hence the frequent occurrence in the case books of the phrase "Neither prefect nor district magistrate could solve the case and referred it to the capital".

Moreover, next to the government also the accused himself or his relatives could apply for a re-trial, but only to a judicial authority higher than the one who had dealt with the case. Re-trial on the same administrative level was apparently not permitted; Case 67-B describes how a magistrate had to evolve a complicated scheme in order to be able to deal with a case that had already been disposed of by his colleague in the neighbouring district. Cf. also, however, Case 20-A.

Finally it must be remembered that in the Chinese governmental hierarchy promotion was largely based on actual performance. Nepotism and political favouritism did also play a role, but mainly in the higher strata of the administration. A conscientious and diligent judicial official could reasonably expect regular promotion, whereas inefficient or wantonly cruel ones risked their position, if not their very life. Since appointments in the lower and middle strata lasted an average of three years, most judicial officials tried to acquit themselves of their duties as well as they could—hoping to be promoted in due course to a less onerous and risky position.

Therefore it can be stated that, all circumstances considered, the old Chinese judicial system worked tolerably well. As I remarked already elsewhere [1], the most flagrant violations of the principles of justice recorded in Chinese history concerned cases of political and religious persecution—and in this respect our own record in the West is none too clean.

The most serious shortcoming was that the system functioned satisfactorily only under a strong central government. During the periods of turmoil and political confusion that intervened between the great dynasties the central authority temporarily disintegrated, and the executive prerogative shifted from the center to local civil and military officials. In such times the normal checks ceased to operate, and the administration of justice became very summary, if not arbitrary; I refer, for instance, to Case 14-B of the TYPS. But who are we, Westerners of this advanced age, to criticize such abnormal conditions in times of stress? Case 44-B, describing how in the 10th century under the military dictator of Szuchuan Province the entire population was in the iron grip of the secret state police, and "no one dared to say a word fearing lest the man standing by his side was a secret agent" have still so familiar a ring for us in the West that one hesitates to pronounce hasty judgements.

The 144 cases recorded in the TYPS give a good idea of the great variety of cases dealt with by the lower and higher courts of justice; they run through the entire scale of civil and criminal cases, from disputes about one sheet of silk and the theft of onions till first degree murder and high treason.

This variety seems intentional. Kuei Wan-jung apparently wished to place before his judicial colleagues at least one example of each of the more common crimes and offenses, so as to make his book as complete a manual as possible. Therefore the TYPS presents an instructive cross-cut through Chinese daily life and its problems. Next to the familiar themes of murder, theft, robbery, disputes about land and inheritance suits, one finds there also peculiarly Chinese cases relating to lack in filial piety—in old China a capital crime (Case 14-A, 14-B and 25-A), to magic (Case 27-A, 53-A) or solved by supernatural means (Case 29-A and B, 44-A), while in the passages on jurisprudence the degree of implication of the criminal's relatives—of supreme im-

[1] On page XXIII of the Introduction of "Dee Goong An" (cf. p. 51, note 1).

portance in Chinese law—receives special attention (Case 58-A, 59-A, 61-A, 62-B, 63-B). These typical Chinese features shed interesting light on the differences between Western and Chinese customs and behaviour.

On the other hand a perusal of this case book at the same time focusses attention on striking similarities; for instance, there as here the well known trio passion, greed and revenge prove to constitute the main motives leading to capital crimes. Thus this 13th century document underlines again the fundamental uniformity of human nature regardless of colour and race—a truth that can never be sufficiently stressed.

THE CONTENTS OF THE T'ANG-YIN-PI-SHIH, ARRANGED IN CHRONOLOGICAL ORDER

Pre-Han: 12-B, 16-A

Western Han (Hsi-han) 206 B.C.-24 A.D.: 3-B, 4-B, 25-B, 35-B, 43-A, 61-B

Eastern Han (Tung-han) 25-220 A.D.: 16-B, 41-A, 46-B, 66-B

Eastern Wu (Tung-wu) 220-280 A.D.: 18-B, 57-A, 60-A, 68-B

Former Wei (Ch'ien-wei) 220-265 A.D.: 32-A, 32-B, 49-B, 70-B, 72-B

Former Chin (Ch'ien-chin) 265-316 A.D.: 2-A

Eastern Chin (Tung-chin) 317-420 A.D.: 42-A

Northern Wei (Pei-wei) 386-534 A.D.: 4-A, 9-B, 26-B, 27-A, 70-B

Southern Liang (Nan-liang) 502-557 A.D.: 51-B

Former Ch'in (Ch'ien-ch'in) 350-394 A.D.: 29-A, 43-B

Former Sung (Ch'ien-sung) 420-479 A.D.: 18-A, 26-A, 47-B, 61-A, 63-B, 72-A

Southern Ch'i (Nan-ch'i) 479-502 A.D.: 58-B

Northern Ch'i (Pei-ch'i) 550-557 A.D.: 13-A, 19-A, 19-B, 22-B

Northern Chou (Pei-chou) 557-581 A.D.: 13-B, 51-A, 68-A

T'ang 618-907 A.D.: 2-B, 8-B, 14-A, 17-A, 17-B, 20-A, 20-B, 22-A, 24-A, 33-A, 33-B, 35-A, 37-A, 37-B, 38-A, 42-B, 45-A, 49-A, 54-A, 54-B, 57-B, 60-B, 62-A, 62-B, 65-A, 65-B, 67-A, 67-B, 70-A, 71-A, 71-B

Shu Kingdom 907-926 A.D.: 30-A, 44-B

Later Chou (Hou-chou) 915-960 A.D.: 30-B, 53-B

Later T'ang (Hou-t'ang) 923-936 A.D.: 69-B

Southern T'ang (Nan-t'ang) 937-976 A.D.: 44-A

Later Chin (Hou-chin) 936-946 A.D.: 14-B, 24-B, 55-A

Later Han (Hou-han) 947-950 A.D.: 9-A, 64-A

Northern Sung (Pei-sung) 960-1127 A.D.): 1-A, 1-B, 3-A, 5-A, 5-B, 6-A, 6-B, 7-A, 7-B, 8-A, 10-A, 10-B, 11-A, 11-B, 12-A, 15-A, 15-B, 21-A, 21-B, 23-A, 23-B, 25-A, 27-B, 28-A, 28-B, 29-B, 31-A, 31-B, 34-A, 34-B, 36-A, 36-B, 38-B, 39-A, 39-B, 40-A, 40-B, 41-B, 45-B, 46-A, 47-A, 48-A, 48-B, 50-A, 50-B, 52-A, 52-B, 53-A, 55-B, 56-A, 56-B, 58-A, 59-A, 63-A, 64-B, 66-A, 69-A

CONCORDANCE OF WU NO'S ABBREVIATED EDITION OF THE T'ANG-YIN-PI-SHIH, AND THE TRANSLATION OF THE COMPLETE TEXT

Wu No: Case no.	Complete text: Case no.	Wu No: Case no.	Complete text: Case no.
(1)	61-B	(41)	27-B
(2)	14-A	(42)	27-A
(3)	62-A	(43)	45-B
(4)	59-A	(44)	45-A
(5)	11-A	(45)	49-A
(6)	60-B	(46)	56-A
(7)	52-A	(47)	47-A
(8)	5-A	(48)	54-B
(9)	1-B	(49)	15-A
(10)	1-A	(50)	15-B
(11)	7-A	(51)	36-A
(12)	7-B	(52)	10-A
(13)	28-A	(53)	57-A
(14)	16-B	(54)	26-A
(15)	8-A	(55)	60-A
(16)	8-B	(56)	66-B
(17)	23-A	(57)	42-A
(18)	64-A	(58)	42-B
(19)	2-B	(59)	51-A
(20)	2-A	(60)	43-A
(21)	70-A	(61)	18-A
(22)	11-B	(62)	30-A
(23)	18-B	(63)	9-A
(24)	36-B	(64)	9-B
(25)	39-A	(65)	20-B
(26)	39-B	(66)	68-A
(27)	40-A	(67)	71-A
(28)	40-B	(68)	71-B

Wu No: Case no.	Complete text: Case no.	Wu No: Case no.	Complete text: Case no.
(29)	64-B	(69)	35-A
(30)	32-A	(70)	35-B
(31)	69-B	(71)	24-A
(32)	69-A	(72)	13-B
(33)	17-B	(73)	67-A
(34)	17-A	(74)	37-B
(35)	31-A	(75)	34-A
(36)	31-B	(76)	34-B
(37)	6-B	(77)	38-A
(38)	23-B	(78)	38-B
(39)	33-A	(79)	50-B
(40)	24-B	(80)	46-A

PART II
ANNOTATED TRANSLATION

T'ANG-YIN-PI-SHIH

ANNOTATED TRANSLATION

Liu Li's Preface

"Collections of difficult judicial cases date from far back; but the collection now selected and arranged by the police official Kuei Wan-jung is particularly detailed, it is in truth a magic mirror for deciding judicial cases. This is a book that should be studied carefully by those charged with the function of magistrate or prefect; they should not merely say: 'These affairs are the responsibility of the jail officers [1].

Formerly Judge Yü said himself that after he had accumulated 'occult virtue' by solving cases he suddenly had his gate built higher [2]. And also Judge Ch'ien [3] of our present dynasty acquired his ability of solving cases by skilful questioning only after he had become Prefect. Since Mr. Kuei completed this book already while

[1] For the term *p'i-han* see page 54 above.

[2] Yü-kung 于公 "Judge Yü" was the father of Yü Ting-kuo (于定國 109-40 B.C.), who was also a famous judge of the Western Han Dynasty; cf. Balazs note 28 on page 100. Yü-kung is referred to in Yü Ting-kuo's biography in *Han-shu* ch. 71; when his gate was being repaired he said: "Make it a little higher so that a carriage with a high covering and drawn by four horses can pass through; by my solving of criminal cases I have accumulated much 'occult virtue', I have never wronged a man; (therefore) my sons and grandsons will certainly reach eminent positions (and thus will need a house with a gate sufficiently high for letting chariots of high officials through)" 少高大門閭。令容駟馬高蓋車。我治獄多陰德。未嘗有所寃。子孫必有興者. *Yin-te* means literally "hidden merit", and is generally used regarding persons whose meritorious deeds remain unknown. Since, however, the wise decisions of a magistrate can hardly be called "hidden", I think that here the term refers to credit accruing to a living person in the books kept by the judges of the Other World; *yin* denotes also the Nether Region, in contrast to *yang*, the world of the living. This agrees with the reference to the prosperity of the sons and grandsons, conferred upon them by the Powers on High as a reward for the merits of their father c.q. grandfather. Hence I translated *yin-te* as "occult virtue".

[3] For Ch'ien Jo-shui see the note to Case 1-B.

still a small officer, who can surmise what heights he shall attain later in his career?

I hastily order to engrave this book on the printing blocks, so as to make it circulate widely.

Written on fullmoon's day of the tenth moon of the year 1213, by Liu Li of Pu-t'ien, in the Prefectural Library of Chin-ling (Nanking)."

Kuei Wan-jung's Preface

"In the spring of the year 1207, having been appointed Sheriff of the district Yü-kan in Jao Prefecture, I proceeded to the prefectural office. The outgoing official [1] was Sun Ch'i-yü, a native of Wu-ling; he entertained me one whole day. When we came to speak of the task of a judge, he said: 'All officers charged with judicial cases are indeed the guardians of the people; the favour of Heaven and the fortunes of the State depend upon them. Those who are charged with this office need be more diligent than all others. Recently a judicial official of I-yang was murdered by some one. It happened towards the evening, and no one knew who had done it. The officer charged with finding the criminal arrested a man called Yü Ta and had him arraigned. Complete evidence was adduced and the man confessed, while moreover three others [2] were implicated. All concerned were unanimous in their verdict; but I alone could not but doubt. I myself went to the Prefect and begged to have the case adjourned. I again issued an offer of rewarding (informers), and sent my secret agents everywhere, in order to catch the real criminal. And before long I indeed caught a man called Kung Li who was duly executed. If not, four innocent people had been wantonly sent to their death; if their wrong had never been redressed, whose fault would it have been?'

When I heard this I was startled and filled with awe. With a sigh I remembered that our Master Confucius in the book he read so often

---

[1] *shu-man* 書 滿 means that the term of his office stated in the documents relating to his appointment had been completed. *T'ou-ts'ao* 科 曹 "Yellow-robed officer" is an elegant expression for officials in general.

[2] TYPS-I reads *san-wan* 三 彎 ; TYPS-III splits up the character *wan* into *kung-shou* 弓 手 "archer". I follow TYPS-II which replaces *wan* simply by *jen* 人 .

that he had to change its cords three times [1], mentions especially in the illustrative explanation (*hsiang*) of the 61st hexagram Chung-fu that '(the Superior Man) discusses criminal cases in order to remit death sentences'. The Superior Men of old devoted themselves wholeheartedly to the exact application of the immutable criminal laws [2]. Mr. Sun is indeed an example of this.

After I had returned East and had been provisonally appointed Police Inspector of Chien-k'ang, I often meditated on this subject, as if suffering from a painful sorrow [3]. Then, in hours of leisure, I took the *I-yü-chi* by Ho Ning and his son, and utilizing also the *Che-yü-kuei-chien* by Cheng K'o from K'ai-feng, I selected parallel cases and added titles thereto, together seventy-two rhyming phrases; I called this compilation *T'ang-yin-pi-shih*. All like-minded persons will by these examples be able, on the one hand, to realize the spirit of compassion prevailing (among the judges) of succeeding generations, and on the other to investigate the exemplary zeal that animated them. Subtlety in detection and extreme carefulness (in pronouncing judgements), these must not be taken as empty words. Then the Confucian ethics will be apparent under the pear tree, and under the jujube tree there will be no sounds of crying at night [4]. How great will then be the happiness [5] derived from the genuine respect of the people!

[1] Refers to the *I-ching*, the Classical Book of Divination; Confucius said that he read it so often that the cords or leather thongs that held the wooden tablets together had to be renewed three times.

[2] Quoted from the chapter *Wang-chih* 王 制 of the "Book of Rites", section III, 15: "Criminal law is like a body: a body must be complete, and being one complete whole it can not be changed. Therefore the Superior Man devotes his entire heart (to its correct application)" 刑 者 佀 也 。 一 成 而 不 可 變 。 故 君 子 盡 心 焉 。

[3] Quoted from the ode *Po-chou* 柏 舟 in the section Kuo-feng 國 風 of the Book of Odes; the commentary there explains *yin* 隱 as *t'ung* 痛 .

[4] See the remarks on page 48 above.

[5] *To-li chih hsing* 多 禮 之 幸 refers to a passage in the works of the philosopher Yang Hsiung (揚 雄 53 B.C.-18 A.D.) who replied to a swordsman who advocated the power of brutal force: "Can prison officials force people (by their cruel punishments) to have a genuine respect for them?" 狴 犴 使 人 多 禮 乎 . The editor of TYPS-II did not recognize the quotation and changed 禮 to *fu* 福 , which is unwarranted.

Therefore, not shunning the doubtful credit accruing from it [1], I intend to have this book engraved on the printing blocks, in order to have it circulate widely.

Preface written by Kuei Wan-jung from Szu-ming, on the 15th day of the intercalary month of the year 1211 [2]".

1. *Vice-President Hsiang searches out a criminal;*
   Ch'ien Jo-shui finds a hidden slave girl.

A.

"When the Ministerial Vice-President Hsiang Min-chung was serving as judge in the Western capital there was a monk who when passing a village house (at night) asked for a lodging; the master of the house refused. Then the monk accommodated himself for the night (in an empty cart) outside the gate. In the middle of the night he suddenly saw a robber who climbed over the wall and departed with one of the wives and stolen goods. The monk fled, fearing that the next day the master of the house would (suspect him of the deed and) apprehend him. Crossing a plot of waste land (in the dark) he accidentally fell into a disused well. The absconding woman had been killed by her abductor (immediately after their flight) and her dead body had been deposited in the same well. Her husband followed the (monk's) traces (to the well), apprehended him and brought him to the tribunal. The monk could not stand the questioning under torture and wrongly confessed. He stated (that he had violated the woman and fled with her, subsequently killing her fearing that she might denounce him; that while throwing her body in the well his foot had slipped so that he fell into it too;) that he had left the stolen goods and the knife by the side of the well, and that some one must have taken those away. When the case against the monk had been completed only Hsiang Min-chung had doubts because neither the stolen goods nor the weapon had been found. He questioned the monk repeatedly but he answered only that in a former existence he must have been

---

[1] *Chin-ming* 近 名 refers to the first alinea of the chapter *Yang-sheng* 養 生 in *Chuang-tzu*, where it is said: 爲 善 無 近 名. "Doing good does not necessarily imply getting due credit for it".

[2] *Ch'ung-kuang hsieh-hsia* 重 光 協 洽 indicates the cyclical signs *hsin-wei* 辛 未.

predestined to take this woman's life, and that he could adduce nothing in his defense. But after thorough questioning the monk at last told the truth. Thereupon Hsiang Min-chung secretly sent out a constable to search for the (real) culprit. When the constable was having a meal in an eating house in that village, there was an old woman who had heard that he came from the city but did not know that he was a constable; she asked him how the case against the monk was standing. The constable falsely answered: 'Yesterday he was flogged to death on the market place'. The old woman asked: 'If now the (real) criminal were caught, what would happen?' The constable answered: 'Since the Prefect would have wrongly decided the case, he would not further dare to question him'. The old woman then said: '(In that case there is no harm in telling you) The murderer is a certain youth from this village'. The constable asked where he lived, and there found him together with the stolen goods''.

(From the *Su-shui-chi-wen*)

CYKC ch. 2, page 16; SF no. 1; IYC ch. 4, no. 68; YP no. 10.

The *Su-shui-chi-wen* 凍水記聞 is a collection of miscellaneous notes in 16 ch., compiled by the Sung scholar Szu-ma Kuang (司馬光 1019-1086 A.D.); it is reprinted in the *Ts'ung-shu-chi-ch'eng* 叢書集成 of the Commercial Press, first series, no. 2744. In ch. 7, page 74 a much more elaborate version of this case is given; the supplementary words and phrases placed between brackets in my translation are borrowed from that version.

Hsiang Min-chung (向敏中 948-1019 A.D.) was an able scholar-official who was appointed at Court after having served in several places as district magistrate and Prefect. Cf. his biography in *Sung-shih*, ch. 282; the present case is not given there.

B.

"When Ch'ien Jo-shui was serving as Prefectural Judge of T'ung-chou, a slave girl of a wealthy house ran away. Her father and mother brought this case before the Prefect (since the wealthy family was responsible for their daughter). The inspector (serving under Ch'ien) had borrowed money from the wealthy family, he (therefore) made no attempt at locating the slave girl but accused the rich man and his son of having killed her and thrown her body into the river; no matter who of those two had planned the deed and who actually committed it, both deserved the death sentence. When the case (against the wealthy man and his son) had been completed, only

Ch'ien Jo-shui had doubts. He adjourned the case without pronouncing a verdict. Everyone, high and low in the Prefecture, thought this very strange. The Inspector wrongly accused Ch'ien of having accepted a bribe (from the wealthy family), but Ch'ien only denied this with a smile. After about ten days Ch'ien went to the Prefect and said to him in private: 'I adjourned the case because I wanted to find that slave girl; now she has been discovered'. After she had been brought to the Prefecture, the Prefect unexpectedly pushed her from behind a curtain and confronted her with her parents. Greatly startled both her father and mother acknowledged that she was their daughter. Then the wealthy man and his son were acquitted. The Prefect wanted to report Ch'ien Jo-shui's merit to the Throne but he steadfastly declined. But the Court came to hear about it and he was immediately promoted''.

(From the *Su-shui-chi-wen*)

CYKC ch. 2, page 17; IYC ch. 4, no. 67; YP no. 9.

Ch'ien Jo-shui (錢若水 960-1003 A.D.) was an official known for his good administration and his acumen in judicial matters. He served in T'ung-chou ca. 985 A.D. Cf. his biography in *Sung-shih*, ch. 266; there this case is not recorded.

2. *Ts'ao Ch'u clears a widow of suspicion;*
P'ei Chün obtains the acquittal of a husband

A.

"When Ts'ao Ch'u, styled Yen-yüan, of the (Western) Chin Dynasty (265-316 A.D.), was magistrate of Lin-tzu, there was a widow who looked after her mother-in-law with great care. Since the widow was still young, her mother-in-law urged her to remarry; but the widow kept to her decision to remain single. The mother-in-law was so mortified about this that she secretly committed suicide. Her family thereupon falsely accused the widow (of having murdered her). The widow could not stand the questioning under torture in the tribunal and wrongly confessed. Ts'ao Ch'u who then had just taken up his office suspected that the woman was being wronged. He instituted a thorough inquiry and found out the real facts of the case. The people of that time praised his perspicacity''.

CYKC ch. 1, page 1; IYC ch. 5, no. 83; YP no. 20.

Ts'ao Ch'u (曹攄 died 308 A.D.) was well known as an able and just

administrator. It is said that when serving in Lin-tzu he solved a number of
difficult cases. On New Year's day he once released several prisoners in order to
give them an opportunity for visiting their family, and all came back to the prison
on the appointed day. He was killed in battle, and people mourned for him as
for their father and mother. Cf. his biography in the *Chin-shu*, ch. 90, where this
case is related.

B.

"In the T'ang Dynasty, when P'ei Chün was Military Commander
of Hsiang-yang, the wife of a villager in his district had illicit relations
(with her neighbour). She feigned to suffer from bone-fever and said
to her husband: 'The doctor needs the meat of a hound. When I eat
that, I shall recover. (Her husband answered: 'We have no dogs in the
house, so what can I do?') His wife said: 'The dog of our Eastern
neighbour always comes here to snatch food. You can catch and
slaughter him!' The husband did as she had said and gave the meat
to his wife. She ate some of it, the rest she concealed in a clothes box.
When her husband had gone out, she told the neighbour to report it,
and the case (of the husband's theft of the dog) was thus brought
before P'ei Chün. When the husband came to the tribunal he related
the wish of his wife. P'ei Chün observed: 'The wife must have a
paramour, and therefore wishes to involve her husband into trouble'.
He instituted an investigation and found that that was indeed
the case. The wife and her paramour were both punished and the
husband was acquitted."

CYKC ch. 5, page 75; IYC ch. 2, no. 43; YP no. 19. Source unknown.

P'ei Chün served 裴 均 seived as Regional Commander of Ching-nan 荆
南 . In the Yüan-ho era (806-820 A.D.) he was promoted to Right Executive
of the Ministry of Personnel. Afterwards he was sent out again as Regional
Commander, and was ennobled as Duke of Hsün 郇 . Cf. his biography in the
Hsin-t'ang-shu, ch. 108; there this case is not related.

According to the descriptions given in old Chinese medical books, *ku-cheng*
骨 蒸 , here translated as "bone-fever", was probably tuberculosis; cf. *Chung-
kuo-i-hsüeh-ta-tz'u-tien* 中 國 醫 學 大 辭 典 , vol. I page 2413.

The phrase 夫 曰 吾 家 無 犬 奈 何 , placed between brackets in
the translation, is added from the TYPS-II and the CYKC version; IYC has a
phrase of the same meaning. TYPS-I and III wrongly omit it, hence there we
read two times "The wife said....".

3. Ch'eng Hao interrogates a greybeard;
   Ping Chi submits a child to a test

A.

"When the Investigating Censor Ch'eng Hao was Prefect of Chin-ch'eng in Tse-chou, there was a son of a wealthy man called Chang. Shortly after his father's death, an old man came to his house and said: 'I am your (real) father, I have come to live with you'; he related the circumstances. The son was startled and suspected (the old man's story); he took him to the tribunal for an official pronouncement. The old man stated: 'I am a physician who once had to visit a patient in a far-away place. (During my absence) my wife gave birth to a son. Since she was poor she could not raise the child and decided to give it to the Chang family. On a certain day of a certain year and month someone took the baby there and it was accepted'. Ch'eng Hao said: 'All this happened long ago, how can you state those exact dates?' The old man answered: 'The date was written at the end of my prescription book. Thus I came to know this when I had returned from my journey'. He then produced the prescription book as evidence. There was written: 'On a certain day of a certain year and month, some one brought the child to the old gentleman Chang San'. Ch'eng Hao then asked Chang's son how old he was; he said thirty-six. Ch'eng Hao asked: 'How old was your father when he died?' The son said that he had been seventy-six. Thereupon Ch'eng Hao said to the old man: 'When this man was born, his father was only forty years. How could he be referred to in your prescription book as the old gentleman Chang San?' The old man became frightened and confessed his guilt".

(Heard from the elders)

CYKC ch. 6, page 87; IYC ch. 5, no. 105.

Ch'eng Hao (程顥 1032-1085), famous Sung writer who greatly influenced the Neo-Confucianist philosopher Chu Hsi. He was appointed Investigating Censor in the beginning of the Hsi-ning period (1068-1077). Cf. his biography in *Sung-shih* ch. 427, where this case is related in a slightly abbreviated form. Cf. also Case 36-A.

B.

"In the reign of Emperor Hsüan (73-49 B.C.) of the Han Dynasty, there lived in Ch'en-liu and old man of over eighty, who was wealthy but had no sons. From his first wife (who had died), he only had one daughter who had already been given in marriage. Later the old gentleman married again, and this wife bore him a son. After several years, when the old gentleman had died the daughter of the first wife wanted to acquire all the property, and said falsely that the son of the second wife was not begotten by her father. The local officials could not solve this problem, and it was referred to the metropolitan authorities. Ping Chi who at that time served as Head of the Jail observed 'I have heard that a son begotten by an aged father cannot bear cold, and that in the sun his body will cast no shadow'. At that time it was the 8th moon. Ping Chi assembled a number of young children of the same age (as the subject of the dispute) and had them all clad in single garments; then only the child of the old man changed countenance. Then Ping Chi made him stand in the sun (together with the other children), and only he had no shadow. Thereupon the daughter was punished for having calumniated her stepmother".

CYKC ch. 3, page 27; IYC ch. 2, no. 24. Source unknown.

Ping Chi (丙 吉 died 55 B.C.) was a Han official famous for his probity and acumen in legal matters. B.D. No. 1651 reproduces the following anecdote: "One spring day he came upon a crowd of brawlers, among whom were several killed and wounded; but he took no notice of them and passed on. Soon afterwards he saw an ox panting violently, and at once showed the greatest concern. 'For', as he explained, 'the brawlers can be left to those whose business it is to deal with such matters; whereas an ox panting in spring means that heat has come before its time, and that the seasons are out of joint, thus opening a question of the deepest national interest'.

4. *Li Ch'ung returns Hsün T'ai's child;*
   Huang Pa reprimands an elder sister

A.

"When during the Later Wei Dynasty (386-534 A.D.) Li Ch'ung was Prefect of Yang-chou, there lived in one of the districts a man called Hsün T'ai whose three year old son became lost. Later Hsün T'ai discovered the boy in the house of a man called Chao Feng-po. Both Hsün and Chao maintained that the child was theirs and produced supporting testimony of their neighbours. Neither the authorities of the district nor those of the prefecture could decide the case. Li Ch'ung had Hsün, Chao and the child confined separately. After a few days he unexpectedly sent a prison official to Hsün and Chao who said: 'The child has suddenly died'. When Hsün T'ai heard this he was nearly out of his mind from grief, while Chao Feng-po only sighed without showing real sorrow. Thereupon the child was given back to Hsün, and Chao confessed".

CYKC ch. 6, page 90; IYC ch. 1, no. 2; YCTI no. 11.

Li Ch'ung (李 崇 died 583 A.D.) was a well known scholar-official who served as Prefect in several places, widely respected for his probity and his skill in solving difficult cases; his nickname was Wo-hu 臥 虎 "Sleeping Tiger". Cf. his biography in *Pei-shih* ch. 43, where this case is given in a more elaborate version. B.D. No. 1120 also quotes the case related here.

Cf. also Case 27-A.

B.

"In the (Western) Han Dynasty (206 B.C.-24 A.D.) there was in Ying-ch'uan a wealthy family, headed by two brothers who shared the family residence. Their wives became pregnant at the same time; the elder brother's wife had a miscarriage but the wife of the younger gave birth to a son. The wife of the elder brother appropriated the baby and said it was her own. After having quarreled about this for three years the case was brought before Huang Pa. He had a constable carry the child into Court and told the two women that she who could get hold of it might have it. The elder brother's wife tried to grab it with violence, but the younger one feared lest the child might get hurt. Huang Pa then reprimanded the elder one saying: 'You coveted the family's property (that would in due time revert to the eldest son) and therefore wanted this child. Had not you better be careful, lest it gets hurt?' He then returned the child to the wife of the younger brother".

(From the *Feng-su-t'ung*)

CYKC ch. 6, page 89; IYC ch. 1, no. 14.

Huang Pa 黃 霸 was a judge of legendary fame who in his youth had made a profound study of the law, and as an official distinguished himself by opposing the cruel punishments that were used in that time. He died in 51 B.C. Cf. his biography in *Han-shu* ch. 89; also the extensive note in Balazs, page 100-101.

Later versions of the *Feng-su-t'ung* do not include this story, but quotations in two older sources show that originally it formed part of that text. Cf. *Le Fong*

Sou T'ong Yi, avec un appendice contenant les fragments du texte perdu cités en d'autres ouvrages (published by "Centre franco-chinois d'études sinologiques", Peking 1943), vol. I, page 108.

5. *Ou-yang exposes a left-handed criminal;*
Ch'ien proves guilt by a man's right arm

A.

"When the Metropolitan official Ou-yang Yeh was Prefect of Tuan-chou, a military guard from Kuei-yang was beaten to death during a quarrel over a boat. The case remained pending during a long time, no one being able to decide (who among the crowd involved in the brawl was guilty of the manslaughter). Ou-yang Yeh had all the suspects taken out of the prison and gave them a meal; thereafter he sent all of them back to prison save one. This man showed signs of fear. Ou-yang said to him: 'You are the killer'. The prisoner did not understand how he had been found out. Ou-yang Yeh said: 'I observed that when eating all used their right hand, only you used your left. Now the wounds of the victim were all on the right side of his body, which proves clearly that you (being left-handed) killed him'. The prisoner thereupon confessed".

(From his tomb inscription composed by Ou-yang Hsiu)

CYKC ch. 6, page 96; IYC ch. 8, no. 149; YP no. 8.

For the meaning of *tu-kuan*, here translated "metropolitan official", cf. des Rotours, pp. 117-120. Ou-yang Yeh 歐 陽 曄 (*yeh* being a taboo character is written in various later editions 煜) must have been a relative of Ou-yang Hsiu (歐 陽 修 1007-1072 A.D.), the famous Sung writer who composed the tomb inscription.

B.

"When Ch'ien Wei-chi was Prefect of Ch'iang-chou there was a vender of mulberry bark; a robber tried to take his wares by force, but he failed to obtain them. Then the robber (out of spite) cut his own right arm and falsely accused the vender of attempted murder. None of the local officials could solve this case. Ch'ien Wei-chi questioned the robber and let him partake of some food in front of him; then the thief lifted his spoon with his left hand. Ch'ien Wei-chi said: 'When a man inflicts a wound upon another, the upper section of the cut is deep and the lower shallow. But in the present case the lower section is deep and the upper shallow. Furthermore, you cut your right arm with your left hand'. The slanderer confessed".

(From his biography)

CYKC ch. 3, page 35; SF no. 4; IYC ch. 8, no. 143.

Ch'ien Wei-chi 錢惟濟 served as Deputy Regional Commander of the Wu-ch'ang Army in the reign of Jen-tsung (1023-1063 A.D.). As a judge he was extremely harsh, it is said that he remained unmoved by the most cruel executions. Cf. his biography in *Sung-shih* ch. 480, which reproduces this case in an identical version.

6. *Shen K'uo on throat and larynx;*
Li Nan-kung and the criminal's nose

A.

"The Han-lin Academician Shen K'uo says: 'At present people make a (kind of) whistle from bamboo, wood, ivory or bone. If it is placed in a man's throat and he breathes through it he can produce speech; this is called a larynx whistle. There was a person suffering from dumbness who when oppressed by someone was distressed because he was unable to explain his wrong himself. The judge then tentatively used that whistle and placed it in his larynx. He then produced sounds resembling those of marionettes, one could grasp here and there what he wanted to say and thus his wrong was set right".

CYKC ch. 2, page 25.

The text of TYPS-I, II and III is corrupt; my translation is based on the original text as found in ch. 13 of the *Meng-hsi-pi-t'an:* 世人以竹木牙骨之類爲叫子。置人喉中吹之。能作人言。謂之頦叫子。嘗有病瘖者爲人所苦。煩冤無以自言。聽訟者試取叫子。令頦之。作聲如傀儡子。粗能辨其一二。其冤獲申。

The *Meng-hsi-pi-t'an* 夢溪筆談 is a collection of miscellaneous notes compiled by the Sung scholar Shen K'uo (沈括, 1030-1094 A.D.); *nei-han* 內翰 is an elegant expression for the Han-lin Academy. For other quotations from the *Meng-hsi-pi-t'an* cf. Case 46-A, 50-B, 52-A, 59-A and 63-A.

The instrument described would work satisfactorily in the case of persons whose dumbness is due to hysteria, which is one of the most common causes of this defect. Western specialists in laryngology also insert a tube through the vocal chords of patients whose dumbness is caused by hysteria, whereupon they suddenly start to produce sounds. It is interesting to note that as early as the 11th century the Chinese had discovered this device.

Sang 顙 "forehead" must be an old copyist's mistake for *sang* 嗓 "larynx".

B.

"When the Minister Li Nan-kung was Judicial Intendant in Ho-pei, a minor official had committed a crime and was put in prison. When interrogated he did not confess, keeping his mouth closed he did not eat for more than a hundred days. The prison officials did not dare to question him under torture lest they come to harm in the extreme case (of the weakened prisoner dying on their hands). Li Nan-kung said: 'I can make him eat immediately'. He had the prisoner brought before him for questioning and said: 'I shall stop up your nose with something; then will you be able to continue refusing to eat?' The man was greatly afraid, he started eating again (and finally confessed his crime). Now that man was expert in 'feeding on air'; but if his nose were stopped up, his breathing would be obstructed and the air would cease to circulate. Therefore he confessed".

CYKC ch. 3, page 43; IYC ch. 8, no. 163; YP no. 37.

Li Nan-kung 李南公 served under the Emperor Shen-tsung (1067-1085 A.D.) as Auxiliary Academician of the Lung-t'u Pavilion. Cf. his biography in *Sung-shih* ch. 355. He figures again in Case 39-A. Neither of these two cases is recorded in his biography.

For the Taoist discipline of "feeding on air" cf. Maspéro, *Le Taoisme* (Mélanges Posthumes sur les Religions et l'Histoire de la Chine, II), Paris 1950, page 98 sq.

7. *Ch'eng Lin on stoves;*
   Ch'iang Chih on curtains

A.

"When the Palace Councillor (*hsüan-hui*) Ch'eng Lin was Prefect of K'ai-feng, a fire broke out in the palace grounds and spread to the Two Palaces. The eunuchs thoroughly questioned the (Palace) tailors (who use a brass pan with glowing coals as a flat iron), who wrongly confessed. They were sent to the Prefectural office for trial. Ch'eng Lin came to the conclusion that the men were not guilty. He ordered a draughtsman to draw a map of the course of the fire. Then he observed: "In the Imperial harem there are many inmates and their quarters are cramped. The wooden wall near their portable stoves, when parched too long, is liable to catch fire. This should be called a calamity of Heaven that cannot be blamed on human beings'. The Emperor agreed to show lenience and no one was condemned to death".

(From his biography. A *wei-tsao* is a portable stove; 煨 is pronounced *wei*).

CYKC ch. 2, page 20; IYC ch. 8, no. 150; YP no. 11.

Ch'eng Lin (程 琳 988-1056 A.D.) was an able and learned official who after service in the provinces occupied a series of high Court functions, i.a. Censor and second Privy Councillor. He was also appointed Prefect of K'ai-feng, and Academician of the Han-lin Academy and of the Lung-t'u Pavilion. He ended his career as Regional Commander. Cf. his biography in *Sung-shih* ch. 288, where the present case is not recorded.

The title *hsüan-hui* refers to the Hsüan-hui-yüan 宣 徽 院 , an office established in the T'ang Dynasty and dealing with Palace affairs; it was mostly filled by eunuchs. During the Sung Dynasty its importance increased, and its members had the status of Ministers of State.

B.

"When the Head of the Sacrificial Section (of the Ministry of Rites) Ch'iang Chih served as Intendant of the Imperial Guards in K'ai-feng, oiled curtains had been left piled up in the open air, and one night they caught fire. According to the law the men responsible for guarding them were all to be executed. At the preliminary hearing of the case Ch'iang Chih conceived doubts about the cause of the fire. He summoned the workmen who had made the curtains and questioned them. Those artisans said: 'When making the curtains (the oil) must be mixed with some drug; when they have been lying piled up for a long time, they may start burning when they get moist'. When Ch'iang Chih reported this to the Emperor Jen-tsung (1023-1063 A.D.), His Majesty suddenly obtained an idea and said: 'The fire that recently occurred in the mausoleum of the Emperor Chen-tsung (998-1022 A.D.) started in oiled garments. So that was the cause!' The keepers were let off with a lighter punishment.

(From the record of Ch'iang's career)

"Chang Hua thought that the fire that formerly during the (Western) Chin Dynasty (265-289 A.D.) occurred in the Armoury originated in the oil accumulated there; in fact it was the same cause as mentioned here (i.e. spontaneous ignition of oiled garments stored there)".

CYKC ch. 2, page 21; IYC ch. 8, no. 151; YP no. 12.

Ch'iang Chih 强至 served as district magistrate in various places and thereafter became a member of the suite of the statesman Han Ch'i (韓琦 1008-
1075 A.D.; cf. BD no. 610); when Han Ch'i had become Prime Minister, he gave
Ch'iang the appointment in the Ministry of Rites referred to here. Ch'iang Chih
was well known as a writer; he composed i.e. a biographical account of Han Ch'i.

Hsi 夕 in the fourth column is a copyist's mistake for *chiu* 九 .

TYPS-II prints the remark about Chang Hua as part of Cheng K'o's commentary. That remark of Chang Hua (張華 232-300 A.D.) is found near the end
of ch. 3 of his *Po-wu-chih* 博物志 ; he says there: "If a full hundred catties
of oil are accumulated, the oil will be subject to spontaneous ignition. The fire in
the Armoury that occurred in the T'ai-shih era (265-274 A.D.) of the of reign Emperor Wu (265-289 A.D.) was caused by accumulated oil" 積油滿百石。
則自然生火。武帝泰始中武庫災。積油所致。
Dr. Joseph Needham, the well known authority on the history of science,
kindly informs me that the "drug" mentioned by the workmen to Ch'iang Chih
was probably quick lime, perhaps used as a whitening agent. Although the
feasibility of igniting oil by the heat generated by quick lime on contact with
water has often been denied, it has been proved to be possible, given the right
conditions. On the other hand, certain kinds of oiled cloth are liable to ignite
spontaneously when close together, without the previous addition of any chemical.
Needham further refers to a passage in T. Thomson's *History of Chemistry*
(London 1830, vol. I, page 293) where it is stated that two accidental spontaneous combustions occurred in Russia in the reign of Catherine II (1729-1796)
and were ascribed to treason. The Empress alone suspected that the combustion
was spontaneous, and experiments made by her orders proved that her surmise
had been correct. This provides a curious parallel to Ch'iang Chih's case. It may
be added that this property of oiled cloth is at present well known in technical
circles, and instructions against piling it up are issued to all army and navy store-
keepers.

8. *A concubine and a constable poison Mr. Sung;*
   The slave girl Yü-su poisons Mr. Kuo

A.

When the Minister Fan Ch'un-jen was Prefect of Ho-chung, (his
subordinate) the Executive Inspector Sung Tan-nien became ill after
a banquet held in his house, and during the night he suddenly died.
This was because one of his concubines had illicit relations with a
minor officer (and therefore the pair was arrested for further investigation of their possible connection with the sudden death of Sung).
Fan Ch'un-jen, knowing that it had not been a natural death, ordered

the local officials to investigate. During the autopsy it was found that blood had flown from the nine openings of the body. The concubine and the officer said: 'We put poison in the turtle mincemeat'. Fan Ch'un-jen asked during which course the mincemeat had been served; (when he learned that this had occurred early in the banquet) he said: 'How could the poisoned man have sat through the entire banquet? This is certainly not the truth!' He ordered a further investigation. Then it transpired that when the guests were leaving, the accused had murdered Sung by placing poison in his wine cup. Since Sung did not eat turtle meat and since the other guests had rejected it also, the criminals had hoped that later the case would have to be reopened on different premises and that they thus would escape the death penalty".

(From the *Record of the Words and Works of Fan Ch'un-jen*)

Substantially the same text in CYKC ch. 6, page 85, YP no. 15, and SF no. 8. IYC ch. 4, no. 74 has a different version which reads: "When the Minister Fan Ch'un-jen was Prefect of Ch'i-chou, (his subordinate) the Executive Inspector Sung Tan-nien died suddenly from poison. Fan found the criminal, and had him punished according to the law. Fan first heard about this case when, after Sung had given a banquet, members of his suite suddenly came to report that he had died. Fan sent the younger members of his household to see the burial. They noticed that when the corpse had been dressed, blood was coming forth from its mouth and nose, soiling the shroud. Fan then suspected that Sung had not died a natural death. (Upon further investigation) it indeed transpired that a favourite concubine of Sung had illicit relations with a small officer; when questioned in the tribunal they confessed that they had utilized the banquet to put poison in the turtle meat. Fan then asked: 'During which course was that meat served? How could Sung have sat through the entire banquet after he had eaten the poison?' He ordered a second investigation. It was then proved that Sung Tan-nien had not eaten of the turtle meat, and neither had his guests. But when the guests were leaving returning home intoxicated, they had put poison in Sung's wine cup and thus murdered him. They had first said that they had put poison in the turtle meat, hoping that later the case would have to be reopened on different premises, thus planning to escape the death penalty. Everyone opined that Fan possessed superhuman skill in discovering evil and detecting secret plots; if Fan Ch'un-jen had not happened to be there, the wrong of Sung Tan-nien in the Nether World would not have been righted".

丞相范純仁知齊州時。　錄事參軍宋儋年中毒暴卒。公得罪人。置於法。初宋君因會客罷。是夜門下人遽以疾告。公遣家人子弟。視其喪事。宋君小殮。口鼻血出。漫污幎帛。公疑其死不以理。果為寵妾與小吏為姦。付有

司。按治具伏。因會客置毒鱉肉中。公曰。肉
在第幾巡。豈有中毒而能終席耶。命再劾之。
宋君果不食鱉肉。同坐客亦然。及客散醉歸。
置毒酒杯中而殺之。承置毒鱉肉者。覬他日
獄變爲逃死之計也。 人以爲公發姦摘伏如
神明。若非遇公。 則宋君之寃無以申於地
下矣。

This IYC-version is evidently the result of attempts by the Ming editor at rewriting in an intelligible manner the original text, which has been transmitted in a badly mutilated form. The interesting point in this case is that the criminals hoped to have their death-sentence commuted by stating that they had committed the crime in a manner that could be proved to have been impossible. It faintly suggests that in the Sung Dynasty common law admitted a rule resembling our Western principle of *ne bis in idem;* but this concept is to the best of my knowledge never referred to in the Chinese Code. It is more probable, therefore, that the criminals just meant to confuse the issue. The editors were apparently puzzled by the term *fan-i* 翻異 in the TYPS and CYKC text. The SF changes it into *fan-an* 翻案 "to reverse the case", and IYC into *yü-pien* 獄變 "to change the case". "To reopen the case on different premises" seems the most logical translation.

Fan Ch'un-jen (1027-1101 A.D) was a native of Soochow who became *chin-shih* in 1049, and occupied various high offices under the Sung Emperors Che-tsung and Hui-tsung; he was known for his honesty and his love of learning. Cf. his biography in the *Sung-shih*, ch. 314; there this case is not related.

B.

"In the T'ang Dynasty, when the State Secretary Kuo Cheng-i conquered Pyong-yang (the capital of the N. Korean Kingdom Kao-li), he there obtained a Korean slave girl called Yü-su, who was of great beauty; he put her in charge of his treasury. When Kuo Cheng-i wanted rice gruel in the night, he always insisted that it was prepared by her. Yü-su then poisoned him (putting the poison in the gruel). (The authorities) searched for a long time for the slave girl and the gold and silver articles (from Kuo's treasury which she had taken along with her) but could not find her. When the Throne had been informed of this case, Shih Liang, Sheriff of the Wan-nien sector of Ch'ang-an, was ordered by the Emperor to arrest her. Shih Liang's Chief of Police Wei Ch'ang had a plan. He summoned the young slaves of the Secretary and selected from among them three whose heads he covered with a piece of cloth. Then they overpowered four of Kuo's guards. Wei Ch'ang asked them: 'Who has come during the last ten days to look for the Secretary's house?' The guards answered: 'There was a naturalized Korean who left a note to be handed to the Secretary's groom. When we examined the note it said: In the Chin-ch'eng quarter there is an empty house. There was written nothing else'. Shih Liang went there and searched the quarter. They found a house that was tightly closed. He had the door broken open and found there the slave girl and the naturalized Korean; the girl had been hidden there by the Korean and the groom. On Imperial command they were beheaded on the Eastern market''.

CYKC ch. 7, page 117; IYC ch. 2, no. 33; YP no. 16. Source unknown.

TYPS-I and III abbreviate the first sentence, leaving out the information that Yü-su was a Korean girl and obtained in Pyong-yang. I follow the reading of TYPS-II and CYKC, reproduced on Fig. 2 and Plate II.

The editor of the CYKC observes in a note that Kuo Cheng-i 郭正一 was never in Korea and was never involved with a slave girl, and that the story is evidently borrowed from T'ang fiction. However, the case shows so many typical features that it could hardly be an imaginary tale; probably it did actually happen to some other Chinese official who took part in a campaign against Korea, perhaps the one of 668 A.D. when the Chinese occupied and sacked Pyong-yang. Unfortunately only a bare skeleton of the case is given. But is seems clear that the background is supplied by a Korean scheme of vengeance on the Chinese conqueror, else the import of Wei Ch'ang's plan would remain a mystery. It must be assumed that the Chinese official brought back with him from his Korean campaign not only the beautiful slave girl but also a number of servants, including his guards and his groom. Wei Ch'ang realized that it would be no use to interrogate in the tribunal the Korean members of the household, because they would side with the slave girl. Therefore he selected three of the murdered man's

Chinese servants (hence the epithet *tuan-cheng* 端正 "upright, loyal" added in the TYPS-II and CYKC version), and they all made it appear as if they were Korean patriots, thus ensuring that the guards would tell them the truth. Doubtless Wei used for this purpose servants of the house instead of his own men, because the former would be able to check whether or not the guards gave genuine information.

9. *Yen-ch'ao feigns a burglary;*
   Ch'ien-chih deceives a crook

A.

"When Mu-jung Yen-ch'ao of the (Later) Han Dynasty (947-950 A.D.) was Commander of Yün, he established an official pawnshop.

Then there was a crook who pawned two false silver bars for 100.000 cash; the officer in charge of the storehouse discovered this only after a considerable lapse of time. When Mu-jung heard this he secretly instructed the officer in charge to make in the night a hole in the wall of the storehouse, and to transfer all the gold and other valuables to another place; then this was announced as a burglary. Mu-jung had an official notice put up in the market place, summoning people to catch the thief, adding that everyone who could assess what he had pawned would be compensated accordingly. All the people vied with each other to announce what they had pawned, and thus in the end they caught the man who had pawned the false silver bars. He was arrested and confessed".

CYKC ch. 7, page 113; IYC ch. 3, no. 56; YP no. 63.
  TYPS-I and III, and also IYC give a version that is abbreviated to such a degree that it is difficult to see the point. Therefore I have based my translation on the version in TYPS-II and CYKC which follows closely the text of Mu-jung's biography in the *Hsin-wu-tai-shih*, ch. 53:

漢慕容彥超爲鄆帥日。置庫質錢。有奸民以僞銀二鋌。質錢十萬。主吏久之乃覺。彥超知之。陰教主吏夜穴庫墙。盡徙其金帛於他所。而以盜告。彥超即牓于市。召人收捕。乃使民自占所質以償之。民皆爭以所質物自言。已而得質僞銀者。執之服罪。

  Mu-jung Yen-ch'ao was a military official of the later Han Dynasty, famous for his prowess. He is said to have had a black face and a long beard, and was therefore nicknamed "The Blackamoor". Being defeated in battle by the founder of the Later Chou Dynasty, he committed suicide together with his wife.

B.

"In the Later Wei Dynasty (386-534 A.D.) when Kao Ch'ien-chih, styled Tao-jang, was magistrate of Ho-yin, a man filled a bag with gravel. He made people believe that it was gold and thus purchased a horse, whereupon he disappeared. When the order came to arrest the thief, Kao put a prisoner in a cangue and made him stand on the horse market, with an official placard by his side stating that he was a welsher about to be punished. Then he secretly made his officers mix with the crowd and listen to their private talk. There was one man who said happily: 'From now on there is nothing to fear!'

That man was arrested and interrogated, whereupon also all the members of the band (of horse thieves) were caught".

CYKC ch. 7, page 113; IYC ch. 1, no. 17; YP no. 64.

Kao Ch'ien-chih was famous for his filial piety. He was appointed magistrate of Ho-yin in the Hsiao-ch'ang era (525-527 A.D.) and earned the reputation of an able administrator. Cf. his biography in *Pei-shih* ch. 50; the present case is related there.

10. *Sun Fu has paddy pounded;*
Hsü Yüan burns a boat

A.

"When the Academician-in-waiting (of the T'ien-chang Pavilion) Sun Fu served as judge in Hua-chou, the paddy in the Government granary proved to be bad; the officer in charge would have had to make good several million cash. The Fiscal Intendant Li Hung handed the officer over to Sun Fu (for trial). Sun Fu ordered one bushel of the rejected paddy pounded, and found that only one or two tenths were bad. He made a second test, with the same result. The officer was released and had to make good only a few 100.000 cash. Li Hung therefore recommended Sun Fu (for promotion)".

(From his tomb inscription composed by Tseng Kung)

CYKC ch. 8, page 130; IYC ch. 9, no. 170; YP no. 52.

Sun Fu (孫甫 998-1057 A.D.) was appointed in Hua-chou shortly after he had obtained the degree of *chin-shih*. Thereafter he occupied various posts in the capital and the provinces. He left a considerable literary oeuvre. Cf. his biography in the *Sung-shih*, ch. 295; there this case is not recorded.

Tseng Kung (曾鞏 1019-1083 A.D.) was a scholar-official known as a brilliant writer.

B.

"When the Academician-in-waiting (of the T'ien-chang Pavilion) Hsü Yüan, in the beginning of his career was Intendant of Exchange, he was greatly distressed by the fact that most of the official boats (proved unworthy because the contractors) used less nails than they charged for. [Since all badly constructed boats had sunk, there was no means for checking the amount of nails actually used; thus the contractors could practise this deceit.] One day Hsü Yüan gave orders that a newly constructed boat be burned. (After having raked the ashes) the nails were weighed and found to represent but one-tenth of the amount paid for. He then fixed the exact amount to be used".

(From the *Tung-hsien-pi-lu* by Wei T'ai)

CYKC ch. 8, page 129.

Hsü Yüan 許元 was an official well known for his cleverness, especially in financial matters. Between 1041-1048 A.D. he was appointed Intendant of Exchange of the Chiang-huai area, which post he occupied for 13 years. He died after having served thrice as Prefect. Cf. his biography in *Sung-shih* ch. 299; there this case is not related.

The *Tung-hsien-pi-lu* 東軒筆錄 is a collection of notes on contemporary affairs in 15 ch., compiled in 1094 A.D. by the scholar-official Wei T'ai 魏泰. The reprint of a Ming edition of this book in the *Hu-pei-hsien-cheng-i-shu* 湖北先正遺書 does not contain the present case, although Hsü Yüan is mentioned in ch. 11, page 9/a.

The passage between square brackets I borrowed from TYPS-II: 蓋以陷於水中。不可稱盤。故得為姦。 CYKC reads *mu* 木 instead of *shui* 水, but the latter is better because *hsien-shui* is a common compound.

P'o 破 seems to mean here "to charge" rather than "to spend"; Cheng K'o says in his commentary: "I find that Hsü Yüan's not punishing the crime of 'empty charges' but confining himself to fixing the correct amount (of nails) was permissible" 按元不治虛破之罪而但立為定額可也。 It all depends upon *who* practiced the deceit, the local officials or the contractors; my translation is based on the assumption that the latter were the culprits.

The editor of CYKC explains the term *ting-chü* 釘鞠 as a synonym of *ting-chiao* 釘鉸, which seems doubtful; probably it is a local dialect term for "nails".

11. *Ma Tsung-yüan and the provisional arrest;*
   Wei T'ao proves that a person died by accident.

A.

"When the Academician-in-waiting Ma Tsung-yüan was still young, his father Ma Lin hit a man and was arrested provisionally till the degree of his guilt would have been determined; when the man he had hit died, Ma Lin was going to be executed. But Ma Tsung-yüan calculated that reckoning from the hour of the fight, the time-limit (within which the death of the injured man would be fully charged to the man who hit him), had expired one hour before the victim's death. He reported this to the Prefect and obtained a pardon for his father. He became famous because of this feat".

CYKC ch. 4, page 51; IYC ch. 8, no. 147; YP no. 5. Source unknown.

Ma Lin 馬麟 was a famous painter of the Sung dynasty; about Ma Tsung-yüan 馬宗元 I could find no further information.

Shou-ku 守辜 (also *pao-ku* 保辜) is a legal term which has no counterpart in English. It applies only in the case of a person who dangerously wounds another. He is placed under arrest pending observation of the development of the wounded man's condition. If the victim dies within a set time-limit, the other is prosecuted for murder c.q. manslaughter; if not, his sentence is commuted. Cheng K'o adds a brief commentary discussing the time-limit (quoted also in TYPS-I, II and III), and YP and IYC add a long commentary on the rules for those time-limits in the Ming and preceding dynasties. For the Ch'ing Dynasty rules cf. Alabaster, "Notes and Commentaries on Chinese Criminal Law" (London 1899), page 229 sq.

B.

"When the Court-appointee Wei (T'ao) was magistrate of the Yung district in I-chou, two men who had a feud started a fight during which one of them was wounded. After the fight had ended and the participants gone home, the wounded man died. Wei T'ao inquired after the cause of death but before he could learn it, the son of the deceased brought the matter before the Circuit Intendant who became angry and sharply criticised Wei T'ao (for not taking immediate action against the accused). Wei T'ao said with a sigh: 'My post can be taken away from me, but the prisoner (whose guilt has not been established) must not be killed'. Later the true facts of the case became known. When the wounded man was going home that night, he fell from his horse when he had reached his gate and died thereof. When this was clearly established by the testimony of the neighbours, the false accusation was exposed".

(Fom his tomb inscription composed by Ch'en Shih-tao)

CYKC ch. 3, page 38; IYC ch. 8, no. 154; YP no. 22.

About Wei T'ao 魏濤 I could find no further details. The term *ch'ao-feng* 朝奉 refers to persons directly appointed by the Emperor; probably, however, it is here an abbreviation of *ch'ao-feng-ta-fu* 朝奉大夫, one of the 29 honorary court ranks listed in ch. 169 of the *Sung-shih*.

Ch'en Shih-tao 陳師道, styled Wu-chi 無已, was a writer whose biography is given in *Sung-shih,* ch. 444.

12. *Commander Sang keeps the palisade closed;*
   Su Ch'in is executed on the market place

A.

"At the end of the Ming-tao era (1032-1033 A.D.) the region West of the capital suffered from a drought and locusts, and it was infested by twenty or thirty robbers. The Bureau of Military Affairs summoned the Military Inspector of Yung-an called Sang I and, giving him the names of the robbers, ordered him to arrest them. Sang I reasoned: 'The robbers have respect for my name, they will certainly disperse (as soon as they hear that I have been assigned to the case). Therefore I must first seem to be afraid'. When he had arrived on the spot, he kept the palisade (of his camp) closed (i.e. he remained inactive feigning to be afraid). He cautioned his officers not lo leave camp. The men under his command begged several times to be allowed to go after the robbers themselves, but Sang I refused all their requests. Then, one night he disguised himself and a few soldiers as robbers and trailed the robbers to a place which they used to frequent. When they entered a farmer's house, young and old all fled; only one old woman remained and prepared for them food and drink, just as if she were serving the robber band. After three days he again visited the old woman bringing food from which he let also the old woman partake. She being convinced that they were real robbers, he started to talk with her. Coming to speak of the robber band she said: 'When they heard that Commander Sang had come they all dispersed. But when recently they heard that the commander kept his camp closed and did not come out after them, they gradually came back. This one lives here, that one lives there'. Three days later Sang I once more went to see her, and rewarded her liberally. Then he told her the truth saying: 'I am Commander Sang. I want you to find out for me the real hiding place of the robbers, do not let my plan leak out!' Then he divided his soldiers into separate groups, and caught all the robbers".

(From his biography)

CYKC ch. 7, page 118.

Sang I 桑懌 was a military official famous for his bravery. In the beginning

of the Pao-yüan era (1038-1039) he was killed in battle when the Hsi-hsia Prince
Li Yüan-hao revolted (for more details about this Prince cf. page 136 below).
Sang I's biography is found in the *Sung-shih*, ch. 325, where this case is recorded
in a more elaborate form.

B.

"When Su Ch'in served (as counsellor) in the state of Ch'i, the high
officials of that state used to vie with him in obtaining the favour of
the King. They sent a man to murder him but he had to flee without
having attained his object. The king tried to find the murderer but
failed. When Su Ch'in was about to die, he said to the King of Ch'i:
'After I have died you must have my body be torn asunder between
chariots and have it exposed on the market announcing that I tried
to create disturbances in Ch'i on behalf of the State Yen. Then you
will certainly catch my murderer'. The King did as Su Ch'in had said;
his murderer actually came forward (to claim a reward) and he was
duly executed".

(Formerly contained in the *Ch'un-ch'iu-hou-yü*)

CYKC ch. 7, page 119; IYC ch. 3, no. 65.

Su Ch'in 蘇秦 was a semi-legendary diplomat of the period of the
Warring States; cf. H. Maspéro, *Le Roman de Sou Ts'in*, in "Études Asiatiques",
Hanoi 1925.

The *Ch'un-ch'iu-hou-yü* is a small work in 1 ch., by the Chin scholar K'ung Yen
(孔衍, 268-320 A.D.). Cf. the text reprinted in the *Han-hsüeh-t'ang* 漢學
堂 ts'ung-shu, where this story is related on page 9 b.

13. *Kao Chieh shows a stolen boot;*
    Yang Chin recovers stolen silk

A.

"In the Northern Ch'i Dynasty (550-557 A.D.), when (Kao) Chieh,
Prince of Jen-ch'eng, was Prefect of P'ing-chou, a married woman was
washing clothes on the bank of the River Fen. There came a traveler on
horseback who (violated her or committed another offense and) rode
away after he had changed his old boots for her new ones. The woman
took one old boot with her and went to the Prefect to report the case.
The Prince summoned all old women of the city. He showed them the boot
saying falsely: 'A man on horseback was robbed with violence on the
road. This is one of his boots found there. Is there not a relative of him

among you?' One old woman started beating her breast and wailed: 'My son wore those when yesterday he went to visit his wife's family!' Thus the criminal was found and arrested".

CYKC ch. 7, page 111; IYC ch. 2, no. 47.

Kao Chieh 高湝 was the 10th son of Kao Huan (高歡 ; BD no. 954) who laid the foundation of the N.Ch'i Dynasty; Chieh's brother Kao Yang (高洋 ; BD no. 964) became the first Emperor. Kao Chieh was known as a just and lenient administrator. Later he acquired merit when mobilising the Ch'i army against Chou but was captured by the enemy and died together with his brother Kao Yang. Cf. his biography in *Pei-shih*, ch. 51, where this case is told.

B.

"When Yang Chin, styled Lo-han, of the Northern Chou Dynasty (557-581) was Prefect of Chi-chou, there was a man who because of military prowess was rewarded with three hundred bolts of silk. When he was at a distance of ten *li* from the city, he was badly wounded by a robber who made off with the silk. Shortly afterwards a messenger on horseback passed by there and the wounded man could describe his assailant to him (before he died). The messenger went to the Prefecture and reported the case. Yang Chin had publicly announced that a man wearing robes of such-and-such colour, and riding such-and-such a horse, had been murdered ten *li* East of the city; that his identity was unknown, and that if he had any relatives they should immediately come to view and take the body. Then an old woman came forward and said crying: 'He is my own son!' Thereupon the robber was apprehended, and all the silk recovered also".

CYKC ch. 7, page 120; IYC ch. 5, no. 95; YP no. 72.

Yang Chin 楊津 served as Prefect in Chi-chou and Hua-chou 華州 , and between 525-527 as Prefect of Ting-chou 定州 . After the advent of the Chou Dynasty he became prominent as a general. Cf. his biography in the *Pei-shih* ch. 41; there this case is included.

14. *Li Chieh makes people purchase a coffin;*
     Chung-jung reprimands and shoots a person

A.

"In the T'ang Dynasty, when Li Chieh was Governor of Ho-nan (i.e. the Eastern Capital Lo-yang), a widow accused her son of unfilial behaviour. [The son would adduce nothing in his defense, he only said: 'I have offended against my mother, I gladly submit to the death penalty']. Li Chieh studied the complaint but could find no proof of unfilial behaviour. He then said to the widow: 'You are a widow and you only have this one son. For the present crime he must be put to death. Don't you feel remorse?' The widow answered: 'A disobedient son, why should he be spared?' Li Chieh said: 'Then I thus decide the case. Go to buy a coffin and bring it here to receive your son's body (after he has been executed)'. Then he ordered an officer to watch the woman. (The officer noticed that when the woman had left the tribunal) she said to a Taoist monk: 'The affair is settled!' Soon she came back (to the tribunal) with a coffin. Li Chieh still hoped that she would reconsider but the widow stuck firmly to her former decision. At that time the Taoist monk was waiting (again) outside the gate. Li Chieh had him secretly arrested. He confessed as soon as he was interrogated, saying: 'I had illicit relations with the widow, but we were always hindered by the son; therefore we wanted to get rid of him'. Li Chieh thereupon had the Taoist monk and the widow beaten to death, and their bodies placed in the coffin''.

CYKC ch. 5, page 63; IYC ch. 1, no. 22; YP no. 2.

Li Chieh 李 傑 was especially famous as a perspicacious judge; he was appointed Governor of Ho-nan in 712 A.D., and ended his career as Censor-in-chief in the Capital. Cf. his biography in *Hsin-t'ang-shu* ch. 128; the case related here is also found there.

The words of the son—placed between square brackets in the translation—occur in the version of this case in TYPS-II.

B.

''In the Later Chin Dynasty (936-946 A.D.), when An Chung-jung was Commander of Heng-chou, a man and his wife accused together their son of unfilial behaviour. An Chung-jung reprimanded the son in front of his parents; drawing his sword he ordered them to kill their son themselves. The father wept and said he could not bear to do it. But the mother cursed the son, took the sword and set upon him. An Chung-jung questioned her, whereupon it turned out that she was the son's stepmother. He reviled her, then he put an arrow on his bow and shot her dead. This gladdened the heart of all who heard about it''.

CYKC ch. 5, page 64; IYC ch. 3, no. 61.

An Chung-jung 安 重 榮 was an able general who fought against the Ki-tans; for his exploits see Franke, vol. IV, page 47 sq.

This case is related in his biography in the *Hsin-wu-tai-shih* ch. 51.

15. *Su Ts'ai's request regarding common burial;*
Chia Yen dismisses a man who deferred mourning.

A.

"At the time when Su Ts'ai served as Reviewing Official in the High Court of Justice there was a man whose mother remarried after his father had died. When he heard later that his mother had died and had been buried, he stole the coffin and interred it in his father's tomb. According to the law he would have to be executed (being guilty of desecrating a grave). Su Ts'ai alone said: 'A son who steals his mother's coffin in order to bury her in his father's tomb, this can in no way be compared with desecrating a grave in order to loot it'. On his request the son's death sentence was commuted".

CYKC ch. 4, page 55; IYC ch. 8, no. 167; YP no. 49.

Su Ts'ai 蘇 寀 occupied several official functions under the Sung Emperor Ying-tsung (1064-1067 A.D.) and was well known as an expert in judicial matters. Cf. his biography in the *Sung-shih*, ch. 331, where this same case is related.

B.

"When the Reader-in-waiting (of the Han-lin Academy) Chia Yen was serving in the Bureau of Executory Personnel, Cheng Tse, Pre-fectural Judge of I-chou had served in Szuchuan Province for three years without knowing that his father had died. He only went to arrange the burial when the time of his transfer had arrived, and when the official in charge of personnel changes did not issue the documents (relative to his new post). As soon as Cheng Tse had completed the mourning, he requested to be admitted to the periodical examinations of officials. Chia Yen observed: 'For three years not having inquired after his father, although this cannot be branded as concealing one's parent's death (in order to retain office), it can hardly be called filial behaviour!' Thus in the end Cheng Tse was punished by being dismissed and sent back to his native place".

(From his tomb inscription composed by Wang Kuei)

CYKC ch. 4, page 56; IYC ch. 8, no. 168; YP no. 50.

Chia Yen 賈黯 was an official known for his strictness and his courageous memorials to the Throne. Cf. his biography in *Sung-shih* ch. 302. where the present case is reproduced in a slightly abbreviated form.

TYPS-II gives the name of the unfilial official as *Sang* Tse 桑澤 ; the characters *sang* and *cheng* 乘 resemble each other in cursive writing.

Wang Kuei (王珪 1019-1085 A.D.) was a scholar-official known for his excellent literary style; when serving at Court, all important proclamations were drafted by him. He left a literary collection, the *Hua-yang-chi* 華陽集 in 100 ch.

In accordance with an old-established and strictly enforced rule, officials in mourning should resign from their post for the duration—three years in the case of the death of one's father or mother. As a rule such a respite from the exacting duties of active service was not unwelcome, for many officials the periods of mourning were the only vacations they had in their entire career; many scholar-officials utilized the periods of mourning for devoting themselves to their literary work. However, for those who placed ambition before everything else, those spells of forced inactivity meant delay in promotion and loss of emoluments; hence one reads occasionally about attempts at evading the rule, as referred to in Chia Yen's remark.

16. *Cheng recognizes evil;*

   Yen suspects crying

A.

"Once Cheng Tzu-ch'an (when riding in his chariot) heard a woman cry (by the side of the road); he had his men arrest and interrogate her. It came out that she had indeed murdered her husband. His charioteer asked Cheng how he had known this. He answered: 'If a relative is ill, one sorrows; if he is going to die one is in fear, and after he has died one is sad. Now I noticed from the way that woman cried after her husband had died that she was afraid rather than sad. Thus I knew that she had committed a crime'."

(From the *Tu-i-chih*)

CYKC ch. 5, page 69; IYC ch. 2, no. 41.

Cheng Tzu-ch'an (鄭子產 581-521 B.C.) was a contemporary of Confucius. He was famous as an expert in judicial matters, and is credited with the compilation of a Penal Code. Confucius wept when he heard that Cheng had died. Cf. BD no. 1029.

The *Tu-i-chi* 獨異志 is a small work in 3 ch. by the T'ang writer Li Jung 李冗 . The fragments reprinted in SF do not contain this story.

B.

"When Yen Tsun was Prefect of Yang-chou he once made a tour of inspection in the territory under his jurisdiction. Suddenly he heard some one crying in fear rather than in sadness. He halted his chariot and interrogated that person. She answered: 'My husband had an accident with fire and burned to death'. Yen Tsun suspected her and had a constable watch the dead body. He noticed that flies congregated on the top of the dead man's head. He parted the hair and looked: he found (the head of) an iron nail (that had been driven into the skull). Then it transpired that the woman had together with her paramour murdered her husband, and their guilt was established".

CYKC ch. 5, page 69; IYC ch. 1, no. 16; YP no. 14.

All TYPS editions give the name of the Prefect as *Chuang* Tsun 莊遵, but IYC has *Yen* 嚴. CYKC ch. 1, page 12 gives another case solved by the same Prefect; the editor there shows that *Chuang* Tsun is a mistake for *Yen* Tsun who served as Prefect in Yang-chou in the Eastern Han Dynasty and was known as an able administrator.

The "nail murder" is a famous motif in Chinese crime literature, and it has been utilized several times by later Chinese novelists. The point of these stories is always that the judge is baffled by the fact that although there are strong reasons for suspecting the widow, the dead body of her husband does not show any signs of violence. The reasoning that leads to the final discovery of the nail's head is elaborated in various ways. Cf. the 18th century detective novels *Shih-kung-an* 施公案 (cases solved by the Ch'ing scholar-official Shih Shih-lun 施世倫 1659-1722) and *Wu-tse-t'ien-szu-ta-ch'i-an* 武則天四大奇案, partially published by me in English translation under the title *Dee Goong An, Three murder Cases solved by Judge Dee* (i.e. the famous T'ang statesman Ti Jen-chieh 狄仁傑 630-700), Tokyo 1949. A different version is given by Rev. Macgowan in his *Chinese Folklore Tales*, London 1910, under the title "The Widow Ho", and another by G. C. Stent in the *China Review* of 1881 (vol. X, pp. 41-43) under the title of "The Double Nail Murders". The latter is an interesting variation of the motif. When the coroner fails to discover any trace of violence, his own wife suggests to him to look for a nail in the head. When the judge has convicted the murdered man's widow on that evidence, he has also the coroner's wife brought before him, since her knowledge of such a subtle way of committing a murder seems suspicious to him. When it is found that the coroner is her second husband, the coffin of her first husband is opened, and a nail discovered inside the empty skull. Both women are executed.

TYPS-III, first line, has 聞一哭聲, which is a better reading than 一聞哭聲 in TYPS-I; TYPS-II has 忽聞哭聲, which I have adopted here.

17. *Szu-ching deceives a retainer;*
  An official slanders P'ei Kuang

A.

"During the reign of Empress Wu (684-704 A.D.) of the T'ang Dynasty, some one accused the Imperial son-in-law Ts'ui Hsüan of planning a revolt. The Empress ordered the Censor Chang Hsing-chi to investigate. Now the accuser had first enticed one of Ts'ui Hsüan's concubines (to join the plot) and hid her. Thus (when the case was heard) the accuser said: 'Since the concubine was going to denounce the planned revolt, Ts'ui Hsüan murdered her'. Chang Hsing-chi conducted an investigation but could not formulate a case (against Ts'ui Hsüan). The Empress was angry and ordered a second investigation, but still no concrete facts were brought to light. Then the Empress said: 'If that concubine is not found, how could he prove that he is innocent?' Chang Hsing-chi then pressed Ts'ui Hsüan's family to find the concubine. Ts'ui Hsüan's second cousin Szu-ching promised a large reward (to whomsoever would give information about her whereabouts), but learned nothing. Then (Szu-ching found out that) all the deliberations conducted inside the Ts'ui residence were immediately known to the accuser in prison, and he suspected that the latter had an accomplice in the Ts'ui household. Therefore he said falsely (in a family council): 'We must hire a professional stalwart to kill the accuser'. Having said this, he went the next morning to watch beside the tribunal. Then there came a retainer who for a long time had enjoyed the trust of the T'sui family; he offered a bribe to the guard at the gate for delivering a message to the accuser. Szu-ching (came forward) and scolded that man saying: 'You betrayed Ts'ui Hsüan, we must kill you!' The retainer thereupon led Szu-ching to the accuser's accomplices, and the concubine was discovered with them. Then only Ts'ui Hsüan was released".

CYKC ch. 3, page 31; IYC ch. 1, no. 18; YP no. 34.

The editor of the CYKC states in a note that this case does not agree with historical facts, and that it must be derived from T'ang fiction.

TYPS-III reads in the 7th column of page 13 *ku* 顧 instead of *ku* 雇, and in the last line *ch'i* 妻 instead of *ch'ieh* 妾 .

It should be noted that in serious cases, such as high treason, both accuser and accused are put in prison; if the latter can prove his innocence, the accuser is executed.

B.

("When in the T'ang Dynasty, in the year 685, false accusations became rampant), Chiang Shen, a subordinate official of Hu-chou, took a document written by the Prefect P'ei Kuang, and cut out a number of characters; these he joined together so as to form a new text, falsely constituting a rebellious letter sent (by P'ei Kuang) to Hsü Ching-yeh, and then accused P'ei. A Censor was sent to investigate this matter. P'ei Kuang stated: 'The characters are indeed my writing, but the letter was not written by me'. The case was tried thrice, but no decision could be arrived at. Then Empress Wu ordered to despatch a capable man to investigate, saying: 'Chang Ch'u-chin should be able to arrive at a decision'. (Chang investigated the case, but) P'ei Kuang stuck to his former statement. Deeply distressed he lay down on his back (on a couch) facing the window. He saw the sunlight filter through the (paper) window panes (and this gave him a hint). He examined (the rebellious letter) against the light, and (thus discovered that) it consisted of characters patched together. Chang thereupon (called a session of the tribunal and) ordered Chiang Shen to throw the letter in (a bowl filled with) water; then the characters came apart one by one. Chiang Shen knocked his head on the floor and confessed his crime. The Empress had him beheaded".

CYKC ch. 3, page 31; IYC ch. 1, no. 19; YP no. 33.

The source of this case is unknown. The editor of the CYKC observes that there is a discrepancy in the dates.

The opening sentence 唐垂拱年羅織事起 is given only in TYPS-II; I added it in the translation because it indicates the background of such trumped-up charges. The cruel persecution that was inaugurated by Empress Wu in the year 692—mainly because she had become afraid after the rebellion of Hsü Ching-yeh (cf. BD no. 770)—is graphically described in the section on criminal law in the *Chiu-t'ang-shu;* cf. Bünger, pp. 106-107. In the capital a special Court of Inquisition *T'ui-shih-shih-yüan* 推事使院 was instituted where the notorious Lai Chün-ch'en 來俊臣 and other inquisitors encouraged false accusations of rebellion, and had hundreds of innocent people executed.

Lai Chün-ch'en is said to have written a book called *Lo-chih-ching* 羅織經 "Manual for ensnaring persons in the law", which explains the various methods of involving innocent people in law cases and of fabricating false accusations. The term *lo-chih* in the first line of this case refers to the title of this book.

Chang Ch'u-chin 張楚金 was Vice-Minister of Justice from 676-678 A.D., and was charged i.a. with revising the then existing criminal laws.

18. *Fu Yen and the beans in a chicken's crop;*
    Chang Chü and the ashes in a pig's mouth

A.

"When Fu (Yen, styled) Chi-kuei of the (Former) Sung Dynasty (420-479 A.D.) was magistrate of Shan-yin, two men got involved in a dispute about the ownership of chickens (and brought the case before him for a decision). Fu Yen asked: 'What do you feed the chickens in the morning?' One man said beans, the other said rice. Fu Yen had one chicken killed and its crop cut; it contained beans. He thereupon fined the man who fed rice to his chickens".

CYKC ch. 6, page 95; IYC ch.1, no. 8.; YP no. 61.

Fu Yen 傅琰 served as magistrate in Wu-k'ang 武康 and Shan-yin and earned fame as an able and just administrator. He was later appointed Prefect of I-chou 益 州 , and in the Yung-ming era (483-493 A.D.) Chief Administrator of the Prince of Lu-ling. Cf. his biography in *Nan-ch'i-shu*, ch. 53, where this case is recorded.

Cf. also Case 26-A.

B.

"When Chang Chü of the Wu Dynasty (220-280 A.D.) was magistrate of Chü-chang, a woman murdered her husband and thereafter set fire to the house so that it burned down, falsely stating that her husband had burned to death. Her husband's family suspected her, and accused her before the authorities. The woman denied and would not confess her crime. Chang Chü then took two pigs. One he had killed, the other he let live; then he had both pigs burned on a heap of faggots. On investigating (the differences of the two burned pigs he found that) the pig previously killed had no ashes in its mouth, while the mouth of the pig burned alive was full of it. Then it was verified that there were no ashes in the dead man's mouth. When she was confronted with this evidence the woman indeed confessed".

(Source unknown)

CYKC ch. 6, page 94; IYC ch. 1, no. 6; YCTI no. 15; YP. no. 23.

TYPS-II, and IYC read the first line 張 舉 吳 人 也 "Chang Chü, a native of Wu"; TYPS-I and III, and YP read 吳 張 舉 "Chang Chü of the Wu Dynasty". I agree with the editor of CYKC that the latter reading is the better one. Since as far as I could ascertain there is no record of a person called Chang

Chü who would fit the present case, it is difficult to check the point; but the reading "Chang Chü of the Wu Dynasty" accords better with the style of the other cases, most of which begin with a similar phrase.

The YCTI text starts the case with the phrase 文章舉爲句章令 which is evidently corrupt.

It is interesting that Chang Chü chose pigs for his experiment; for it is well known that the anatomy and general size of a pig are very similar to those of the human body.

19. *The Prefect of Ting-chou has a hide recognized;*
The Prefect of Ts'ang-chou has meat bought

A.

"When in the Northern Ch'i Dynasty (550-557 A.D.) (Kao) Yu, Prince of P'eng-ch'eng, was Prefect of Ting-chou, a man's black cow with a white spot (on its back) was stolen. The Prince then falsely announced that the Prefectural stores would pay double the price for cowhides. When the lots of hides started arriving, he let the owner of the (stolen) cow indicate its hide. Thus the thief was caught".

CYKC ch. 7, page 111; IYC ch. 1, no. 12.

Kao Yu 高洨 was the fifth son of Kao Huan (cf. the note added to Case 13-A). He served as Prefect of Ting-chou in the Wu-ting era (543-550 A.D.), and after the Ch'i Dynasty had been established he was made Prince of P'eng-ch'eng. He enjoyed the reputation of a wise and discerning official. Cf. his biography in *Pei-shih*, ch. 51, where both this case and the next are included.

All texts read 黑牛上有白毛; but the text in the *Pei-shih* adds the character *pei* 背 between *niu* 牛 and *shang* 上, which I have adopted here.

B.

"When the same Prince was Prefect of Ts'ang-chou, there came a man from Yu-chou leading a mule that carried a load of dried deer-meat. Having arrived at the boundary of Ts'ang-chou—walking slow because of a foot ailment—he happened to meet a man who accompanied him on the way. This man made off with the mule and the dried meat. The following morning the merchant reported this to the Prefecture. The Prince ordered his assistants and the officers of the tribunal to go out each man by himself and buy dried dear meat, not haggling over the price. (When looking over these purchases) the owner recognized his own deer meat, and thus the thief was caught".

CYKC ch. 7, page 111; IYC ch. 1, no. 11.
   Cf. also Case 22-B.

20. *Chang accepts a case outside his district;*
    P'ei Tzu-yün orders a quick confession

A.

"In the T'ang Dynasty, when Chang Yün-chi was magistrate of Wu-yang, he instructed those under him by his virtuous example, and the common people cherished him. In the neighbour district of Yüan-wu, a man left one of his cows for eight or nine years with the family of his wife; during that time the cow had more than ten calves. When the man was going to move to another place, his wife's family did not give him the cows. The magistrate of that district heard the case several times but could not solve it. The man then crossed the district boundary and laid a plaint before Chang Yün-chi. Chang said: 'You have your own magistrate, why should you come here?' The man wept and would not go. When he had explained the facts of the case, Chang ordered his assistants to bind the man and throw a piece of cloth over his head (so that he could not be recognized). They took him to the village where his wife's family lived (and told the people there that) they were arresting cow thieves; they began a minute inquiry as to where all the cows in that village had come from. The wife's family, not knowing the reason behind it, were afraid that they might become involved (in the investigation of the cow thefts). Therefore they said: 'These cows belong to our daughter's husband'. Chang thereupon ordered to remove the cloth from the man's head, and said: 'This is your son-in-law! You must give him back his cows!'".

CYKC ch. 7, page 101; YCTI no. 12.

   Chang Yün-chi 張允濟 first served under the Sui Dynasty as magistrate of Wu-yang, where he acquired the reputation of a strict administrator. After the advent of the T'ang Dynasty, he occupied various official posts; in the Chen-kuan era (627-649 A.D.) he was Prefect of Yu-chou 幽州. Cf. his biography in *Hsin-t'ang-shu* ch. 197, were this case is recorded.
   Cf. also Case 22-A.

B.

"In the T'ang Dynasty P'ei Tzu-yün was magistrate of the Hsin-hsiang district in the Wei Prefecture. When Wang Kung, a man of that district, was leaving for military service on the border, he left six cows with Li Chin, his maternal uncle. (Li Chin looked after the cows) five years, during which time they had thirty calves, (worth ten thousand strings of cash or more). When Wang Kung came back, he asked for the cows. His uncle said: 'Two of your cows have died. I return to you only four old cows'. Wang brought this case before the tribunal. P'ei Tzu-yün had Wang put in prison, and ordered the arrest of Li Chin as an accomplice in the cow theft. When Li Chin arrived, P'ei scolded him saying: 'The thief mentioned you as having stolen thirty cows together with him, all the animals are concealed on your farm. I shall now call the thief and confront him with you!' He made Wang, whose head had been covered with a piece of cloth, stand by the Southern side of the dais, and ordered Li Chin to confess immediately. Li then said: 'The thirty cows were all calved by cows belonging to my nephew, they were truly not obtained by theft!' P'ei thereupon removed the cloth from Wang's head. He ordered Li Chin to return all the cows but five, which were given to him as a reward for his trouble (in taking care of the cows during Wang's absence)".

CYKC ch. 7, page 102; IYC ch. 1, no. 20; YCTI no. 13; YP no. 65.

It seems that P'ei Tzu-yün's fame rests entirely on this one case; beyond this, I could find no details about his career.

21. *Wang Chih opposes an acquittal;*
    Ma Liang commutes a death sentence

A.

"When the Academician-in-waiting (of the T'ien-chang Pavilion) Wang Chih was Prefect of Lu-chou, a robber killed a member of his band and stole his money. He was arrested by a patrol, and Wang Chih proposed the death sentence for him. The Fiscal Intendant Yang Kao opposed this saying: 'If a robber kills another robber, he should be exempted from the death penalty'. Wang Chih said: 'If a robber kills another robber, he may be exempted provided that he gives himself up to the authorities. But in this case he killed the man, stole his money, and did not give himself up but was arrested. If he were exempted from the death penalty, how could that be in accordance with the spirit of the law?' He several times sent memorials to the Throne but no sentence was pronounced. Then he was degraded to Supervisor in Ling-hsien-kuan in Shu-chou. But the next year, when Han Ch'i was heading the Bureau of Judicial Investigation (in the capital) he submitted that a robber who kills another robber and does not give himself up must not be exempted".

(From his biography)

CYKC ch. 4, page 52.

Wang Chih (王 質 1001-1045) was a scholar-official, known for his acumen in juridical matters. Cf. his biography in *Sung-shih*, ch. 269, where this case is related in detail; it is added there that after the pronouncement of Han Ch'i (see above, the note of Case 7-B), Wang Chih was again given a high post.

Yang Kao 楊 告 was a famous jurist; cf. his biography in *Sung-shih*, ch. 304.

B.

"When the President (of the Ministry of Public Works) Ma Liang was Prefect of Tan-chou, there was in a district under his jurisdiction an army deserter who, attacking and robbing the villagers, caused great trouble to them. Some plotted his murder, and four of those would according to the law have to be executed. Ma Liang said: 'To apply the death sentence as retaliation (for a murder) to persons who (by that murder) proved able to eradicate an evil on behalf of the public weal, how could this be the intention of the law?' The death sentence of all four was commuted".

CYKC ch. 4, page 51.

Ma Liang (馬 亮 959-1031) had a long and distinguished career, being known especially for his just administration. His detailed biography in *Sung-shih* ch. 298 relates many instances of his setting free innocent persons, i.a. the case given here.

TYPS-I and III add here a brief comment by Cheng K'o.

22. *Chang Yün-chi smells onions;*

   A Prince inscribes vegetables

A.

"When Chang Yün-chi was magistrate of Wu-yang, he noticed by the side of the road an old woman planting onions; she had built a hut to watch them. Chang Yün-chi told her: 'You need not trouble to watch them. Should they be stolen, come and report to me'. The old woman followed his advice. The next morning onions proved stolen, and the old woman reported this to Chang. He summoned all the people who lived near the onion field. One by one he had their hands smelled. Thus he found the thief".

CYKC ch. 7, page 107.

For Chang Yün-chi, see above Case 20-A. This case also is recorded in his biography in *Hsin-t'ang-shu* ch. 197.

B.

"When (Kao) Yu, Prince of P'eng-ch'eng in the Northern Ch'i Dynasty (550-557 A.D.) was Prefect of Ts'ang-chou, an old woman had planted vegetables; these vegetables were repeatedly stolen. The Prince ordered his assistants to go and write secretly some characters on the leaves of the vegetables. Thus the next day these vegetables could be recognized on the market, and the thieves arrested".

CYKC ch. 7, page 111; IYC ch. 1, no. 13.

For Kao Yu, see Case 19-A above. The present case also is related in his biography.

23. *Lü and the woman with the cut-off hands;*
   Pao and the cow with the cut-off tongue

A.

"When the Reader-in-waiting (of the Han-lin Academy) Lü Kung-cho was Prefect of K'ai-feng, there was a soldier's wife whose husband had gone on a far expedition. One night a robber entered her quarters; he departed after having cut off her hands. This crime caused much alarm among the citizens of the capital. Lü Kung-cho thought that only a personal enemy of the husband would thus give himself satisfaction. He despatched mounted guards to interrogate the husband. (Having elicited from him the name of his enemy, and reported this to the Prefect), it proved to be his camp-mate Han Yüan. He was convicted of depravity and executed".

(From his tomb inscription, composed by Wang Kuei)

CYKC ch. 6, page 93; IYC ch. 8, no. 153; YP no. 17.

Lü Kung-cho 呂 公 綽 became Corrector of the Han-lin Academy in the

T'ien-sheng era (1023-1031), later Reader-in-waiting; thereafter he occupied various other high posts, i.a. Academician of the Lung-t'u Pavilion. Cf. his biography in *Sung-shih*, ch. 311; there several of his wise judgements are related, but not the present case.

For Wang Kuei see above, Case 15-B.

B.

"When the Assistant Commissioner (of Military Affairs) Pao Ch'eng was in the beginning of his career magistrate of the T'ien-ch'ang district of Yang-chou, some one reported that a robber had cut off the tongue of his cow. Pao ordered him in secret to go home, slaughter the cow and sell its meat. Soon a man came to the tribunal reporting that the victim had clandestinely slaughtered a cow. Pao interrogated the informer saying: 'Why did you first cut off the tongue of so-and-so's cow, and on top of that now accuse him?' This took the man by surprise and he confessed".

(From his biography)

CYKC ch. 7, page 103; IYC ch. 4. no. 72; YP no. 38.

Pao Ch'eng 包拯 (999-1062 A.D.) is one of the most famous judges in Chinese history; he is also the hero of the famous Chinese play *Hui-lan-chi* 灰闌记 "The Chalk Circle". After having obtained his *chin-shih* degree he became a Judicial Investigator of the High Court, then served as magistrate of the Ch'ien-ch'ang 建昌 district. Under the Emperor Jen-tsung he was appointed Auxiliary Academician of the Lung-t'u Pavilion, and ended his career as Executive Secretary in the Ministry of Rites. In later ages he became the centre of a cluster of detective stories, collected and published under the title of *Lung-t'u-kung-an* 龍圖公案. He also figures largely in the Chinese theatre, where "Judge Pao" Pao-kung 包公, with his black face and long beard is a familiar figure. He is known to young and old as the great master-detective. Cf. BD no. 1621, and his detailed biography in *Sung-shih*, ch. 316, where this case is quoted at the very beginning.

No cattle could be slaughtered without official permission; cf. the T'ang Code, ch. 15 article 8.

Cf. also Case 46-A.

24. *Ts'ui investigates a treasury;*
Chang enters through a tunnel

A.

"In the T'ang Dynasty, when Ts'ui Yen was Military Commander in

Hu-nan there was a depraved youth who was not tolerated any more by the people of his village. He thereupon inflicted upon himself (as it were) the punishment of 'shaving his head and putting a iron band round his neck', and took refuge with the Buddhist religion. He served as a menial, and falsely pretending to practice the Buddhist disciplines he tricked and deceived the ignorant laymen, and thus assembled wealth that was counted by the ten-thousand strings of cash. When Ts'ui Yen took up his office this monk feared that his doings would be found out. Therefore he gave up his monk's certificate and asked to be allowed to shed the fetters (of the priesthood) and return to the state of layman. Ts'ui Yen asked: 'How much money have you earned during these three years of teaching the Doctrine?' He answered: 'Just enough for my daily needs, I do not recall the exact amount'. Ts'ui Yen asked again: 'How much money have you spent for your expenditure?' The monk answered: 'A little over three thousand strings of cash'. Ts'ui Yen then said: 'Since you know exactly how much you spent, while you do not remember how much you earned, there must be some hidden deceit!' He searched the monk's accumulated wealth and found his quarters full of wives and children. Thereupon the monk's deceit and knavery were established, (he was punished and) his wealth was distributed among the poor''.

CYKC ch. 5, page 64; IYC ch. 5, no. 87; YP no. 71. Source unknown.

Ts'ui Yen 崔黯 became *chin-shih* in 828 A.D., and in the K'ai-ch'eng era (836-840 A.D.) was appointed Investigating Censor. He ended his career as Policy Critic-adviser of the Throne. Cf. his biography in *Chiu-t'ang-shu* ch. 117, where this case is not related.

K'un-ch'ien 髡鉗 is the technical name of an ancient punishment, the criminal's head being shaved (k'un) and an iron band placed round his neck (ch'ien); cf. Hulsewé, page 129. Here the term is evidently used figuratively, to suggest the fetters of the priesthood, and implying also the ruffian's show of penitence.

TYPS-I and III have *ch'i-nu* 妻孥 "wife and children", IYC has *ch'i-tzu* 妻子, with the same meaning. TYPS-II has *ch'i-nu* 妻帑; the Yüan editor observes in a note that *nu* should be read *t'ang*, meaning "treasury". Since *ch'i-nu* is a fixed binom, this gloss seems a mistake. In the title of the case, on the other hand, *nu* 帑 might well be read *t'ang*, and I have translated it as such.

TYPS-I and III have *lung-su* 龍俗, an elegant expression for "the ignorant crowd"; TYPS-II changes this into *yü-su* 愚俗, which is unnecessary.

B.

"In the Later Chin Dynasty (936-946 A.D.) there was in a Buddhist temple in the Hua village of the Kuan-shih district in Wei-chou an iron statue of the Buddha, more than one fathom high, and hollow inside. One day it was announced that this Buddha could speak. Both gentry and commoners assembled there like clouds, and their rich gifts piled up. The magistrate of the district reported this to the Prefecture. The Emperor Kao-tsu, who then was Commander of Yeh, could not fathom the mystery. He ordered Shang Ch'ien, an officer of the tribunal, to offer incense (in that temple) and take part in the service, at the same time investigating the phenomenon. The guardsman Chang Lu asked to be allowed to accompany the officer, in order to investigate this wizardry. Soldiers surrounded the temple and drove all the monks from their quarters and made them assemble in the main hall. Chang Lu then secretly opened the monk's quarters, and discovered there a tunnel. He entered it and found that it led to the socle of the iron Buddha. From inside the hollow body he enumerated in a strident voice the evil deeds of the monks. The officer of the tribunal thereupon ordered the arrest of the leaders of the monks, several people. When this was reported to the Emperor, he ordered them to be executed forthwith, and promoted Chang Lu to the post of Registrar of the district Ch'ang-ho".

CYKC ch. 5, page 64; IYC ch. 3, no. 59; YP no. 40. Source unknown.

Kao-tsu's name was Shih Ching-t'ang (石 敬 瑭 892-942 A.D.; cf. BD no. 1706). He was a general of Turkish descent, who later founded the N.Chin Dynasty. His career is described in detail in Franke, vol. IV, pp. 38-39 e.a.

TYPS-I and III give Chang Lu's rank as *san-ch'uan* 三 傳 ; IYC and CYKC omit this. I have followed TYPS-II which reads *san-wei* 三 衛 .

25. *Tu Hao on the destruction of a portrait;*
    Huang Pa has three men summarily executed

A.

"When the elder brother of the Executive Secretary Tu Hao was serving as judge in Chiang-nan, a son destroyed the painted portrait of his father, and therefore was accused by his relatives (of unfilial behaviour). (Tu Hao's brother) doubted whether there was a law that could be applied for deciding this case. At that time Tu Hao was still young, but he said immediately: 'This case should be tried as a parallel to those of Buddhist or Taoist monks destroying an image of their deities'. His elder brother greatly marveled (at this clever solution) and pronounced judgement accordingly".

CYKC ch. 4, page 51; YCTI no. 8.

Tu Hao 杜鎬 was employed in the Imperial Archives in the reign of T'ai-tsung (976-997 A.D.), and ended his career between 1008-1016 as Executive Secretary of the Ministry of Rites; he was known as a good classical scholar. Cf. his biography in *Sung-shih* ch. 296, which gives the present case in practically the same words.

B.

"Huang Pa, styled Tz'u-weng, was minister during the reign of the Han Emperor Hsüan (73-49 B.C.). In the boundary region of Yen and Tai, three men had married one and the same woman, who bore them a son. When the men wanted to separate, each of them claimed the child as his own. They brought their case before the Grandee Secretary asking Huang Pa to decide it. Huang said: 'Men who do not behave as human beings should be treated as animals!' The three men were beheaded and the child returned to its mother.

I find that the philosopher Hsün-tzu said: 'Those whose behaviour falls within the scope of the law should be judged according to the law. Those for whose behaviour the code gives no written rules should be judged according to (the nearest) parallel'. Thus, when Huang Pa had the three men executed, and when Wang Tsun had the stepson killed, they acted according to the nearest parallel. The law does not forbid animals to copulate indiscriminately, but if a man kills these animals he does not commit a crime. Therefore it was permissible that the judges mentioned here killed those persons (who behaved like animals'.

CYKC ch. 4, page 46; IYC ch. 2, no. 25; YCTI no. 5.

TYPS-II and IYC do not have the second alinea.

For Huang Pa see above, Case 4-B. Hsün-tzu was a famous philosopher of the 3d century B.C., who devoted special attention to the difference between men and animals; cf. Feng Yu-lan, *A History of Chinese Philosophy*, translated by Derk Bodde (Peking 1937, vol. I), more especially p. 296.

The story regarding Wang Tsun 王尊 is not found in TYPS, but CYKC relates it as appendix to the present case. It says: "In the time of the Emperor Yüan (48-33 B.C.), when Wang Tsun was magistrate of Huai-li, at the same time taking care of the affairs of the Mei-yang district, there was a woman of that district who accused her stepson of unfilial behaviour, saying: 'My son always has me as his wife, and he reviles and whips me'. When Wang heard this he sent his constables to arrest him. When interrogated he confessed. Wang Tsun said: 'The code has no law against incest with one's mother, because the Sages (of old) could not bear to write about such (awful) things. This man is what the Classics call an inventor of a (new) crime'. Thereupon he rose from his seat, had the unfilial son's body cut open and had him suspended on a tree. Then he had five of his mounted guards draw their bows and shoot him dead".

元帝時王尊守槐里令。兼行美陽令事。美
陽女子告假子不孝曰。兒常以我爲妻。詬笞
我。尊聞之。遣吏收捕。驗問辭服。尊曰。律
無妻母之法。聖人所不忍書。此經所謂造獄
者也。尊於是出坐廷上。取不孝子懸磔著樹。
使騎吏五人。張弓射殺之。

Wang Tsun was a famous judge; cf. his biography in *Han-shu*, ch. 76. This case is also discussed in Balazs, page 105, and referred to by Hulsewé, page 111.

Hulsewé, page 98 note 43, refers to the same case as attributed here to Huang Pa, described in the fragments of the *Hou-han-shu* by Hsieh Ch'eng 謝成 as having been solved by Fan Yen-shou 范延壽, who served 27-19 B.C. as Commandant of Justice. Hulsewé points out that there it is wrongly stated that the case occurred in the reign of Hsüan-ti. This mistake is doubtless due to the text quoted by the TYPS and that of the *Hou-han-shu* having become mixed up. It may be added that the *Hou-han-shu* reads 燕趙之間 "in the boundary region of Yen and Chao".

26. *Fu Yen has silk flogged;*
    Li Hui has salt beaten out

A.

"In the (Former) Sung Dynasty (420-479 A.D.), when Fu (Yen, styled) Chi-kuei was magistrate in Shan-yin, there were two (old women), one of whom sold sugar and the other needles. They had a quarrel over the ownership of a ball of silk, and brought the matter before Fu Yen. He ordered to hang the silk against a pillar and to flog it; then some iron filings dropped from it. He thereupon fined the woman who sold sugar".

CYKC ch. 6, page 96; IYC ch. 1, no. 7; YP no. 54.

For Fu Yen see Case 18-A above; this case is also recorded in his biography in the *Nan-ch'i-shu*.

B.

"When Li Hui of the Later Wei Dynasty (386-534 A.D.) served as Prefect of Yung-chou, a salt carrier and a wood carrier quarreled about a lamb-skin, each claiming it as the very one he used to wear on his back. Li Hui ordered one of his officers: 'Question this skin under torture, then you will know its owner'. All the officers were dumbfounded. Li Hui had the lamb-skin placed on a mat, and had it beaten with a stick; then grains of salt came out of it. He showed them to the contestants, and the wood carrier confessed".

CYKC ch. 6, page 95; IYC ch. 1, no. 15.

Li Hui 李 惠 was the father-in-law of the Emperor Hsien-wen (466-470 A.D.); he proved himself an able administrator and eminent general. Cf. his biography in *Pei-shih* ch. 80, where the present case is recorded.

27. *The Prefect of Yang-chou has a sorceress flogged;*
Hsüeh Hsiang has a Turkish merchant arrested

A.

"In the Later Wei Dynasty (386-534 A.D.) when Li Ch'ung was Prefect of Yang-chou, an exile from Ting-chou called Chieh Szu-an deserted from the military corvée and failed to return. His elder brother Chieh Ch'ing-pin (knowing that he would be held responsible) decided that (his absconding brother's) name had better be deleted in the records. He therefore claimed a dead body found outside the city and falsely stated that it was his younger brother, murdered by Su Hsien-fu and Li Kai (two men against whom Chieh Ch'ing-pin had apparently a grudge). (To strengthen his case he had) a sorceress called Yang make a ghost in a séance relate his younger brother's bitter fate. (When interrogated in the tribunal) Li Kai and the other man could not stand the torture, and both confessed. Li Ch'ung suspected that this was not the truth. He sent two of his own men who feigned to have come from the border region. They said to Chieh Ch'ing-pin: 'When we were staying in Pei-chou, one night a man stayed overnight in our inn; he said that he was a deserter from the military corvée, called Chieh Szu-an. We wanted to deliver him to the authorities but he begged us urgently to desist. He added that he had an elder brother called Chieh Ch'ing-pin who lived in Yang-chou. If we would pity him and go for him to report to his brother, his brother would certainly give us a generous reward. Now we have come to ascertain this. If you let us go without the money, it is not too late yet to report your brother to the authorities'. Hsieh Ch'ing-pin then was sad and appeared greatly embarrassed. (When this was reported to Li Ch'ung) he had him arrested and interrogated him, and he confesssed. A few days later Chieh Szu-an was caught by someone and brought before the tribunal. Li Ch'ung had the sorceress given hundred lashes, and Li Kai and the other man were released".

(From his biography in the *Pei-shih*)

CYKC ch. 1, page 5; IYC ch. 5, no. 82; YP no. 42.

For Li Ch'ung see Case 4-A above; also this case is recorded in his biography in the *Pei-shih*, in a slightly enlarged form.

B.

"When the Commissioner of Military Affairs Hsüeh Hsiang at the beginning of his career was Finance Inspector of the Metropolitan area he concurrently controlled the trade taxes. There was a Turkish merchant who when passing the Tax bureau produced a box filled with silver; on it was written: 'Sent by the Commissioner of Military Affairs to the Director General of the Circuit Ching-yüan'. Hsüeh Hsiang said: 'This is certainly an attempt at deceit (in order to avoid paying the tax on the silver); how could there be a high official who when he wishes to send a present to some one, employs a Turkish merchant for forwarding it?' He had the merchant arrested and took him to the Prefecture for trial; the man then indeed confessed his deceit".

(From his tomb inscription composed by Lü Ta-fang)

CYKC ch. 5, page 79; YP no. 41.

Hsüeh Hsiang 薛向 served first as Registrar of Yung-shou 永壽. In the beginning of the Yüan-feng era (1078-1085 A.D.) he was appointed to the Military Affairs Bureau, distinguishing himself as an expert in financial matters. He ended his career as Prefect of Sui-chou 隨州. Cf. his biography in *Sung-shih*, ch. 328, where this case is recorded.

Lü Ta-fang (呂 大 防 1027-1097) was a prominent scholar-official of the Sung period.

28. *Ch'eng K'an and the gate of the enemy's house; Pi Chung-yu and the Commander's residence*

A.

"When the Palace Councillor Ch'eng K'an was Prefect of Ch'ien-chou, there was a man who had an inveterate enemy. One day his sons said secretly to their mother: 'You are old and sickly, we fear that you will not live long after this. We beg leave to kill you, since through your death we shall be able to avenge our father'. They then killed their mother and laid her dead body in front of their enemy's gate. Then they accused him in the tribunal. The enemy could not clear himself of this charge. But Ch'eng K'an was in doubt. Some one said that there was no cause for any doubt. But Ch'eng K'an said: 'When one has murdered some one and then leaves the body in front of one's own gate, is this not sufficient cause for doubt?' He himself took charge of the investigation, and discovered the original plot".
(From his tomb inscription by Wang Kuei)

CYKC ch. 3, page 36; IYC ch. 8, no. 152; YP no. 13.

Ch'eng K'an 程戡 after having occupied several official posts was appointed Academician-in-waiting of the T'ien-chang Pavilion. In the reign of Jen-tsung he was appointed Prefect of I-chou, then returned to the capital as Academician of the Tuan-ming Hall 端 明 殿 . Under the Emperor Ying-tsung (1064-1067) he earned fame in his dealings with the barbarians. Cf. his biography in *Sung-shih*, ch. 292, where the case related here is briefly alluded to.
For Wang Kuei see Case 15-B above.

B.

"When Pi Chung-yu was Judicial Intendant of Ho-tung, the Ministerial Vice-President Han Chen was appointed Commander of T'ai-yüan. Then one of the Commander's house slaves, a Turkish boy, reported that a soldier had robbed him of his clothes, right beside his official residence. Han Chen was angry and ordered his officers to have the soldier branded in the face. But Pi Chung-yu observed that the garments of a young boy are thin and few, and that it seemed against human nature to dare to steal them near the very mansion of the

Commander, the former Vice-President. He had another official investigate, and it proved indeed to be a case of slander".

CYKC ch. 3, page 38.

Pi Chung-yu 畢 仲 游 was a well-known scholar-official who in the Yüan-yu era (1086-1093 A.D.) served in the Directorate of Military Supplies. Thereafter he was appointed Judicial Intendant of Ho-tung, and in the reign of Hui-tsung (1101-1125 A.D.) was appointed Division Chief in the Ministry of Rites. Cf. his biography in *Sung-shih* ch. 281, where this same case is related.

Han Chen (韓 縝 1019-1097) was a high official, known both for his skill in poetry, and his impetuous character.

TYPS-II quotes as the source of the present case Pi Chung-yu's tomb inscription, composed by Ch'en T'ien 陳 恬 , a writer of prose and poetry who flourished ca. 1080 A.D.

29. *Fu Yung on the ablutions and the pillows;*
    A Court officer has wooden clogs washed

A.

"In the Former Ch'in Dynasty (350-394 A.D.), Fu Yung, styled Po-hsiu, excelled in solving difficult criminal cases. A man called Tung Feng had been away three years for study, and when he returned stayed in the house of his wife's family. That first night an unknown person murdered his wife. Her elder brother suspected Tung Feng (and accused him before the tribunal). Fu Yung asked him: 'Did not you previously have some strange experience about which you consulted the oracle?' Tung Feng said: 'One night I dreamt that I entered into a river riding on horseback and going North; then again I went from North to South. Looking down I saw two suns reflected in the water, and noticed that the left flank of my horse was wet. The soothsayer (whom I consulted about this dream) said: There is the anxiety of getting involved in a criminal case. Keep far from the two ablutions (in the morning and the night) and shun the two pillows (of the conjugal couch). When I had returned my wife prepared a bath and at night arranged the pillows; but remembering the words of the soothsayer I refused both. Thereupon my wife took a bath herself and arranged her pillow, and then went to sleep on our couch'. Fu Yung said: 'In the Book of Divination (*I-ching*) the triagram *k'an* means *water* and *north*, the triagram *li* means *horse* and *south*. If a horse crosses the river in the North, and then passes from North to South, that means that the triagrams *k'an* and *li* should be three times changed, which produces a hexagram where the middle stroke of *li* indicates *woman* and that of *k'an* indicates *man*. As regards the left flank of the horse being wet, this means *water* on left and *horse* on right, that is the character *feng* 馮 ; two suns form together the character *ch'ang* 昌 . Would this mean that a man called Feng Ch'ang has murdered your wife?' He had a man called Feng Ch'ang arrested, and on being interrogated he confessed. He had illicit relations with Tung Feng's wife, and they had planned to murder Tung when he had gone to sleep after his bath; but he had (in the dark) killed Tung's wife by mistake''.

CYKC ch. 1, page 2.

Fu Yung derives from the dream two triagrams *k'an* and *li*; if *k'an* is placed on top of the other, they form together the 63d hexagram *Chi-chi* 既濟 , which indeed supplies a very good key to the situation. This hexagram implies a warning for impending danger; the *I-ching* adds i.a. the phrase: ''The Superior Man, keeping in mind (possible) calamities, prepares to ward them off''. 君子以思患而豫防之 . The central stroke of *li* means 'woman', and in a certain position this particular stroke is explained as ''The married woman (rides in a chariot) without curtains'' 婦喪其茀 , which suggests a woman of loose morals. For further details about the method of constructing hexagrams in the process of divination, see Richard Wilhelm, *I Ging, das Buch der Wandlungen*, Jena 1924.

Fu Yung 苻融 was the brother of the Chin Emperor Fu Chien (苻堅 337-384 A.D.), and known as an able general; more details in BD no. 579, and Franke, vol. II, pp. 92 sq. Cf. his biography in *Chin-shu* ch. 114, where a more elaborate version of this case is given. For another case solved by Fu Yung cf. Case 43-B.

TYPS-III gives Fu Yung's style as 博林 , which is an error of the copyist; TYPS-I reads Po-hsiu 博休 , which is correct.

B.

''In the High Court of Justice in Chiang-nan there once was investigated a murder case, but the true facts could not be found. A minor officer of the Court was greatly worried about this. Then he burned incense and prayed (asking for divine guidance). He dreamt that having found a dry river bed he ascended a high mountain. When he woke up he reasoned: 'A *river* without *water*, that leaves the character *k'o* 可 ; and a high mountain is represented by the character *sung* 嵩 .

Now K'o-sung, that is a Buddhist monk's name!' In the Ch'ung-
hsiao Temple there was indeed a monk of that name. He reported
this to his superior officer, and the monk was arrested. But when
the monk was interrogated, no proof of his having committed a crime
could be obtained. Suddenly the officer noticed that the wooden
clogs of the monk showed ink blotches. When asked how the ink
came there the monk said: 'It are just a few splashes (that soiled my
clogs when I was rubbing ink prior to writing). He was made to take
off his clogs, and when they were examined closely it appeared that
the ink had been (intentionally) painted on there. The monk showed
signs of fear. The ink was washed off, and underneath bloodstains
were found. When interrogated about this the monk confessed (having
committed the unsolved murder)".

(From the *Pi-ko-hsien-t'an*, by the Revisor Wu Shu)

CYKC ch. 6, page 82.

Wu Shu (吳 淑 947-1002 A.D.) was a well known Sung literatus. His
Pi-ko-hsien-t'an 祕 閣 閑 談 is included in SF, but the present story is not
found there.

30. *Hsü Tsung-i unrolls silk;*
    Kao Fang compares cloth

A.

"In the time of the Kingdom of Shu (10th century A.D.), Hsü
Tsung-i served in Chien-chou. A man recognized the features of a
ruffian (who broke into his house in the night) as revealed by the lamp
light, and in the morning reported this to the tribunal. A constable
arrested a man (indicated by the victim) and found with him the
stolen goods, namely balls of silk thread and rolls of white silk. The
victim of the theft stated that those goods were his. The (alleged) thief
could not stand the questioning under torture and wrongly confessed. Thereupon he was forwarded to the Prefecture. When Hsü Tsung-i
had the prisoner brought before him for reviewing his case, he said that
those goods were his own property, but that he had previously had
an argument over the ownership with the accuser. Hsü Tsung-i had
the spindles used by the accused and the claimant brought to the
tribunal, and moreover asked the two men: 'When you rolled up the silk,
what kind of roller did each of you use?' The accused said that he had

used sticks of prune wood, the other said that he had used tiles. Hsü had the rolls opened, and they proved to be rolled on sticks of prune wood. Then he had the balls of silk thread placed on the spindles in order to measure them, and they proved to fit exactly those of the accused. Thereupon the victim of the (alleged) theft was pronounced guilty of falsely stating that he had recognized the accused, and the constables were found guilty of having forced a decision by torture. Thus this wrong was set right".

CYKC ch. 2, page 15; IYC ch. 3, no. 60; YP no. 62.

About Hsü Tsung-i 許宗裔 I could find no further details. For the Shu Kingdom cf. the note to Case 44-B.

TYPS-I and III read *kung* 舡 instead of *k'uang* 舼 "spindle", the latter being a Sung-taboo.

B.

"In the time of Shih-tsung (954-959 A.D.) of the (Later) Chou Dynasty (915-960 A.D.), when Kao Fang was Prefect of Ts'ai-chou, a man of that place called Wang I was robbed with violence. Five men were arrested, put in prison and thoroughly interrogated. When the stolen goods were indeed found with them all five (confessed and) were going to be submitted to the supreme penalty. Kao Fang, however, had the stolen goods brought and examined them. Summoning Wang I he asked him whether the garments he had lost were made out of one piece of cloth or not. Wang I stated that they had been made out of one piece. Then Kao Fang had the size and texture (of the component parts) of the (recovered) garments checked and found that they were different. The prisoners then declared that they had been falsely accused. When Kao Fang asked them why they had confessed, they stated that they had been unable to stand the flogging, and only had desired to die quickly. After a few days the real robber was apprehended and the five men were acquitted. Kao Fang later served under this (i.e. the Sung) dynasty, and ended his career as Executive assistant of a Minister".

(From his biography)

CYKC ch. 2, page 16; IYC ch. 8, no. 142.

Kao Fang (高防 905-963 A.D.) served in the Chou Dynasty on the staff of a Regional Defense Commander, and was commended for his bravery in fighting the Kitans. After the foundation of the Sung Dynasty he became Auxiliary

Academician of the Bureau of Military Affairs, and died as Prefect of Feng-hsiang 鳳翔. Cf. his biography in *Sung-shih* ch. 270, which does not give this particular case; it does contain, however, Case 53-B.

31. *Chiang distinguishes the outside and the inside of paper;*
    Chang P'in notes the difference between red and black ink

A.

"In the Jen-shou district of Ling-chou there was a village clerk of the surname Hung who wanted to profit from the field of his neighbour. Deceiving him the clerk said: 'I shall pay the taxes for you and get you exempted from the corvée'. The neighbour was glad that he could pay less taxes, and had the piece of land registered with the authorities. After twenty years had passed the clerk made a forged contract (ceding the land to him), and soaked the paper in tea so as to make it appear very old. Then he brought the matter before the tribunal (in order to have his ownership of the land confirmed). The magistrate, a Division Chief of the surname Chiang took the contract and having crumpled it up smoothed it out again (so that the inside of the paper showed along the fold marks). He said: 'If this were old paper, the inside would be white. Since in this case inside and outside are of the same colour, it is a forgery'. He interrogated Hung who indeed confessed".

(Chiang was a native of K'ai-hua in Ch'ü-chou; his personal name is now lost. This case is related in his tomb inscription composed by the Registrar Li T'ai-po)

CYKC ch. 5, page 79; IYC ch. 8, no. 161; YP no. 35.

Chu Hsü-tseng, the editor of TYPS-I, states in an additional note at the very end of the book that he has checked Chiang's identity in the *K'ai-hua-hsien-chih* 開化縣志 and other literary sources, and found that it was the scholar-official Chiang Hao 江鎬, who became *chin-shih* in 1012 A.D. Chu verified that his tomb inscription was indeed written by the Sung scholar Li T'ai-po 李泰伯.

As to the method of detecting artificially aged paper, the point is that in the case of genuine old paper its surface has become darkened by age, while its inside retains of course the original colour; paper "aged" artificially by soaking it in tea or exposing it to thick smoke will be darkened through and through. Sung connoisseurs of antique paintings—i.a. the famous Mi Fu—often refer to this method.

B.

"When the Palace Censor Chang P'in was magistrate of the Chiu-lung district in P'eng-chou, there was a man called Sun Yen-shih of a prominent family of Mei-chou, who by means of a forged contract appropriated the land of a member of his clan. This case remained pending for a long time. The Fiscal Intendant entrusted Chang P'in with examining and deciding it. (Chang P'in studied the contract and) said: 'The writing is done over the red ink (of the seal impression); Sun Yen-shih evidently first used his relative's seal clandestinely, and afterwards wrote the text of the contract'. Thereupon Sun confessed. But before Chang had reported his findings, Sun's family again brought the case before the Fiscal Intendant who ordered Huang Meng-sung, magistrate of the Hua-yang district in I-chou, to review the case; he came to the same conclusion. Because of this decision Huang was promoted to Investigating Censor, while Chang P'in was punished for delaying the completion of the case, being degraded to Supervisor of the production of spirits in Ch'ing-chou".

(From his biography. Chang was in 1034 A.D. sent on a mission to the Kitans and died on the road).

CYKC ch. 5, page 78; IYC ch. 8, no. 261; YP no. 36.

Chang P'in 章 頻 became *chin-shih* in the Ching-te era (1004-1007 A.D.). He served as magistrate in several places, and was known as a perspicacious judge. After his degradation he again served as magistrate, of Ch'ang-chou 長 洲 , and ended his career as Division Chief in the Ministry of Justice. Cf. his biography in *Sung-shih* ch. 301, where this case is related.

The seals authenticating a deed or other document are impressed with red seal ink across the signature and dates, often also across other important parts of the text. Thus the red seal ink appears on top of the writing which is done with ordinary black ink. Sun Yen-shih must have induced his relative under some pretext or other to impress his seal on a blank sheet of paper, and later written on that paper the text of the contract; thus his writing ran over the seal.

In order to prevent unauthorized use, the Chinese usually keep their seals carefully locked away, or carry them on their person.

32. *Hu Chih assembles the neighbours;*
   Kao Jou observes a criminal's mien

A.

"In the (Former) Wei Dynasty (220-265 A.D.) when Hu Chih,

styled Wen-te, was Prefect of Ch'ang-chou, a man called Lu Hsien, from Tung-kuan, was murdered and the criminal could not be found. Hu Chih said: 'This gentleman has no enemies, but he has a very young wife; she must be the cause of his death!' He assembled all the young men living in that neighbourhood. Among them there was one called Li Jo, who showed signs of fear when he was being interrogated. Upon an exhaustive examination he himself confessed his crime".

CYKC ch. 6, page 92; IYC ch. 2, no. 28; YP no. 30.

Hu Chih 胡 質 started his career as a military official; he was appointed Prefect of Tung-kuan in the Huang-ch'u era (220-226 A.D.), and kept that office nine years. Cf. his biography in the *Wei-chih* of the *San-kuo-chih*, ch. 27, where the same case is told.

The second character *chih* 志 is superfluous.

B.

"In the (Former) Wei Dynasty when Kao Jou was Commandant of Justice, a soldier of the Army Protector's camp called Tou Li went for a short walk and did not return to the camp; it was thought that he had deserted. His wife *née* Ying and their sons and daughters complained that they were being wronged (according to the law the wife and children of a deserter would be made government slaves. Transl.) and brought their case before the (military) authorities. When no one could solve this affair, they went to the Commandant. Kao Jou asked the woman: 'How do you know that your husband has perished?' She said weeping: 'My husband was not an irresponsible man who did not care for his wife and children!' Kao Jou asked again: 'Did your husband have any enemies?' She replied: 'My husband was a righteous man, he had no enemies'. (Finally Kao Jou asked:) 'Did your husband ever lend money to some one?' She answered: 'He once lent money to his camp-mate Chiao Tzu-wen; my husband asked him to return it but he would not give it'. At that time Chiao Tzu-wen happened to have been put in jail for another offense. Kao Jou had him brought before him and questioned him about that offense. Suddenly he asked him: 'Did you ever borrow money?' Chiao answered: 'I am single and poor, and would not dare to borrow money'; but Kao noticed that he looked uneasy. He asked again: 'Since you took money from Tou Li, how can you deny having borrowed money?' Chiao, bewildered that the affair had become known, could not give a coherent answer. Kao Jou spoke: 'You have murdered Tou Li, you had better confess now!' Chiao then knocked his head on the floor and confessed his crime".

CYKC ch. 6, page 92; IYC ch. 2, no. 26.

Kao Jou (高柔 174-263 A.D.) was a straightforward official who served as Censor under Emperor Wen (220-226 A.D.); under Emperor Wen's successor he became Commander-in-chief. Cf. his biography in the *Wei-chih* of the *San-kuo chih*, ch. 24, where the present case is recorded in detail. TYPS-I and III abbreviate it to such an extent that the point of Kao Jou's questioning is entirely lost: he immediately asks the woman whether her husband had lent money. TYPS-II gives a better abbreviated version which leaves out only immaterial details; this version is translated above. The Chinese text follows.

魏高柔爲廷尉。護軍營士竇禮近出不還。營以爲沒身。其妻盈氏及男女稱冤自訟。莫有省者。乃詣廷尉。高柔問。何以知夫亡。盈氏泣對曰。夫非輕狹。不顧室家者。又問。汝夫不與人有讎乎。曰。夫良善。與人無讎。汝夫不與人交錢物乎。曰。嘗出錢與同營焦子文。求不得。時子文適坐事繫獄。柔乃召問所坐。語次問曾舉人錢否。對曰。單貧不敢舉人錢。察其色動。遂復問。汝曾舉竇禮錢。何言否耶。子文怪知事露。應對不次。柔詰之曰。汝已殺竇禮。便宜早服。子文於是叩頭服罪。

33. *Chiang Ch'ang has an old crone spied upon;*
    Han Szu-yen assembles a crowd of young boys

A.

"In the (Chen-kuan era, 627-649, of the) T'ang Dynasty, the wife of an inn keeper of Pan-ch'iao (in Wei-chou 衞州) called Chang T'i, went to visit her parents. That day Wang Wei, Yang Cheng and a third man stayed overnight at the inn and departed early the next morning, in the fifth nightwatch (i.e. about three o'clock a.m.). In the night there had come a man who took Wang Wei's knife and murdered Chang T'i. (After the deed) he put the knife back in its scabbard, without

Yang Cheng or the others waking up. In the morning the servants of the inn (having discovered the murder) went after Yang Cheng and his party; (searching them) they pulled the knife from its scabbard and found it all covered with blood. (Yang Cheng and the two others were arrested). When interrogated (under torture) they wrongly confessed. (When their death sentence was submitted to the Throne for approval), the Emperor had doubts and sent the Censor Chiang Ch'ang to review the case. After his arrival Chiang examined thoroughly all the people of the inn, more than fifteen persons, but their number was insufficient (for finding a suspect among them). He let them go away, detaining only one old woman. In the evening he let her go also, but ordered an officer of the tribunal to (follow and) watch her secretly, saying to him: 'If some one accosts her (to inquire what happened in the tribunal), mark him well!' The next day Chiang gave the same instructions, and also the third day; each day it was the same man (who accosted the old woman). Then Chiang summoned more than three hundred men and women and ordered (the woman) to select from among them the man who had spoken to her. When interrogated this man confessed: he had illicit relations with Chang T'i's wife and therefore murdered him".

CYKC ch. 1, page 8; IYC ch. 1, no. 4; YP no. 39. Source unknown.

When the Censor failed to find a likely suspect among the inn people, he had to look for the murderer among the population of the entire village. In order to entice that man to betray himself, after the session he detained the oldest woman he could find among the personnel of the inn, and let her go after dark; he reasoned that since she was so old, and since the darkness acted as further protection, the criminal would approach her for obtaining news about the progress of the investigation. It is not clear, however, why the Censor did not have that man arrested after he had approached the woman the third time. Neither is it clear why the Censor chose to assemble the population of the entire village. The only explanation would seem to be that the Censor wished to strengthen his case in order to obviate criticism from the Throne that he had concocted a case against an innocent man. It should be noted that the editor of CYKC leaves out the passage about the three hundred people, and makes the Censor arrest the criminal after he had accosted the old woman on the third day.

The date in the first line I took over from the version in TYPS-II.

About Chiang Ch'ang 蔣 常 I could find no further details.

B.

"In the T'ang Dynasty, when Han Szu-yen was serving in P'ing-chou, a robber murdered a man, and the identity of the murderer could not be established. Then (the constables) arrested a drunken Turk who carried a knife covered with blood; when questioned under torture he confessed. Han Szu-yen suspected this confession. In the morning he assembled several hundred young boys in the tribunal, and released them in the evening. This he did three days in succession. Then he asked the boys: 'When you left, was not there some one who asked you what happened here in the tribunal?' The boys all said that there had been such a man. Han Szu-yen had that man traced, and interrogated him. Then the real murderer was indeed caught".

CYKC ch. 1, page 9.

Han Szu-yen 韓思彥 was an able and honest official who flourished ca. 700 A.D. His biography in *Hsin-t'ang-shu* ch. 112 says that when he served in I-chou (Szuchuan Prov.) he had to decide a lawsuit between two brothers that had been going on for a number of years. Han Szu-yen had a cup of milk brought from the kitchen and made both drink from it, implying that two persons who had been suckled by the same breast should not seek to harm each other. The two brothers understood, and a reconciliation took place. The present case too is given in Han's biography.

34. *Liu Hang and the testimony of the neighbours;*
    Han I and the testimony of the wet nurse

A.

"When the Assistant Secretary Liu Hang was Prefect of Heng-chou, there was a man of a prominent family called Yin who wanted to purchase a plot of land from his neighbour, but could not obtain his assent to the sale. Since that neighbour was old and had only one young son, Yin prepared a forged deed of sale; after the neighbour had died, Yin drove the son from the property. The son brought a suit (against Yin), but for twenty years he could not get his wrong righted. When Liu Hang arrived, the son again accused Yin. Yin then produced the receipts of taxes (paid by him for the land) covering many years as proof (of his ownership). Liu Hang said: 'You have a hundred acres of land, why did they specially give you tax receipts for this particular plot? And when the deed of sale was drawn up, did you ask the neighbours to witness it? Many of those people must be still alive, I can summon them to testify'. Yin could answer nothing, and confessed.

"I find that it was the ancient rule that when a piece of land was sold the neighbours were asked to act as witnesses, and the deed was drawn up in their presence. In recent years the authorities, just to please themselves, changed this rule; they probably did not realize (that in doing so they lost a useful means for checking disputed deeds)".

CYKC ch. 6, page 86; IYC ch. 9, no. 171; YP no. 75.

Liu Hang 劉沆 became *chin-shih* in 1030 and was appointed judge in Shu-chou 舒州 where he solved in a few days a difficult criminal case that had been pending for years; thereafter he was appointed Prefect of Heng-chou. Later he occupied various important posts in the capital and the provinces. Cf. his biography in *Sung-shih* ch. 285, where the present case is recorded.

TYPS-II gives the second alinea as a separate remark by Cheng K'o.

B.

"When the Assistant State Councillor Han I was Prefect of Yang-chou, the local tyrant Li Chia, when his elder brother had died, had forced his widow to remarry (so that she forfeited her share in the inheritance); then he falsely said that her son (of the first marriage) was a bastard (so that he would not inherit either), in order to appropriate all the property. The tyrant's sister-in-law sued him repeatedly, but he at once bribed the officials and had her beaten till she stated that her claim was unfounded. (When) Han I (had taken up office there he) examined the old records (of this case), and found that the wet-nurse (of the son that was allegedly a bastard) had never been summoned for delivering testimony. One day he had Li Chia and his entire clique brought before him, and confronted them with the wet-nurse. None of them could say anything (against her testimony), and the widow's wrong was righted".

CYKC ch. 6, page 97; IYC ch. 4, no. 71; YP no. 76.

Han I 韓億 served as prefect in several places, and earned the name of a just administrator. In the reign of Jen-tsung (1023-1063 A.D.) he was appointed Assistant State Councillor, and ended his career as Junior Tutor of the Heir Apparent. Cf. his biography in *Sung-shih*, ch. 315, where the present case is related. It is also found in ch. 11 of the *Tung-hsien-pi-lu* (cf. the note to Case 10-B).

35. *Yuan Tz'u melts gold;*

   Sun Pao weighs cakes

A.

"In the T'ang Dynasty, when Li (Mien), Duke of Ch'ien was Military Commander of Feng-hsiang, there was a farmer of a district in that region who when hoeing his field found a jar filled with solid lumps of gold; the villagers brought this jar to the magistrate of that district, for drawing up a forwarding letter in order to have the jar deposited with the Prefecture. The magistrate, thinking that the official treasury was not safe enough, had the jar placed in his private strongbox. When the next day he opened the jar and looked, it was filled only with lumps of clay; he reported this to the Prefecture. There this matter was discussed and all suspected that a crook had effected the exchange. Thereupon an official was despatched to investigate the matter. The magistrate could not prove his innocence, and wrongly confessed that he had replaced the gold (by clay). When pressed to indicate where he had concealed the gold, he first said that he had hidden it under offal (but that some one had subsequently stolen it), later he said that he had sunk it in the river (but had forgotten the place). When this was reported to the higher authorities, Li Mien was very angry. On the occasion of a banquet the conversation turned to this affair, and all the guests were greatly amazed (at the depravity of the magistrate). Then the (later) Minister of State Yüan Tz'u was a member of Li Mien's staff; he alone nodded his head and made no comment. When Li Mien questioned him, Yuan Tz'u said: 'I suspect that injustice is being done in this case'. Li Mien then referred the case back to the local authorities and ordered Yüan Tz'u to deal with it. Yüan had it verified that the jar contained about 250 lumps of clay. He ordered gold bars from a number of shops, had them melted and made into lumps of the same size as the pieces of clay. When half the total number of lumps had been produced, they weighed already more than three hundred catties. Then he investigated who had first brought the jar to the magistrate's office; it was found that it had been two farmers who had carried the jar on a large bamboo pole. Yüan then calculated that two men could never have carried the whole weight (of gold lumps) on a bamboo pole. Thus it was proved that the gold had turned into clay already when it was being brought to the magistrate. Thereupon the entire case was cleared up, and the magistrate was acquitted".

(From the *Chü-t'an-lu*)

CYKC ch. 1, page 10; IYC ch. 2, no. 35; YCTI no. 1; YP no. 69.

Li Mien 李 勉 was an able official who served as Censor under the Emperor

Su-tsung (756-763 A.D.), and as Regional Commander under Tai-tsung (763-780 A.D.); he was also known as a great art collector.

Yüan Tz'u 袁 滋 was a scholar-official known for his wide learning, who served as Prefect and Regional Commander in several places. Cf. his biography in *Chiu-t'ang-shu* ch. 185 and *Hsin-t'ang-shu* ch. 151; both contain a brief reference to this case: 部 官 以 盜 金 下 獄。滋 直 其 冤: "A local official was put in prison for stealing gold, but Yüan Tz'u righted his wrong."

In the last line but one I read *chi-shih* 即 是 instead of *tu-ch'i* 度 其, following CYKC.

This would be a better story if one took it that one of the villagers who brought the jar to the tribunal had stolen the gold on the way. But the text says clearly "the gold had *turned into* clay" 金 已 化 爲 土, and nothing is said about a villager being prosecuted for the theft. Thus we must assume that the lumps of gold were fakes to begin with, being made of gilded lumps of clay that the finder mistook for real gold.

The *Chü-t'an-lu* 劇 談 錄 is a small work in 3 ch. by the T'ang writer K'ang Pien 康 駢 who flourished ca. 880 A.D. The text reprinted in SF does not give this case.

B.

"In the (Western) Han Dynasty (206 B.C.-24 A.D.), when Sun Pao was Governor of the capital, there was a vender of *huan-san* — which at present are called 'ring-shaped cakes'. On the market in the capital a villager accidentally bumped into him, and the cakes fell on the ground and all broke to pieces. The villager was perfectly willing to compensate the loss of fifty cakes, but the vender insisted that there had been three hundred. They brought their dispute before the Grand Administrator. Sun Pao had them brought before him and questioned them but could obtain no clear proof. Thereupon he had one *huan-san* cake bought elsewhere, and weighed it. Then he had all the broken cakes weighed together. This total he divided by the weight of one cake (and thus the correct number was clearly established). The vender then admitted that he had made a false statement".

CYKC ch. 6, page 94; IYC ch. 3, no. 62; YP no. 70.

Sun Pao 孫 寶 was i.a. Prefect of I-chou 益 州 and Chi-chou 冀 州, and Military Commander of Kuang-han; thereafter he was appointed Prefect of Ching-chao. He occupied high Court functions under the Emperors Ai (6-1 B.C.) and P'ing (1-5 A.D.); but he had to retire because he opposed the policies of Wang Mang (BD. no. 2203). Cf. his biography in *Han-shu* ch. 77.

TYPS-II adds to this case an interesting note by Cheng K'o, relating that Sun

Ch'üan (孫 權 181-252 A.D., founder of the Wu Dynasty; BD no. 1803) had an elephant and wanted to ascertain its weight; no one of his assistants knew a method for determining it. Then some one advised to let the elephant stand in a boat, and make a mark on the outside of the hull, indicating how far the boat had sunk into the water. Then the elephant was put ashore again, and the boat filled with blocks of ballast of known weight till the water reached the spot previously marked.

36. *Registrar Ch'eng and old money;*
Wang Chü and an old document

A.

"When the Investigating Censor Ch'eng Hao in the beginning of his career served as Registrar of the Hu district in the Metropolitan area, there was a man who lived in a house he had rented from his elder brother; (after his brother's death) he dug up in the garden a cache of money. His elder brother's son brought this case before the tribunal, stating that the money had been buried there by his father. The magistrate said: 'Since there is no proof, how can this case be decided?' Ch'eng Hao observed: 'That can be easily determined!' He asked the son: 'How many years ago did your father bury the money?' The answer was twenty years previously. Then Ch'eng sent an officer to bring a thousand cash from the cache. Examining these cash he said: 'The cash minted by the present government have spread all over the Empire within the space of five or six years. How do you explain that these cash were all minted scores of years before your father was born?' The son thereupon admitted his guilt".

(From his tomb inscription composed by Ch'eng I)

CYKC ch. 6, page 98; SF no. 9; IYC ch. 9. no. 169; YP no. 51.

For Ch'eng Hao see Case 3-A above. Ch'eng I (程 頤 1033-1107 A.D.) was his younger brother, whose literary name was I-ch'uan 伊 川 . The present case is recorded in Ch'eng Hao's biography in *Sung-shih* ch. 427.

B.

"When the High Court Assistant Wang Chü was magistrate of Chung-lu in Hsiang-(yang-)chou, there was an (arrested) robber whose crime could not be found out despite long questioning. Then Wang Chü accidentally found in the robber's bag an old letter. When this letter was publicly displayed, a merchant from Fang-ling came for-

ward and said that that letter had been stolen from him. The robber
then confessed".

(From his tomb inscription composed by Wang Kuei)

CYKC ch. 6, page 96; IYC ch. 8, no. 155; YP no. 24.

About Wang Chü 王璩 I could find no further details.
For Wang Kuei see the note to Case 15-B above.

37. *Liu Kung-cho has coffins broken open;*
Lü Yüan-ying arrests a funeral procession

A.

"The *Liu-shih-hsü-hsün* says: When Liu Kung-cho was Regional
Commander of Hsiang-yang, in a year of famine the scarcity was especially severe in the neighbouring district. A group of people in mourning came weeping (to Liu's headquarters) and presented a petition
stating that they wished to convey twelve bodies of three generations
of relatives to Wu-ch'ang for burial, but that the guards at the ford
would not let them cross the river. Liu Kung-cho immediately ordered
the military police to arrest the men and to break the coffins open;
all were filled with grain. Burying people in a time of scarcity,
they should not have talked about twelve dead of three generations,
for by that their deceit became known".

CYKC ch. 7, page 116

Liu Kung-cho 柳公綽 was a man of stern character who served i.a. as
President of the Ministry of Personnel. The Emperor Hsien-tsung (806-820 A.D.)
employed him as a commander in several campaigns. Under the Emperor Wen-
tsung (827-840 A.D.) he served as Minister of Justice, thereafter as Regional
Commander of Ho-tung. Bünger, p. 202, gives a passage from the *T'ang-hui-yao*
唐會要 which quotes one of Liu's decisions. A mother flogged her stepdaughter who died as the result, and the death penalty was proposed for her.
Liu opposed this on the ground that corporal punishment inflicted by a member
of an older generation is permitted; moreover, since her son (i.e. the stepdaughter's
husband) was still alive, it was against educational principles if a mother would
be punished for an offense against a son's wife. The Emperor decided that the
mother's death sentence would be commuted.

Liu Kung-cho's biography is found in *Chiu-t'ang-shu* ch. 165 where the present
case is not recorded. The book quoted as source I could not trace.

B.

"In the T'ang Dynasty Lü Yüan-ying, styled Ching-fu, when he was Garrison Commander of Yo-yang, once went for a stroll to enjoy the scenery. He noticed a funeral procession halting on the left side of the road, accompanied by five men in mourning. Lü observed: 'To bury the dead far-away is wasteful, to bury them near is thrifty. Those people are certainly a band of robbers out for mischief!' He therefore ordered his assistants to investigate; they found that the coffin was filled with nothing but weapons. The men said that they had planned to cross the river and steal goods; they had taken on the guise of a funeral procession, to prevent the men who ferried them across from becoming suspicious. Lü Yüan-ying ordered an investigation of this affair; then a score of other members of the same band proved to have assembled waiting on the opposite bank of the river. They were arrested and executed".

CYKC ch. 7, page 116; IYC ch. 2 no. 44; YP no. 74.

Lü Yüan-ying (呂 元 膺 749-820 A.D.) was an able official who occupied with distinction a number of civil and military functions. In the Chien-chung era (780-783 A.D.) he was appointed Prefect of T'ung-chou 同 州 . Then he was appointed in the capital Executive Censor, thereafter Guardian of the Eastern Capital, in which function he broke up a dangerous complot. Afterwards he was appointed Regional Commander of Ho-chung, and Executive Secretary of the Ministry of Personnel. He ended his career as Chief Counsellor of the Heir Apparent. Cf. his biography in *Chiu-t'ang-shu* ch. 154, where the present case is not related.

38. *Liu Yün and the dumb slave;*
Wang Han and the crazy woman

A.

"(In the T'ang Dynasty), when Liu Yün was a judge attached to the Regional Supervisor of Kiangsi, a Buddhist monk had been drinking at night (and accidentally) set fire to his dwelling; he accused a dumb slave. The military police officer (who dealt with the case) accepted a bribe and did not examine the accused. When the case (against the slave) was completed, Liu Yün and one of his colleagues, called Ts'ui Yu-fu, reported the wrong that was being done to the slave to the Regional Supervisor Wei Shao-yu; he went there and interrogated the monk who then confessed".

(From his biography)

CYKC ch. 1, page 10; IYC ch. 5, no. 88; YP no. 77.

Liu Yün 柳渾 was a well known scholar who became *chin-shih* in the T'ien-pao era (742-755 A.D.). Later he was involved in a conflict with the Minister Chang Yen-shang (BD no. 126) and retired from official life. Cf. his biography in *Hsin-t'ang-shu* ch. 142, where an identical version of the present case is recorded.

B.

"When the Chief Judge of the High Court Wang Han was Prefect of Tan-chou, there was a mentally deranged old woman who repeatedly came with a complaint to the Prefecture; but there was rhyme nor reason in what she said, and she was mostly driven away by the mounted guards. (When) Wang Han (had taken up office he) ordered to bring her back before him in the court-room. While she was knocking her head on the steps (of the dais) Wang patiently questioned her. Although her language was confused, now and then her argument could be understood. It transpired that originally she had been a married woman; she had not born a son, while her husband's concubine had given him one. After her husband's death she had been driven out of the house by the concubine. When notwithstanding her repeated complaints with the authorities her wrong was not righted, grief had unhinged her mind. Wang Han set this matter right and assigned all the property to her".

(From the *Su-shui-chi-wen*)

CYKC ch. 2, page 25; IYC ch. 9, no. 172; YP no. 78.

Wang Han 王罕 was a paternal uncle of the great writer Wang Kuei (see the note to Case 15-B above). He began his career as Fiscal Intendant in Kuang-tung, and then became Assistant Commissioner in the Ministry of Finance, and Prefect of Tan-chou. Cf. his biography in *Sung-shih*, ch. 312, where this case is recorded. For the *Su-shui-chi-wen* cf. Case I-A.

TYPS-III, 2nd column, writes *t'ing* without the 53 d radical.

39. *Li Nan-kung studies an elm tree;*
    Wang Ch'en recognizes a plant

A.

"When the Minister Li Nan-kung was magistrate of Ch'ang-sha district, two men started fisticuffs; A. was strong and B. weak. (When brought before the magistrate) both men had blue and red spots on their body. Li Nan-kung probed the discoloured spots with his fingertips and stated: 'B.'s complaint is justified, A.'s is false'. Subsequent interrogation proved that this was indeed the case. Now in the South there is a kind of elm tree. If one rubs its leaves on one's skin they will leave blue and red spots resembling the marks of fist blows. If one peels off its bark and places a piece on the skin, then pressing it with a hot flat iron, it will produce marks resembling those left by blows with a stick. These spots can not be washed off with water. However, in the case of genuine bruises the blood will assemble there and grow hard, while faked spots will stay soft".

(Heard among scholars)

CYKC ch. 6, page 89; IYC ch. 8, no. 156; YCTI no. 16; YP no. 25.
For Li Nan-kung see Case 6-B above.

B.

"When the Policy-Adviser Wang Ch'en was Prefect of Fu-chou, an aboriginal of that region wanted to take revenge upon an enemy. One day he first ate wild *Pueraria* beans, and then engaged his enemy in fisticuffs, whereupon he dropped dead. His family falsely accused the enemy. Wang Ch'en asked (the coroner): 'Are his wounds really lethal?' That officer answered: 'The wounds are not very serious'. Wang became suspicious. He started to interrogate the accusers and then obtained the truth".

CYKC ch. 3, page 35; IYC ch. 8, no. 157; YP no. 26.

Wang Ch'en 王 臻 occupied various administrative functions, distinguishing himself as a clever judge. After having served as Prefect of Fu-chou, he was in 1023 A.D. appointed Policy Adviser of the Right, and ended his career as an Executive Censor. Cf. his biography in *Sung-shih* ch. 302, where this case is related in approximately the same words.

40. *Ou-yang Ying recognizes sons as thieves;*
    Sun surmises that an elder brother is a murderer

A.

"When the Division Chief Ou-yang Ying was Prefect of She-chou, a burglar broke into the treasury of a wealthy man. For a long time the culprit could not be found. Ou-yang Ying said: 'Do not try to arrest a robber! Summon the two sons of that rich man, and have them bound in jail!'. When the case was thus investigated the two sons confessed. The officers of the tribunal at first suspected that they had wrongly confessed because they could not stand the torture. But when the stolen goods were found in their possession, they were convinced''.

CYKC ch. 7, page 109; IYC ch. 8, no. 158; YP no. 27.

About Ou-yang Ying 歐 陽 穎 I can give no further details. His biography is given in ch. 18 of the *Sung-shih-i* 宋 史 翼 by Lu Hsin-yüan 陸 心 源 (1834-1894), publ. 1906, which is not at my disposal. TYPS-II, however, states that this case is related in his tomb inscription composed by the famous Sung literatus Ou-yang Hsiu (see the note to Case 5-A), so probably Ou-yang Ying was a relative of his.

B.

"When Sun Ch'ang-ch'ing was Prefect of Ho-chou, a man reported that his younger brother had been murdered by an unknown person. Sun found that his speech betrayed lack of feeling, and asked him: 'To what tax-category does your family belong?' The man answered: 'To the highest'. Sun asked again: 'Of how many persons does your family consist?' The man said: 'Only my younger brother and his wife and son'. Thereupon Sun said: 'You, the elder brother, are the man who murdered him. Was it not because you wanted to acquire his property?' Upon investigation this proved indeed the truth''.

(From his tomb inscription composed by Wang Kuei)

CYKC ch. 5, page 77; IYC ch. 8, no. 159; YP no. 28.

Sun Ch'ang-ch'ing (孫 長 卿 1004-1069 A.D.) served in She-chou ca. 1020 A.D. On several posts he earned fame by his acumen in the solving of difficult cases, and was appointed Academician of the Lung-t'u Pavilion, thereafter Prefect of Ting-chou 定 州 . He was not a very learned man, but chiefly known for his administrative ability. Cf. his biography in *Sung-shih*, ch. 331 where the present case is recorded.

For Wang Kuei see Case 15-B above.

41. *Kuo Kung differentiates between two kinds of errors;*
    Ch'en Hsi-liang helps an official on unauthorized leave.

A.

"In the Eastern Han Dynasty (25-220 A.D.) when Kuo Kung, an officer in a Commanderie, was employed by the 'Three Dukes', two brothers murdered a man together, and it could not be decided how the responsibility should be divided between the two. The Emperor Ming (58-75 A.D.) decided that since the elder brother failed to instruct the younger, the elder should be executed while the sentence of the younger should be commuted. The Gentleman-in-waiting Sun Chang when promulgating the Imperial decision stated wrongly that both brothers should be executed. Thereupon a Minister memorialized the Throne stating that since Sun Chang had falsified an Imperial order, he should be cut in two through the loins. Since Kuo Kung had a clear understanding of the law, the Emperor summoned him to the Palace and asked his opinion. Kuo Kung said: 'Sun Chang must pay a fine'. The Emperor said: 'Sun Chang falsified an Imperial order and (thereby) killed a man. Why should he only pay a fine?' Kuo Kung said: 'The law makes a distinction between an intentional and an unintentional error. Sun Chang's mistake in transmitting the order was indeed an unintentional error; and such errors are punished lightly'. The Emperor said: 'Sun Chang is a native of the same district as the two prisoners. Therefore I suspect that his mistake was intentional' (because he was either a friend of the murdered man, or an enemy of the two brothers). Kuo Kung said: 'The road of Chou is smooth like a whetstone, it is straight like an arrow (quoted from the *Book of Odes*, section *Hsiao-ya* 小雅, the Ode *Ta-tung* 大東). The Superior Man does not anticipate deceit. The (ancient) Emperors and Kings took Heaven as model. Punishments cannot be tampered with and made to suit one's own ends'. The Emperor praised Kuo Kung and promoted him to Director to the Commandant of Justice".

(From his biography)

CYKC ch. 4, page 46.

Kuo Kung 郭躬 was especially known as an eminent judge; he died in the Yüan-ho era (84-86 A.D.). Cf. his biography in *Hou-han-shu*, ch. 76, where this case is related in a more elaborate form.

The "Three Dukes", *san-kung* 三公, were the T'ai-wei 太尉 Grand Marshal, Szu-t'u 司徒 Grand Instructor, and the Szu-k'ung 司空 Grand Master of Works.

For *chung-ch'ang-shih* 中常侍, here translated "Gentleman-in-waiting", cf. des Rotours, page 141.

TYPS-III writes Kuo's family name wrongly as Cheng 鄭.

The distinction between *ku* 故 "intentional mistake" and *wu* 誤 "unintentional error" is discussed in detail by Hulsewé, op. cit. page 251 sq.; there also the present case is briefly referred to.

TYPS-I and III add here a commentary by Cheng K'o.

B.

"When the Minister Ch'en Hsi-liang was Prefectural Inspector of K'ai-feng, a man from Ch'ing-chou called Chao Yü reported to his superiors that (the Hsi-hsia Prince) Li Yüan-hao would certainly revolt. He was punished by being banished and placed at the disposal of the Prefectural Inspector of Education in Fu-chou. The next year Li Yüan-hao indeed revolted. Chao Yü brought a suit (stating that he had been unjustly punished); but the pertinent authorities would not consider it. Then Chao went to the capital without permission. The Assisting Councillor ordered proceedings against him on the basis of the law on leaving one's post without authorization. Ch'en Hsi-liang thereupon memoralized the Throne, submitting that since the Bureau of Nobility had the duty to deal with his earlier report (they were at fault); since his report had proved true, he should not have been punished. Consequently Chao Yü was acquitted".

(From his biography)

CYKC ch. 4, page 55.

Ch'en Hsi-liang 陳希亮 was a benevolent and just official who solved a number of difficult criminal cases. He became *chin-shih* in 1030 A.D., and after the advent of the Emperor Jen-tsung (1064-1067 A.D.) was appointed Junior Lord of the Imperial Sacrifices; he died shortly afterwards. His biography in *Sung-shih* ch. 298 records a number of cases decided by him, including the present one; there, however, the name of the wronged official is written Yü 禹 , and the case is related in a different manner. There it says: "Chao Yü, a man from Ch'ing-chou, reported to the Throne that Chao Yüan-hao would certainly revolt. The Minister of State concerned had Chao Yü banished to Ch'ien-chou (i.e. Ch'ien-an 建安 in Fukien) for having reported unfounded rumours. When Chao Yüan-hao indeed revolted, Chao Yü brought a suit but the pertinent authorities refused to consider it. He then went to the capital without permission in order to justify himself. The Minister was angry and had him put in jail in K'ai-feng. Ch'en Hsi-liang said that Chao Yü ought to be rewarded instead of punished, and would not give up his argument. The Emperor released Chao Yü, and appointed him as Prefectural judge of Hsü-chou, as a reward" 青州民趙禹上書 言趙元昊必反。宰相以禹狂言徙建州。元昊 果反。禹訟所部不受。亡至京自理。宰相怒。

下開封獄。希亮言禹可賞不可罪。爭不已。
上釋禹。賞爲徐州推官。 My translation of the evidently
corrupt phrase 坐責爲文學參軍福州安置 is based on
the information supplied here to the effect that Chao Yü was indeed banished
to Fukien.

Li Yüan-hao (李元昊, also known as Li Nang-hsiao 李曩霄, died
1048 A.D.) was an ambitious Hsi-hsia Prince, upon whom the Sung Emperor
bestowed the Imperial family name Chao 趙; hence he is also referred to as
Chao Yüan-hao. He began a revolt to establish an independent Hsi-hsia Kingdom,
but was defeated. Later he was forgiven and reinstated in his former position.
Cf. Franke vol. IV, pp. 154 sq.

42. *Yin forgives a man who proffers a false statement;
Tou Ts'an opposes leniency because of mourning*

A.

"In the (Eastern) Chin Dynasty (317-420 A.D.) when Yin Chung-
k'an was Prefect of Ch'ing-chou, a man from Kuei-yang called Huang
Ch'in-sheng whose parents had died long before, falsely put on sackcloth
and hemp and said that he was going to bury his father. The officers
of the tribunal would have him publicly executed on the strength of the
existing laws. But Yin Chung-k'an said: 'According to the spirit of the
law he should be pardoned. If when both one's parents are still alive,
one should wickedly aver that they are dead, this is an offense against
human nature too depraved for words, and such a man should indeed
be publicly executed. Now since Huang's parents have died already
he is only guilty of proffering a false statement'. Thereupon his death
sentence was commuted".

CYKC ch. 4, page 47; IYC ch. 2, no. 31; YP no. 57.

Yin Chung-k'an 殷仲堪 was an official known for his high moral
standards. The Emperor Hsiao-wu (373-396 A.D.) appointed him administrator
of three prefectures together, including Ch'ing-chou. Cf. his biography in *Chin-shu*
ch. 84, where a more elaborate version of the present case is given.

TYPS-I and III begin Yin's statement with the words 原此旨, which
are arbitrarily quoted from the longer text in the biography. TYPS-II reads
原此法意, a paraphrase which fits better into the abbreviated text;
this reading I have adopted for the translation.

Since the character *yin* 殷 occurred in the name of a Sung Emperor, TYPS-I,
II and III replace it by *shang* 商. CYKC replaces it by *t'ang* 湯, the other

character used instead of the tabooed *yin*. IYC, however, gives the name in its original form.

B.

"In the T'ang Dynasty, when Tou Ts'an in the beginning of his career was Sheriff of Feng-hsien, a man called Ts'ao Fen and his younger brother who were serving in the Northern Army, while drunk laid hands on their younger sister. Their father tried in vain to save her, and in mortification killed himself by jumping into a well. Tou Ts'an opined that both brothers deserved the death penalty. But their fellow-soldiers asked Tou Ts'an to grant the culprits a stay of execution because they were in mourning (for their father). Tou Ts'an said: 'If a man who has caused his father's death be granted reprieve on the ground that he is in mourning for him, that would be tantamount to patricide going unpunished'. He had both beaten to death".

(From his biography in *T'ang-shu*)

CYKC ch. 4, page 49; IYC ch. 5, no. 86; YP no. 58.

Tou Ts'an 竇 參 was an official expert in juridical science and well versed in administrative problems. He was appointed to the High Court and thereafter as Censor, and distinguished himself by his impartial justice. In 792 A.D. he was appointed Vice-Governor of Pin-chou 彬 州 . Cf. his biography in *Chiu-t'ang-shu* ch. 136, which gives the same version of the present case; *Hsin-t'ang-shu* ch. 145 gives a more elaborate version.

TYPS-I and III add a comment by Cheng K'o.

43. *Hsüeh Hsüan and the quarrel about a silk sheet;*
Fu Yung makes two robbers engage in a race

A.

"In the (Western) Han Dynasty (206 B.C.-24 A.D.) a man went to the market with a sheet of waterproof silk. When it started to rain he unfolded the sheet to cover himself. After a while another man came and asked him whether he might share the shelter; the merchant yielded one end of the sheet to him. When the rain had ceased and the two men were about to part, each claimed that the sheet belonged to him; (they brought this matter before the authorities). The Grand Administrator Hsüeh Hsüan had the sheet cut in two, and gave each man half. Then he ordered his mounted guards to follow them and to hear what they would say. The man (who had come later) said: 'This is a favour from Kung-chün!' (Note in the text: Hsüeh Hsüan's style was Kung-chün). But the owner did not cease shouting that he was being wronged. Hsüeh Hsüan then knew the situation. He questioned the man who had come later and he confessed".

(From the *Feng-su-t'ung*)

CYKC ch. 6, page 90; IYC ch. 1, no. 9; YP no. 60.

Hsüeh ¦Hsüan 薛宣 was an able official who having attracted the notice of

Wang Feng (王鳳 died 26 B.C.; cf. BD no. 2167) was appointed magistrate of Ch'ang-an. Later he became well known as Censor. Cf. his biography in *Han-shu* ch. 83, where this case is not related.

A more elaborate version of this case is found in the fragments of the older *Feng-su-t'ung* version; cf. the edition mentioned in the note to Case 4-B, op. cit. page 107.

TYPS-I and II give the style of Hsüeh Hsiang as Kung-chün 公君 , TYPS-II

as Kung-yüeh 公月 ; the correct form is Kung-chün 贛君 .

B.

"In Ch'i-chou an old woman was set upon by a brigand (on the road) and (before she succumbed from her wounds) cried out that she was being robbed. A passer-by came to the rescue and caught the robber. The latter thereupon falsely accused the passer-by of the crime, and the pair was brought before the Prefect, accusing each other. Fu Yung said: 'Both of you will engage in a running contest. He who first reaches the Feng-yang city gate is innocent'. When they came back Fu Yung said sternly to the loser: 'You are the robber!' He reasoned that if the robber were a good runner, he would certainly not have been caught by the passer-by. In this manner he deducted that the good runner was the man who caught the other".

CYKC ch. 3, page 29; IYC ch. 1, no. 5.

For Fu Yung see Case 29-A above. This case is recorded in his biography in *Chin-shu*, ch. 114.

44. *Hsiao Yen and the cow struck by thunder ;*
Hsiao Huai-wu makes use of secret agents

A.

"According to the decrees of the Sheng-yüan era (937 A.D.) of the Southern T'ang Dynasty (937-976 A.D.), thefts amounting to more than three strings of cash were punished with the death penalty. At that time a prominent man of Chi-chou lost some clean new quilts worth several thousand cash when his clothes were being sunned; he denounced his neighbour as the thief. (Brought before the tribunal) the neighbour could not stand the torture and wrongly confessed. When asked what he had done with the stolen quilts he replied: 'I sold them at random in the market, there is no way to recover them'. But on the day that he was going to be executed (he regretted his confession), his loud wailing that he was being wronged moved everyone's heart. When the official in charge of that district reported this to the Throne, the First Emperor (i.e. Li Pien) ordered the Division Chief Hsiao Yen to review the case. Hsiao Yen fasted and prayed, earnestly desiring to redress the wrong. On the day he arrived in the prefecture (where the case had happened) the clear weather suddenly changed into rain and thunder which killed a cow of the victim of the theft. When its belly was cut open, the lost quilts were found; the cow had eaten them (when they were being sunned in the garden) and they had not yet been digested".

(From the *Nan-t'ang-chin-shih* by Cheng Wen-pao)

CYKC ch. 2, page 15.

Hsien-chu 先主 "The First Emperor", here refers to Li Pien (李昇 died 943 A.D.; cf. BD no. 767), also called Hsü Chih-kao 徐知誥, the founder of the Southern T'ang Dynasty.

About Hsiao Yen 蕭儼 I could find no further particulars.

It should be noted that according to the old Chinese belief it was the thunder that killed living beings, and not the lightning accompanying it. The same idea used to prevail in the West; cf. our expression "thunderstruck".

The *Nan-t'ang-chin-shih* 南唐近事 is a small collection of historical notes in 1 ch., compiled in 977 A.D. by the Sung writer and lute-player Cheng Wen-pao (鄭文寶 953-1013 A.D.). The *Ts'ung-shu-chi-ch'eng* edition (no. 3856) gives on page 7 a much more elaborate version.

B.

"In the time of the Kingdom of Shu, a man called Hsiao Huai-wu was in charge of the 'band that searches out facts', that is the office of military information. He had under him about a hundred men, and each of those trained again ten or more secret agents, who were known as 'dogs'. In every nook and cranny, among horse-healers and wine-waiters, beggars and coolies, even among street urchins selling their wares, they had their men. If people happened to say something about public or private affairs, it was immediately reported. Thus the people's hearts were full of fear, everyone always suspecting that the man standing next to him was a 'dog'. In this manner Hsiao Huai-wu had countless people killed. When Kuo Ch'ung-t'ao entered Shu (at the head of his army) he had Hsiao executed together with his entire family. Thus the man who was charged with discovering hidden evil, himself became guilty of practising hidden evil".

(From the *Ch'eng-tu-ku-chin-chi*)

CYKC ch. 1, page 8.

The short-lived Shu Kingdom was founded by the T'ang General Wang Chien 王 建 ; the T'ang Emperor had made him Prince of Shu (i.e. Szuchuan Province) in recognition of his valour. When the T'ang Dynasty collapsed, Wang declared himself independent, and assumed the title of King of Shu. In 918 A.D. he was succeeded by his son Wang Yen 王 衍 . Wang Yen was defeated by General Kuo Ch'ung-t'ao 郭 崇 韜 of the Southern T'ang Dynasty, and executed.

The *Ch'eng-tu-ku-chin-chi* 成 都 古 今 記 is a small collection in 1 ch. of historical notes on the capital of Szuchuan Ch'eng-tu, compiled by the well known scholar and lute-player Chao Pien (趙 抃 1008-1084 A.D.), who at one time served as Prefect there. The fragments of the text printed in SF do not include the present story.

45. *Chang Tsu covers up part of a forged permit;*
    Lang Chien compares the writing on a document

A.

"In the T'ang Dynasty, when Chang Tsu was Sheriff of Ho-yang, a man called Lü Yüan forged a document (allegedly) issued by the Superintendent of the Government Granaries Feng Shen, and (on the strength of this document) fraudulently sold Government grain. Feng Shen disclaimed having issued the permit, but Lü Yüan maintained that it was genuine. Chang Tsu then took Lü Yüan's written accusation, and having covered up both ends so that only one character in the middle remained visible, he asked Lü: 'Is this written by you?' Lü Yüan said that it was not. Then Chang Tsu removed the covers and showed Lü that it was his own plaint. He was given fifty lashes (for having lied to the magistrate). Then Chang Tsu covered up the forged permit bearing Feng Shen's name, with again only two characters showing; he asked Lü Yüan the same question. Lü said yes. Thereupon Chang removed the covers and showed Lü that it was the forged document. Lü Yüan then confessed his crime''.

CYKC ch. 3, page 32; IYC ch. 3, no. 51; YP no. 44.

Chang Tsu (張 鷟, style Wen-ch'eng 文 成 ca. 660-ca. 741 A.D.) had a chequered official career. Although he earned fame by his brilliant literary style, people took offense at his frivolous character; at one time he was banished to S. China. Later he was reinstated and ended his career as Assistant Chief of the Bureau of Palace Gates (for this post cf. des Rotours, vol. I page 121). His literary works were greatly admired also by the Japanese and Korean envoys who visited the T'ang capital; his erotic novel *Yu-hsien-k'u* 遊 仙 窟 "Visit to the Cave of the Immortals" became very popular in Japan and was preserved in that country.

Cf. also Case 71-A.

TYPS-III writes *kung-tzu* 工 字, a copyist's mistake for *erh-tzu* 二 字.

B.

"When the Executive Secretary Lang Chien was Prefect of Tou-chou, a small official died leaving behind a young son. The son's brother-in-law who was living in the same house forged a document (allegedly written by his deceased father-in-law), on the strength of which he appropriated the young son's land. After his son had grown up he repeatedly accused his brother-in-law (before the local authorities) without getting his wrong redressed. Then he reported the case to the Throne, and the Emperor appointed Lang Chien to investigate. Lang Chien took an old document and showing it (to the brother-in-law) asked: 'Is this the handwriting of your father-in-law?' He said yes. Then Lang Chien took the forged document and showed him that the handwriting was entirely different. The brother-in-law thereupon confessed his crime''.

CYKC ch. 6, page 86; IYC ch. 8, no. 164; YP no. 43.

Lang Chien 郎 簡 became *chin-shih* in the Ching-te era (1004-1007 A.D.) and ended his career as Executive Secretary of the Ministry of Public Works. Cf. his biography in *Sung-shih* ch. 299, where this case is recorded.

46. *Pao Ch'eng has a constable bambooed ;*
Minister Chou has an officer arrested

A.

"When the Assistant Commissioner of Military Affairs Pao Ch'eng was Prefect of K'ai-feng, it was well known that in his severity he had often his own constables bambooed. Once a man had offended against the law and was going to be bambooed as punishment. A constable accepted a bribe from that man and made an agreement with him saying: 'To-day when you are brought before the Prefect he will certainly order me to bamboo you. (I shall beat you lightly but) you must shout loudly in defense of yourself. (The Prefect will find fault with me anyway and) you and I shall have to share the punishment (i.e. bamboo each other); if you hit me hard, I shall also hit you hard!' When Pao Ch'eng had the prisoner brought before him and had finished the questioning, he indeed ordered that constable to bamboo him. The prisoner did as the constable had said and cried incessantly that he was being wronged. The constable shouted at him: 'You can go away after this beating, what does this shouting help you?' Pao Ch'eng then said that the constable had infringed upon his (Pao Ch'eng's) authority (by telling the prisoner that he could go after the beating); he had the constable thrown on the floor and given seventeen blows (by the prisoner). He granted the prisoner special leniency, the blows he gave the officer being subtracted from his own punishment. Pao Ch'eng thought that in this way he could break the power of the constables; but he did not realize that he had been deceived".

(From Shen K'uo's *Pi-t'an*)

CYKC ch. 5, page 74; IYC ch. 9, no. 174; YP no. 80.

For Pao Ch'eng see Case 23-B above; posthumous name *Hsiao-su*.

This story is far from clear. Kuei Wan-jung's version as reproduced in TYPS-I and III is no improvement on the original in ch. 22 of the *Meng-hsi-pi-t'an* (for this book cf. Case 6-A above), and neither is the IYC version which differs only in the opening sentences. I have based my translation upon a modified version in TYPS-II, which is identical with the CYKC text. Hereunder follows first this text, and then the *Meng-hsi-pi-t'an* original version.

包拯副樞知開封府。杖吏號爲嚴明。有民
犯法。罪當杖脊。吏受略與之約曰。今見尹必
付我責狀。汝第號呼自辨。我當與汝分罪。汝

決杖。我亦決杖。旣而拯引囚問畢。果付吏責
狀。囚如吏言分辨不已。吏大聲呵之曰。但受
脊杖出去。何用多言。拯謂其招權。捽杖於庭。
杖之十七。特寬囚罪。止從杖坐。公知以此折
吏勢。不知乃爲所賣也。

　　MHPT: 包孝肅尹京。號爲明察。有編民犯
法⋯⋯何用多言。包謂其市權。捽吏於庭。杖之
七十。特寬囚罪。止從杖坐。以抑吏勢。不知
乃爲所賣。卒如素約。小人爲姦。固難防也。

It is difficult to see the point of the constable's deal with the prisoner if one does not assume that they were to beat each other; for else the constable would have to earn his money by receiving a real bambooing—in the MHPT version even seventy strokes—which does not seem to be a good bargain. I must add, however, that the sentences 'If you hit me hard, I shall also hit you hard' can as well be translated 'You will certainly be bambooed, and I shall also certainly be bambooed'.

However this may be, it is evident that the story is meant as a warning to magistrates to beware of the tricks of their underlings. This is proved by the last sentence of the MHPT version ('The evil practices of small officers are indeed difficult to guard against'), by the note which Cheng K'o added to the story in CYKC, and by a longer commentary in IYC where it is pointed out that even such a perspicacious magistrate as Pao Ch'eng was occasionally fooled by the tricks of his underlings; also the parallel case B. given hereunder points in that direction.

B.

"In the Eastern Han Dynasty (25-220 A.D.) when Chou Yü, styled Wen-t'ung, was Minister of the Marquis of Shao-ling, an officer of the tribunal feared Chou's strictness, and therefore wanted to damage his prestige. Early in the morning he took a dead body that had been found by the roadside (outside the city), and having cut off its hands and feet, set it up against the gate of the tribunal. As soon as Chou Yü heard about this he went there; standing near the body he made as if he were laughing and talking with it. (At the same time) he covertly scrutinized the body and observed that there were dry rice husks in its mouth and eyes. Thereupon he secretly asked the guards at the city gate: 'Who has entered the city (this morning) carrying a load of straw?', and received the answer: 'There was only the officer of the tribunal'. Then Chou asked his groom: 'Was not there outside (the tribunal) one who showed signs of doubt when I was laughing and talking with the body?' He answered: 'The officer of the tribunal doubted you'. Chou Yü had that man arrested, and upon being questioned he confessed".

CYKC ch. 6, page 81; IYC ch. 2, no. 36.

Chou Yü 周紆 served as Prefect in the Chien-ch'u era (76-83 A.D.). He lived in the utmost frugality, and was favoured by the Emperor Chang (76-88 A.D.); he died as Director of Works in the Palace. Cf. his biography in *Hou-han-shu* ch. 107, where this case is related.

47. *Fang Chieh and the list of victims;*
    Emperor Wen and the rebel's handwriting

A.

"When the Senior Lord (of Imperial Banquets) Fang Chieh was Investigator in the Censorate, an army deserter of Li-chou had a feud with a rich man. He falsely accused the rich man of killing twelve people by magic, praying to evil spirits. This case remained undecided for a long time. Then the Emperor ordered Fang Chieh to go there and investigate. Fang Chieh ordered the accuser to enumerate the names of the persons he said the rich man was murdering by magic. He went to see those people to check and found that many of the victims listed were still in perfect health. Thus this case was cleared up".

(From the *T'ien-sheng-ming-ch'en-chuan*).

CYKC ch. 3, page 35; IYC ch. 8, no. 166; YP no. 47.

Fang Chieh 方偕 started his career as a military official; after having served as magistrate he was appointed Investigator in the Censorate, later Censor. He was known as a good administrator, his only weakness being a great fondness of wine; he ended his career—not inappropriately—as Senior Lord of the Imperial Banquets. Cf. his biography in *Sung-shih*, ch. 304, where this case is related in a slightly more elaborate version.

All texts, including that in *Sung-shih*, read *sui-sha* 歲 殺 ; 歲 is doubtless a mistake for 祟, which means 'harm caused by spirits'. Both characters are pronounced *sui* and moreover resemble each other closely in cursive writing.

The *mo-t'o* spirits 摩 駞 神 I could not identify. The term might be a transcription of Sanskrit *mātā* and refer to some Tantrik female deity.

The *T'ien-sheng-ming-ch'en-chuan* 天 聖 名 臣 傳 "Biographies of Eminent Statesmen of the T'ien-sheng era (1023-1031 A.D.)" is not found in the catalogues at my disposal.

B.

"In the (Former) Sung Dynasty (420-479 A.D.), in the twenty-second year of the Yüan-chia era (i.e. 445 A.D.), K'ung Hsi-hsien, Hsü Chan-chih, Hsü Yüeh, Hsieh Tsung and Fan Yeh plotted to place on the throne I-k'ang, Prince of P'eng-ch'eng. Hsü Chan-chih reported this to the Emperor (i.e. Wen-ti, 424-453 A.D.) who thereupon ordered the arrest of Hsieh Tsung and the others. All confessed except for Fan Yeh who would not admit his complicity. When the Emperor had him thoroughly examined several times, Fan Yeh would say only: 'K'ung Hsi-hsien has slandered me'. The Emperor then ordered to show Fan a proclamation (of the rebels) written and corrected in Fan's own hand. Then only Fan Yeh confessed".

(From Fan T'ai's biography in the *Nan-shih*)

CYKC ch. 3, page 41

K'ung Hsi-hsien 孔熙先 was a learned scholar-official whose merits remained unrecognized by the Emperor; he espoused the cause of the degraded Prince of P'eng-ch'eng, also because the latter had bestowed favours on K'ung's father.

Fan Yeh (范曄 398-445 A.D.) is especially known as author of the *Hou-han-shu*, the Dynastic History of the Later Han Period; he was executed for high treason in 445 A.D. The taboo character *yeh* is again written differently in various editions; cf. the note to Case 5-A above.

A more elaborate version of the case is found in Fan Yeh's biography in ch. 33 of the *Nan-shih*, appended to the biography of his father Fan T'ai 范泰.

48. *Ch'en Feng-ku counsels on detaining by force;*
Hu Chih contests the decision on stealing food

A.

"When Ch'en Feng-ku of the Bureau of Guests (in the Ministry of Rites) was Vice-Prefect of Pei-chou, a soldier captured a burglar (who had broken into his house). His mother wanted also to get hold of the burglar but the soldier would not let her and pushed her back. She fell on the floor and died the next day. The soldier was handed over to the local officer who proposed that he be executed in public (as having killed his mother). But Ch'en Feng-ku reasoned: 'Having overpowered a robber, to let him escape is contrary to law. The captor of a robber is entitled in law to resist (any attempt by any person) to get hold of the robber by force. If, when death should result from such resistance, it would be judged in the same way as causing death during a hand-to-hand fight, that would mean that a man acting in self-defense would not be able to overpower a robber. To execute one innocent man (in such circumstances) would establish a precedent (authorizing) a person to liberate a criminal (already captured). This is contrary to the law'. When this opinion had been reported to the Emperor, he decided that the soldier would be punished with a flogging. All praised this as an equitable verdict".

CYKC ch. 4, page 53.

About Ch'en Feng-ku 陳奉古 I could find no further details.

TYPS-III wrongly writes Chü-chou 具州 instead of Pei-chou.

TYPS-II adds the remark that this case is recorded in Ch'en's tomb inscription composed by Wang Kuei (cf. the note to Case 15-B above).

B.

"When the Vice-President of the High Court Hu Hsiang at the beginning of his career was Police Inspector of Yüan-chou, a man stole food and was beaten to death by the owner. The prefectural authorities proposed the death sentence for that man. But Hu Hsiang contested this saying: 'According to the law, the owner should be flogged'. The Prefect did not accept this opinion. When the matter was brought before the Emperor, he decided according to Hu Hsiang's proposal".

(From his tomb inscription composed by Lü Ta-fang)

CYKC ch. 4, page 54.

About Hu Hsiang 胡向 I could find no further particulars.

For Lü Ta-fang cf. Case 27-B above.

TYPS-I and III add here a commentary by Cheng K'o, who observes that this decision is permissible only in cases where it is proved that the accused hit the thief without the intention to kill him.

49. *A Censor loses a written accusation;*
   Kuo Yüan asks for a specimen of writing

A.

"When Li Ching was Prefect of Chi-chou, someone accused him of planning a revolt. The Emperor Kao-tsu (618-626 A.D.) ordered a Censor to proceed (to Chi-chou) to make an investigation. Since the Censor knew that this was a case of slander, he requested to be allowed to proceed there together w'th the accuser. When they had gone as far as several post-stations the Censor said in feigned alarm: 'I have lost the written accusation!' He acted as if in great fear and begged the accuser to write out again his accusation for him. When the Censor examined that document he found that the contents were not the same as those of the original accusation. That same day he went back (to the capital) and reported this to the Emperor. The Emperor was greatly startled, and the accuser was beheaded for having proffered a false accusation. The name of the Censor has been lost".

CYKC ch. 3, page 30; IYC ch. 1, no. 1; YCTI no. 2; YP no. 45.

Li Ching (李 靖 571-649 A.D.) first served under the Sui Dynasty. When the T'ang Dynasty had been established he was condemned to death because his loyalty to the new rulers was doubted; subsequently pardoned, and appointed to high office.

The editor of CYKC observes that the facts of this case do not accord with historical data, and that its source must be sought for in T'ang fiction.

B.

"In the Wei Dynasty (220-265 A.D.) when Kuo Yüan, styled Tzu-ni, was Prefect of Wei, someone sent an anonymous letter slandering (the Emperor T'ai-tsu); the Emperor was very angry and insisted upon knowing who was the writer. Kuo Yüan asked that the letter be left with him and that the occurrence be kept secret. Now the letter contained many quotations from the 'Poetical Essay on the Two Capitals'. Kuo Yüan said to the Counsellor of Merits: 'In this Prefecture there are few scholars. I wish to let (some suitable students) go to the capital and there find a man who can explain (the Essay on the Two Capitals), so that they can learn it from him'. (When the students had found such a teacher) they let him write down something (and forwarded that specimen to Kuo Yüan). He compared the handwriting and found that it resembled that of the slanderous letter. That teacher was arrested and upon being interrogated he confessed".

CYKC ch. 6, page 81; IYC ch. 2, no. 27.

Kuo Yüan 國 淵 was a student of the famous classical scholar Cheng Hsüan (鄭 玄 127-200 A.D.) When General Ts'ao Ts'ao (155-220 A.D.; cf. BD no. 2013) was laying the foundations of the Wei Dynasty (later Ts'ao Ts'ao was called T'ai-tsu, First Emperor of that Dynasty), Kuo Yüan was appointed to high office. Cf. his biography in *Wei-chih* ch. 11, where the case is related with much additional detail.

The missing character in TYPS-III (indicated by a square) is *shu* 書 , as given in TYPS-I; but I read *tu* 讀 , as in the original *Wei-chih* text. In those days books were rare, and very few scholars could afford to have a comprehensive library; hence they mostly concentrated their studies on a limited number of literary texts; their explanations of such a text were more or less a professional secret, communicated only to their direct pupils.

The Essay on the Two Capitals was written by the learned Han scholar Chang Heng (張 衡 78-139 A.D.); it was full of hidden allusions, and it is said that he spent ten years on its composition.

50. *Fan Wei claims Fan Cha as his ancestor;*
Han Chü concentrates on Teng's teachings

A.

"When the Reader-in-waiting (of the Han-lin Academy) Liu Ch'ang was Prefect of Yung-hsing-chün (i.e. Ching-chao-fu, the Metropolitan area), a man of a prominent family called Fan Wei, on the strength of military merit, claimed Fan Cha as his grandfather; he had Fan Cha's tomb opened and his own grandmother buried there together with Fan Cha. During fifty years he evaded the compulsory military service, and he often offended against the law. (Finally) he was sentenced to penal servitude in the border region. But he immediately bought his acquittal. The people of Ch'ang-an were very indignant about this, but no official dared to do anything about it. Liu Ch'ang investigated this case (and found Fan guilty), but he was ordered to some other post before he had completed the case. Thereafter Fan changed his statements repeatedly, and had several hundred persons deliver testimony; the case dragged on year after year without a decision being arrived at. Then the Emperor ordered the Censorate to investigate, and they finally decided that Liu Ch'ang's findings had been correct".

(From his biography)

CYKC ch. 8, page 128.

Liu Ch'ang (劉 敞 1019-1068 A.D.) was an official famous for his wide learning and his excellent literary style. He was Academician of the Chi-hsien Hall 集 賢 院 and also served as judge of the Censorate. Cf. his biography in *Sung-shih* ch. 319, where Fan's offense is summed up in a few characters ("during fifty years he usurped another family's identity" 冒 同 姓 戶 籍 五 十 年); there no further details are given regarding Fan Cha 范 祚 .

B.

"Shen K'uo says in his *Pi-t'an:* 'The people in Kiangsi love law suits. They have a book called *Teng-szu-hsien* that consists entirely of models of documents used in litigation. It starts with teaching how to discredit people by written documents. If one can not trap them with those, one should try to get the better of them by deceit and slander. And should this method fail also, one should cause them to commit an offence and then intimidate them. Teng Szu-hsien is the name of a man. Since he was the first who transmitted this art, the book was named after him. In the village schools they frequently teach the pupils this book.

"When the Head of the Bureau of Nobility (in the Ministry of Personnel) Han Chü was Vice-Administrator of Ch'ien-chou, some people drew up a false complaint and cried and wailed in a most convincing manner. (The Prefect being absent) Han Chü unexpectedly took over the administration. He studied the local customs and investigated the iniquities so that no one under him could practisedeceit. Then the men who had presented the false complaint had to admit themselves that they had suffered no wrong. Han Chü was the elder brother of Han Ch'i (see above, Case 7-B); he ended his career as Fiscal Intendant of North and South Chekiang".

(From his tomb inscription composed by Yin Shu)

CYKC ch. 8, page 127; IYC ch. 9, no. 173; YP no. 79.

The first half of the text is identical with that of *Meng-hsi-pi-t'an,* ch. 25; there it is said that it were the people of Kiangsi 江 西 who were addicted to law suits. But TYPS-I, II and III read Chiang-nan 江 南 ; since Ch'ien-chou is located in Kiangsi, I followed the MHPT reading, as did also the editor of IYC.

Yin Shu (尹 洙 1001-1047 A.D.) was a great scholar, expert on old literature; cf. his biography in *Sung-shih* ch. 295. One of his exploits as a judge is related in Case 56-B below.

51. *Yü has herds driven to the tribunal;*
    Ku Hsien-chih has a cow set free

A.

"In the (Northern) Chou Dynasty (557-581 A.D.) when Yü Chung-wen, styled Tz'u-wu, was Prefect of An-ku in the domain of the Prince of Chao, there were two men of the surname Tu and Jen, each of whom lost a cow. Later a (stray) cow was found, and both contended it was theirs. The local authorities could not solve this case. Then the administrator of I-chou called Han Po-hsi said: 'Yü of An-ku proved clever in detecting in his youth. He must be ordered to decide this case'. Yü Chung-wen had both parties drive their cows to the tribunal. He let loose the stray cow, and it joined Jen's herd. Then he had one of his men inflict a small wound on the cow. Jen sighed with grief while Tu did not show any emotion. Thereupon Tu confessed".

CYKC ch. 6, page 90; YP no. 59.

Yü Chung-wen 于仲文 was a military official under the Later Chou Dynasty who later, under the Sui Dynasty, earned fame in fighting the Kitans, and rose to Commander-in-chief of the Sui Armies. At the end of his career he suffered defeat in the Korean campaign and died in prison. Cf. his detailed biography in *Pei-shih* ch. 23, where this case is related.

For Han Po-hsi 韓伯携 cf. *Sui-shu* ch. 30.

B.

"In the Southern Liang Dynasty (502-557) when Ku Hsien-chih was magistrate of Chien-k'ang, a man's cow was stolen. The thief and the real owner both claimed it as theirs, and no decision could be arrived at. Ku Hsien-chih then ordered to set the disputed cow free and let it wander at will. It walked back to the house of the owner, and then only the thief confessed".

(From the biography of Ku Chi-chih in the *Nan-shih*; Ku Hsien-chih was his grandson)

CYKC ch. 6, page 95; IYC ch. 3, no. 66.

Ku Hsien-chih (顧憲之 died 509 A.D.) was an able and benevolent administrator, who served i.a. in Heng-yang 衡陽, and ended his career as Vice-Governor of Yang-chou 楊州. Cf. his biography in *Nan-shih* ch. 35, appended to that of his grandfather Ku Chi-chih 顧覬之, where this case is recorded.

52. *Chang Sheng investigates a well;*
    Ts'ai Kao stays on the sea-shore

A.

"When the Ministerial Vice-President Chang (Sheng) was Prefect of Jün-chou, a woman's husband went out and after several days had not yet returned. Suddenly it was rumoured that there was a dead body in a well on a vegetable field. The woman went there and wept over the well saying: 'That is my husband!' When this was reported to the authorities, Chang Sheng ordered his officers to assemble the villagers of that neighbourhood and go to the well in order to establish whether the dead man was the woman's husband or not. All said that since the well was deep, they could not recognize the body. Chang Sheng said: 'None of this crowd could identify the body, how could that woman alone know that it is her husband?' She was arrested and brought before the magistrate for questioning. Then it came out that her paramour had murdered her husband, and that he had told the woman (beforehand) about his plan".

(From Shen K'uo's *Pi-t'an*)

CYKC ch. 5, page 77; IYC ch. 8, no. 148; YP no. 7.

Chang Sheng (張 昇 992-1077 A.D.) was appointed Censor in 1055 A.D., and in 1058 Assistant Commissioner of Military Affairs; soon promoted to Commissioner. After having served as Regional Commander, he ended his career as Grand Preceptor of the Heir Apparent. Cf. his biography in *Sung-shih* ch. 318, where this case is not recorded.

Except for a few insignificant changes, the text is identical with that of MHPT ch. 12; there Chang Sheng is referred to by his style Kao-ch'ing 杲 卿. All TYPS editions, and also CYKC, give Chang's personal name as Pien 昪 ; only IYC reads correctly *Sheng*. Since as far as I know *sheng* is not a taboo character, this must be a clerical error.

B.

"When Ts'ai Kao was Sheriff of Ch'ang-hsi in Fu-chou, a woman of that district had two sons who disappeared when fishing on the sea. The woman pointed out a certain man as their enemy, and accused him before the magistrate. The officer in charge made difficulties, saying: 'There was a storm, who can say whether they were really murdered by their enemy? If their bodies are not found, the law can not be applied'. Ts'ai Kao (,however,) instituted a secret search for the enemy, and found his where abouts. Then he promised the woman saying: 'If in ten days the bodies are not found, I shall hold myself responsible for arresting the murderer for you!' He stayed on the seashore for ten days, then the flood washed the two bodies ashore. The autopsy proved that they had been murdered (and had not been drowned). Thereupon the enemy was arrested, interrogated and executed".

(Ts'ai Kao was a younger brother of Ts'ai Hsiang; the case is found in his tomb inscription composed by Ou-yang Hsiu)

CYKC ch. 2, page 23; SF no. 3; IYC ch. 7, no. 125.

Ts'ai Hsiang (蔡 襄 1012-1067 A.D.) was a famous writer whose biography is included in *Sung-shih*, ch. 320; there this younger brother is not mentioned.

For Ou-yang Hsiu see the note to case 5-A above.

TYPS-II and CYKC quote a commentary by Cheng K'o where he states that the bodies were washed ashore in answer to T'sai Kao's earnest desire to solve the case; thus the case is interpreted as an example of divine intervention, which seems to me beside the point. I take it that the murderer concealed the bodies somewhere near the shore, hoping that people would think that they had perished at sea. When he heard that a murder investigation was being initiated and that Ts'ai Kao had stated that he would make an arrest if the bodies were not found, he became afraid and threw the dead bodies in the sea, hoping that the signs of violence would be obliterated by decomposition. This was exactly what Ts'ai Kao had presumed that the murderer would do.

53. *Liu Shih burns a pretended corpse;*
Kao Fang investigates a feigned illness

A.

"When the Keeper of the Imperial Edicts Liu Shih in the beginning of his career was magistrate of Fu-p'ing in Yüeh-chou, a thief robbed someone's son and daughter. After he had been arrested he immediately feigned to be dead, and while his body was being examined he succeeded in escaping. When he had been caught, he again feigned to be dead. Liu Shih had him burned alive".

(From his biography)

CYKC ch. 5, page 67.

Liu Shih 劉湜 served as Judge attached to the Regional Commander of Hunan; then he was appointed magistrate, and transferred to the capital he became Professor of Imperial Sacrifices. Thereafter Palace Censor, and several other high functions; he ended his career as Junior Lord of Imperial Sacrifices. Cf. his detailed biography in *Sung-shih* ch. 304, where this case is related. There we find, instead of *cha-szu* 詐 死 , the proper Taoist term *yang-szu* 陽 死 "suspended animation"; this was one of the accomplishments of the Taoist adept. The Confucianist authors of TYPS and CYKC did not want to employ this Taoist term and hence changed it into *cha-szu*, which robs the story of its point.

TYPS-I and III add here a brief comment by Cheng K'o.

B.

"When Kao Fang in the beginning of his career served under the (Later) Chou Dynasty (915-960 A.D.) as Division Chief in the Ministry of Justice, a man in Su-chou killed his wife with a knife. His wife's family received a bribe (from the man himself or from his relatives) and falsely told the authorities that he was suffering from insanity and could not speak. Therefore he was not questioned under torture and the case was referred to the High Court of Justice. The Court decided that he should be flogged. Kao Fang re-examined the case and said: 'There is no medical attest that this man is insane and cannot speak. On the strength of what testimony is he sentenced to only a flogging? Moreover, did he not ask for drink and food during the months that he was in jail? This case should be re-examined, then we shall certainly learn the truth!' The Emperor followed this advice, and in the end the man was executed".

CYKC ch. 4, page 50.

For Kao Fang see the note to Case 30-B above; this case is related in his biography in *Sung-shih*, ch. 270.

Hsiao 孝 and *hsiang* 相 in TYPS-III are copyist's mistakes for *k'ao* 考 and *tsu* 祖.

In the second column I read *t'ai* 紿 instead of *to* 奪, as in TYPS-I, II and CYKC.

I-kung 醫工 (also *i-chiang* 醫匠) is not a derogatory term for a physician; it implies that a doctor "repairs" a human body in the same manner as an artisan will repair a broken object.

54. *Wang Ngo and an anonymous letter;*
    Li Chih-yüan remembers a surname

A.

"In the T'ang Dynasty when Wang Ngo was Regional Commander of Huai-nan, someone left in the tribunal an anonymous letter (accusing another person). Wang's assistants took it to give it to him, and he put it in his boot (unread), after having bundled it together with other documents. After his officers had withdrawn, Wang took it out and burned the other letters. All thought that Wang had burned all the letters (including the anonymous one); but when Wang had returned home he studied the accusation. Later he involved the man accused in the letter in another case, had him arrested and dealt with on the basis of proof (utilizing the information contained in the letter). Wang thus deceived all his subordinates who praised him for his perspicacity".

CYKC ch. 8, page 126.

Wang Ngo 王鍔, after having occupied various administrative functions was appointed Executive Censor. He was known for his meticulous attention to details and his parsimonious nature. Under Te-tsung (780-804 A.D.) he served as Regional Commander of Ho-tung. Cf. his biography in *Hsin-t'ang-shu* ch. 170 where this case is briefly related; *Chiu-t'ang-shu* ch. 151 gives a more elaborate version, from which it appears that the letter was left by one of Wang's subordinates and that the accusation concerned another of them. The last line reads there *chung-hsia-li* 眾下吏 instead of *chung* 眾; this amplification I followed in my translation.

Cheng K'o states in his commentary on this case in CYKC that Wang Ngo's conduct is to be censured.

B.

"In the T'ang Dynasty when Li Chih-yüan (in his quality of Executive Secretary in the Ministry of Personnel) was in charge of official appointments, he hated small officers serving under him accepting bribes, and had many of those degraded or banished; the officers accordingly respectfully refrained from those activities. But when an official called Wang Chung was going to be dismissed, an officer changed his surname (in the pertaining document) to Shih, in the hope to obtain a reward from him. But Li Chih-yüan said: 'I have dealt with the cases of thirty thousand officials, and none of them bore the surname Shih; this must be Wang Chung!' The officer concerned knocked his head on the floor and admitted his guilt".

(From Li Su-li's biography in *T'ang-shu*; Li Chih-yüan was his grandson)

CYKC ch. 5, page 74; IYC ch. 5, no. 85; YP no. 48.

Li Chih-yüan 李至遠 was an able official who was recommended to Empress Wu for the post in the Ministry of Personnel mentioned here. He ended his career as Prefect of Pi-chou 璧州. The present case is related in his biography in ch. 197 of the *Hsin-t'ang-shu*, appended to the biography of his grandfather Li Su-li 李素立.

It should be noted that the surname *wang* 王 can easily be changed in that o *shih* 士 by obliterating the upper stroke.

55. *Chang Hsi-ch'ung assigns all the property;*
    Chang Ch'i-hsien has both parties move

A.

"In the (Later) Chin Dynasty (936-946 A.D.) when Chang Hsi-ch'ung was Garrison Commander of Fen-chou, a man had been adopted by a family of the surname Kuo, and reared by them from his tender age till manhood; but since he proved wayward and disobedient, later they sent him away. When both Mr. and Mrs. Kuo were about to die, the legitimate heir (i.e. the eldest son) had grown up. (After their death) the relatives then made a secret arrangement with the adoptive son: he would bring a suit averring that he was Kuo's real son; later they would divide together the wealth (which he would inherit). This case was heard several times but no decision could be arrived at. When Chang Hsi-ch'ung had read the documents relative to the case he decided as follows: 'When the plaintiff's father was still alive he left him; when his mother died he did not come (to mourn). Suppose that he is not their real son, he is guilty of ingratitude regarding the twenty years of being reared and fostered; if he is their real son, he is guilty on three thousand counts of the crime of rebellious behaviour. How could a man who has thus gravely offended against the Confucianist ethics be entrusted with the land?' He assigned all the property to the legitimate heir".

CYKC ch. 8, page 126; IYC ch. 3, no. 64.

Chang Hsi-ch'ung 張希崇 started his career as a military official in the T'ien-yu era (904-906 A.D.). Although he acquired military fame by his action against the Kitans, he was at the same time a learned scholar of frugal habits who kept far from wine and women. He served in Fen-chou in the time of the Emperor Ming (926-933 A.D.) of the later T'ang Dynasty; hence the editor of CYKC observes that *Chin* 晉 in the first line should be read T'ang 唐.

Chang's biography is found in ch. 88 of the *Chiu-wu-tai-shih*, where a slightly more elaborate version of this case is recorded. The story is not found in his biography in ch. 47 of the *Hsin-wu-tai-shih*.

Cheng K'o says in his commentary that the term *san-ch'ien-t'iao* refers to *san-t'iao*, the three themes given in the T'ang Dynasty to candidates during the literary examinations, which is far-fetched. It seems better to connect the term with the sentence in *Chung-yung* 中庸 ch. 27, where the "Way of the Holy Man" 聖人之道 is said to embrace "the three hundred rules of ceremony and the three thousand rules of decorum" 禮儀三百威儀三千.

B.

"When the Ministerial Vice-President Chang Ch'i-hsien was Chief Councillor, there developed a quarrel in the quarter of the Emperor's relatives by marriage, about the unequal division (of property). Since this case concerned the Imperial family, the case was brought (directly) before the Emperor; about ten different solutions were proposed, but they were everytime rejected by the contending parties. Chang Ch'i-hsien said: 'This is not a case that can be solved by the Palace Censorate. I request Your Majesty to be allowed to deal with it myself'. (This was granted). One day when he was presiding the State Council, he summoned the two parties and asked each of them: 'Are not you of the opinion that you have been allotted less than the other?' Both parties answered in the affirmative. Chang ordered each of them to write a formal statement to this effect. Thereupon he dispatched two officials to effect an exchange of abode, ordering A. to move to B.'s property and B. to A.'s, leaving all goods and valuables in their original place. Chang then gave to each the other's title-deeds, and the dispute ended then and there".

(From the *Su-shui-chi-wen*)

CYKC ch. 8, page 126; IYC ch. 5, no. 96.

Chang Ch'i-hsien 張齊賢 was originally a poor scholar who attracted the attention of the first Sung Emperor T'ai-tsu (960-975 A.D.). Under the next Emperor he became *chin-shih* and was appointed to several high posts, including that of Policy-critic Adviser (in 984 A.D.). He became the Emperor's trusted adviser, and retained this function under Chen-tsung (998-1022 A.D.). Cf. his biography in *Sung-shih* ch. 265, where this case is recorded as having happened in the reign of Chen-tsung; the fact that Chang had been counsellor of three successive Emperors explains why he was in a position to pass by the Censorate.

Kuan 官 at the bottom of the first line in TYPS-III is a copyist's mistake for *kung* 宮.

For the *Su-shui-chi-wen* see the note to Case 1-A above.

56. *Wang Hsün distinguishes seals;*
    Yin Shu examines old records

A.

"When the Vice-president of the High Court Wang Hsün was Prefect of Chao-chou, someone accused (another person) of having made a false seal of the Prefecture (and impressed it on some old legal document). This case remained undecided for a long time. The official in charge maintained that the impression was not the same (as that of the seal actually used by the Prefecture, and therefore false). (When the case was brought before Wang Hsün), he had old documents dating from before the Ching-te era (1004-1007 A.D.) brought out, and it was proved that the seals on those did not differ in the least (from the disputed seal). The accuser then admitted that he had slandered the other person. Since the document on which the seal was impressed dated from the Ching-te era, the seal had to be compared with that appearing on other documents of that same period. The official in charge did not know that the characters engraved on a seal will change in course of time, and therefore he could not decide the case".

(From his tomb inscription composed by Wang Kuei)

CYKC ch. 2, page 22; IYC ch. 8, no. 165; YP no. 46.

Wang Hsün 王珣 was probably a relative of Wang Kuei; for the latter see the note to Case 15-B.

Official seals are as a rule cast or engraved with an inscription in *chu-wen* 朱文 "red characters", i.e. in thin lines in high relief, which when impressed on the paper leave red characters on a white ground. Regular use will wear down the seal so that there are appreciable differences between old and later impressions of one and the same seal. Seals engraved in *po-wen* 白文 "white characters", i.e. where the inscription is incised in the surface, and which produce a white impression on a red ground, are less liable to change.

B.

"When the Academician of the Lung-t'u Pavilion Yin Shu was magistrate of the I-yang district in Ho-nan-fu, a girl who had become an orphan when very young, claimed to be a daughter of a Mr. Ho (who had adopted her and later died without progeny). A neighbour testified that her claim was false, and all the property of the Ho family reverted to the state. Thereafter, when the said neighbour had died, the woman again brought her case before the tribunal, and claimed the confiscated property. The case remained undecided for a long time. Then Yin Shu (heard the case. He) asked the woman: 'How old are you?' She replied: 'Thirty-two'. Yin Shu then consulted the population register of the Hsien-p'ing era (998-1004 A.D.) and found that Mr. Ho had died in the second year, leaving his widow *née* Liu as head of the family. Yin Shu questioned the woman saying: 'You were

born in the 5th year of that era, how could you be Mr. Ho's daughter?'
The woman admitted her deceit".

(From his biography)

CYKC ch. 6, page 86; IYC ch. 6, no. 126.

For Yin Shu see the note to Case 50-B above; his biography in *Sung-shih* ch. 295 does not refer to this case.

Since the woman was born in 1002 and 32 *sui* when Yin Shu questioned her, the date of the case is ca. 1033 A.D.

57. *Sun Teng compares bullets;*
Li has gold lumps modeled

A.

"When Sun Teng, styled (Tzu-) kao, the eldest son of Sun Ch'üan, was Crownprince, he once went out on horseback; a bullet flew past him. He ordered his assistants to find the man who had shot at him. They happened on a man who was carrying a bow and had (a bag with) bullets hanging on his girdle. All thought that he was the culprit, but on being questioned he denied it. The followers of the Prince asked leave to whip him, but Sun would not have it; he had the bullet that had flown past him located and compared it (with those carried by the suspect). It was found that they were not the same, and the man was released".

CYKC ch. 1, page 1; IYC ch. 1, no. 23; YP no. 53.

Sun Teng 孫登, the eldest son of Sun Ch'üan the founder of the Wu Dynasty (see the note to Case 35-B above), was a man of great talents and a benevolent administrator; his biography in ch. 14 of the *Wu-chih* (where this case is recorded) says that when hunting he always avoided tracts under cultivation, and also in other ways showed his interest in the welfare of the common people. He died at the early age of 32.

Chih 志 in the first line is superfluous. TYPS-I and III omit *tzu* in Sun Teng's style Tzu-kao 子高.

It should be noted that next to the ordinary bow and arrows Chinese hunters use also a bow fitted with a barrel; lead bullets are projected from it by a stick that fits into the barrel and which is propelled by the bow-string. It is interesting that the device of comparing bullets—so important in modern crime detection— was known in China already in the third century A.D.

B.

"In the T'ang Dynasty, when Li Te-yü was Garrison Commander

in West Chekiang, the abbot of the Kan-lu Temple reported that his predecessor had embezzled part of the transmitted temple property, viz. several taels of gold. He adduced the testimony of several former abbots who all had passed on the gold (each time when they handed over the administration of the temple), as proved by the pertaining documents. He added that the weight of the lumps when they were first added to the temple's treasury was clearly stated. But when the day of the transfer came, the lumps of gold were not produced. When the investigation had been completed and the former abbot formally charged with the crime, Li Te-yü doubted his guilt because it could not be established where the accused had spent the money. The accused abbot said: 'My predecessors in this temple always passed on the documents relating to the lumps of gold, but the gold itself was never produced. Because I keep to myself and did not join the profligate monks, they all want to utilize this opportunity for oppressing me.' And he burst into tears. Li Te-yü had several bamboo cages brought and had each of the monks involved sit inside facing the wall, so that they could not see each other. Each was given some clay, and ordered to knead it into the shape of the missing lumps of gold. Since the monks did not know what the (imaginary gold) looked like, each fashioned the clay into a different shape. Li Te-yü angrily pronounced the accuser and the former abbots (who had sustained his accusation) guilty of calumny".

CYKC ch. 3, page 32; IYC ch. 3, no. 58; YCTI no. 3.

Li Te-yü (李 德 裕 787-849 A.D.) was a learned scholar-official who occupied various high posts in the government and played an important role in the political life of that period. Cf. *Chiu-t'ang-shu* ch. 174 and *Hsin-t'ang-shu* ch. 180, where his career is described in great detail; but the present case is not recorded there. For Li Te-yü's political activities cf. Franke, vol. II, page 488 and *passim*, for his views on the examination system ibid. vol. III, page 447. For his part in the administration of justice cf. Bünger, page 171, where his strict views are mentioned: when he was counsellor of the Emperor Wu-tsung (841-846) he advocated that all thefts of more than a thousand cash be punished with death.

The Kan-lu-szu 甘 露 寺 is a famous old Buddhist temple near Chen-chiang in Kiangsu Province. When Li Te-yü was ca. 838 Commander in that region he resided in nearby Yang-chou, and patronized that temple. Hence the occurrence related here must have taken place about that time. In 845 the persecution of Buddhism started, and Li Te-yü took part therein; this is described in the diary of En-nin ,the Japanese monk who then was staying in China (cf. E. O. Reischauer, "Ennin's Travels in T'ang China", New York 1955, pp. 217 sq.)

TYPS I, II and III, and also IYC state that Li Te-yü was Com mander in *Che-yu* 浙右 but CYKC and the *Chiu-t'ang-shu* (Ch'ien-lung edition page 13/b) read *Che-hsi* 浙西.

TYPS-III reads *t'ang-chu-shih-wu* 堂主什物, but all other texts have *ch'ang* 常 instead of *t'ang*; *ch'ang-chu-shih-wu* is a common Buddhist term for the permanent possessions of a temple, including utensils, apparel of the monks etc.

Shu 數 in TYPS-III, second column of page 16, is a mistake for *so* 所.

CYKC gives a more elaborate version of the passage regarding the bamboo cages: "Then he ordered the monks involved to enter a number of bamboo cages to deliver testimony; when they were sitting in the cages, they were all turned with the doors facing the wall, so that the monks could not see each other" 乃 以 圌 子 數 乘。命 關 連 僧 入 對。坐 圌 子 中。門 皆 向 壁。不 得 相 見。

58. *Liang Shih attaches weight to magic spells;*
    Yüan T'uan condemns a pervert crime

A.

"When the Ministerial Vice-president Liang Shih was Deliberating Official of the Bureau of Judicial Investigation, there was a wizard in Tzu-chou called Po Yen-huan who, relying on the help of evil spirits, had devised a method for casting spells on people, several of whom died. When the case was referred to the' capital for a decision, all the judges were in doubt since none of the victims showed signs of violence. But Liang Shih observed: 'If a man kills with a knife, the victim can at least try to ward off the blow, but how can one defend oneself against magic spells?' Finally the death penalty was proposed"
(From his tomb inscription composed by Wang Kuei)

CYKC ch. 4, page 52.

Liang Shih (梁 適 1001-1070) was recommended to the Emperor Chen‑tsung (998-1022) and having served as magistrate in several places was appointed under the Emperor Jen-tsung (1023-1063) to the position mentioned. Cf. his biography in *Sung-shih* ch. 285, where this case is recorded.

For Wang Kuei see Case 15-B above.

TYPS-I and III append to this case a comment by Cheng K'o.

B.

"In the Southern Ch'i Dynasty (479-502 A.D.) Yüan T'uan served as Adviser of the Prince of Lu-ling. When the Prince was Garrison Commander of Ch'ing-chou, a man called Kou Hu-chih, younger brother of Kou Chiang-chih, of the Chiang-ling district in Nan-chün, had a wife who was seduced by a monk of the Tseng-k'ou Temple. When this monk entered the house in the night, Kou Chiang-chih killed him. When this case was investigated by the authorities, Kou Chiang-chih stated that to prosecute the monk would have brought shame upon the entire family, while it was manifestly impossible for him to take a tolerant attitude; and that consequently he had killed the monk. But his younger brother Hu-chih made exactly the same confession. The two brothers thus vied with each other to obtain the death penalty for murder. The magistrate of Chiang-ling reported this case to the Prefect for an opinion on its merits. Yüan T'uan said: 'Neither Chiang-chih nor Hu-chih are violent men by nature; on the day of their trial their righteousness moved even the passersby. When in days of old K'ung Jung took on himself the blame of calumny, he was allowed to escape through the mazes of Justice's net. The disposition of these two brothers corresponds exactly to that of the ancients. If they should perish through a strict interpretation of the law, this would in fact mean that the good are harmed!' The lives of the two brothers were thus saved".

(From the biography of Yüan Chan in *Nan-shih*; Yüan T'uan was the grandson of his paternal cousin)

CYKC ch. 4, page 58.

Yüan T'uan 袁彖 at a tender age already showed great literary talent. After the advent of the Ch'i Dynasty he was appointed Censor, and then attained the position mentioned here. Cf. his biography in *Nan-shih* ch. 26, appended to the biography of Yüan Chan 袁湛 ; there a more elaborate version of this case is given.

K'ung Jung (孔融 153-208 A.D.) was a well known Han writer and poet, here referred to by his style Wen-chü 文舉 ; cf. his biography in *Hou-han-shu* ch. 100, where it is told that in his youth he took the blame for an offense committed by his elder brother Pao 褒 , whereupon both he and his brother claimed the punishment.

59. *A court-officer opposes implicating a murderer's wife;*
K'ung Shen-chih comments on reviling one's mother

A.

"The Han-lin Academician Shen K'uo says: 'In Shou-chou a man killed his parents-in-law, and his wife's elder and younger brothers, altogether several people. The local authorities considered this to belong to the category of inhuman crimes, and hence extended the man's guilt to his wife. A court officer opposed this saying: 'If a man hits his wife's parents, the marriage is considered as dissolved; how much the more then if he kills them! His wife should not be considered as implicated and sentenced as such".

CYKC ch. 4, page 54; IYC ch. 8, no. 146; YCTI no. 9; YP no. 4.
    The text is practically identical with that given in MHPT ch. 11. There this case is recorded together with Case 63-B, evidently because both cases describe a judicial error set right by an anonymous official. In MHPT the passage is preceded by the words *chin-sui* 近 歲 "in recent years", which dates the cases ca. 1050 A.D. *Ts'un-chung* in the first line is Shen K'uo's style.

B.

"In the (Former) Sung Dynasty (420-479 A.D.), when K'ung Shen-chih was First Secretary of the Bureau of Judicial Control of the Ministry of War, in the Ying-ch'eng district of An-lu a man called Chang Chiang-ling together with his wife *née* Wu reviled his mother *née* Huang saying that she ought to die. Mrs. Chang-Huang, in angry mortification, killed herself by hanging. (Chang and his wife) were included in a general amnesty. The law says that any person who kills, wounds or beats his parents shall, in the case of an amnesty, be decapitated and his head publicly exposed (instead of being sliced to pieces); persons condemned to be publicly executed for the crime of insulting their parents shall, in the case of an amnesty, have their sentence commuted. But the law does not provide for the case of a person causing his parent's death by reviling. K'ung Shen-chih said in council: 'If a village (street) bears a name repugnant to the conscience, a man of good character will not enter it. Thus even an odious name is to be avoided. How much more strict should be the relations between individuals! The law forbids the killing or wounding by magic spells, therefore it stands to reason that killing by reviling can never be pardoned. Notwithstanding the amnesty, Chang should be decapitated and his head publicly exposed. The relations of a woman to her mother-in-law being based on duty rather than on natural love, Mrs. Chang-Huang's anger was not roused so much by Mrs. Chang's (behaviour as by that of her son). But if her death sentence were commuted this would be contrary to the correct interpretation of the law'. The Emperor decided according to K'ung Shen-chih's advice, and approved the public execution of Mrs. Chang-Wu".

(From K'ung Ching's biography in the *Nan-shih*)

CYKC ch. 4, page 48.

K'ung Shen-chih 孔深之 occupied the post mentioned here in the reign of the Emperor Ming (465-472 A.D.). His biography in *Nan-shih* ch. 27, appended to that of his father K'ung Ching 孔靖, records this case in a more elaborate version, but gives no further details on K'ung Shen-chih's career.

TYPS-I and III add here Cheng K'o's comment.

TYPS-I and III, and also CYKC, read the last sentence of K'ung's statement 有允正法; I follow TYPS-II which changes 允 into 失.

60. *Sun Liang examines honey;*
   Tu Ya suspects wine

A.

"Sun Liang, the 'deposed Emperor of Wu', when he was once eating fresh plums, told the Chancellor to take a silver vessel with a cover and have the Keeper of the Stores fill it with honey. The Chancellor harboured an old grudge against the Keeper, therefore he took the excrements of a rat and threw them into the honey. Then he reported to the Emperor that the Keeper was careless. Sun Liang summoned the Keeper; he came, bringing the jar the honey was kept in. Sun said to him: 'Since this jar is covered with a lid and moreover sealed with oilpaper, the ordure can not have got inside. Did the Chancellor ever want anything from you?' The Keeper knocked his forehead on the floor and said: 'That man asked me to let him use mats (from the stores), but I would not give them to him'. Sun said: 'That must be it then! We can easily verify it'. He had the rat's excrements broken. Then he said with a smile: 'If the excrements had been in the jar before, they would have been soaked through with honey. Now they are dry inside and wet outside, which proves that there is some mischief!' Thereupon the Chancellor confessed".

CYKC ch. 3, page 28; IYC ch. 1, no. 10; YP no. 55.

Sun Liang 孫亮, youngest son of Sun Ch'üan, the founder of the Wu Dynasty, had been appointed by the latter as his successor before he died in 252 A.D. Sun Liang was a promising youth, but he proved unable to cope with the intrigues of his elder relatives, and was deposed by them in 258 A.D.; hence the designation *fei-ti* 廢帝. Cf. BD no. 1813, and Franke, vol. II p. 14-15. His biography in *Wu-chih* ch. 3 records this case in the commentary.

B.

"In the T'ang Dynasty when Tu Ya, styled Tz'u-kung, was Garrison Commander in Wei-yang, there was a rich man who, shortly after his father's death, started to treat his stepmother without due respect. Thus on New Year's day, when he had congratulated his mother, and she handed him a cup of wine, he feigned to suspect that it was poisoned, and emptied the cup on the floor; the spilt wine then seemed to boil. Thereupon he said that his mother had tried to kill him by poison. His mother said: 'Heaven above knows all, how dare you speak this brazen lie?' Beating her breast she denied everything. When this case was reported to the tribunal, Tu Ya asked the son: 'Where did the wine come from?' He replied: 'The senior lady brought a goblet and gave it'. Tu Ya said: 'Since your wife brought the goblet, it must have been she who put the poison there. How can you slander your mother?' He thereupon took the man apart and questioned him. It transpired that he and his wife had planned to harm their mother (by the false accusation of murder), and both were dealt with according to the law".

CYKC ch. 3, page 33; IYC ch. 2, no. 42; YP no. 6. Source unknown.

Tu Ya 杜亞 served as Policy-critic Adviser under the Emperor Su-tsung (756-762 A.D.), and then as Regional Supervisor in Kiangsi. In 784 he was appointed Executive Secretary in the Ministry of Justice, thereafter Regional Commander of Huai-nan; he ended his career as Defense Commander of the Eastern Capital. Cf. his biography in *Chiu-t'ang-shu* ch. 146 and *Hsin-t'ang-shu* ch. 172, neither of which records the present case.

The term *ch'ang-fu* 長婦, here translated "senior lady", is unusual and apparently puzzled the old editors. TYPS-II suggests that the son used this strange term because he hesitated to admit that it had been his wife; there the following passage is inserted directly after the son's first reply: 母賜爾觴。又從何來。曰。亦長婦所執之爵也。長婦為誰。曰。此子之婦也。

"Tu Ya asked again: 'Where did the cup that your mother offered you come from?' The son said: 'That was filled from the goblet the senior lady held' Finally Tu asked: 'Who is that senior lady?' He said: 'That is my wife'. (Tu ya said: 'Since your wife, etc.)'".

61. *Fu Lung discusses the breaking of family-ties; Emperor Wu defines the position of a stepmother*

A.

"In the time of the (Former) Sung Emperor Wen (424-453 A.D.), a man from Yen-hsien called Huang Ch'u had a wife *née* Chao who killed their son Tsai's wife, *née* Wang; later Mrs. Huang-Chao was included in a general amnesty. The father and mother of the victim Mrs. Chang-Wang were still alive, and she had a son called Ch'eng. According to the law Mrs. Huang-Chao would have to be banished beyond 2000 *li*. Fu Lung, Chief Administrator of the Left under the Grand Instructor, counselled as follows: 'The relationship of father and son is closest of all, they are different shapes developed from the same seed. The relationship between Ch'eng and Tsai is the same as that of Tsai and his mother Mrs. Huang-Chao. Although these people belong to three different generations, in fact they form one body. Although Ch'eng has been caused deep grief, he is in no position to take vengeance on his grandmother; for the ancients have said that one should never place one's father before one's grandfather. If one says that Ch'eng is entitled to kill Mrs. Huang-Chao, how then should one proceed against Tsai? If fathers and sons, grandparents and grandchildren should exterminate each other, this would hardly be in accordance with the enlightened punishments of the ancient Kings, nor with the spirit of the laws instituted by Kao Yao. An old ordinance says: The father and mother of a murderer shall be punished with banishment beyond 2000 *li*; but this does not apply to cases (where the murderer and the victim) are each other's father and son, grandparent and grandchild. Since Mrs. Huang-Chao has to be separated from those relatives who observe a full year's mourning for Mrs. Huang-Wang, she should be banished merely beyond 1000 *li*. On the other hand the law says: 'All close relatives of the same clan-register of banished persons shall be allowed to follow them in exile should they so desire'. Thus, if Mrs. Huang-Chao were banished, then Tsai being her son would certainly have to follow her. And if Tsai went, how could it then be in accordance with the Confucian ethics if (his son) Ch'eng did not follow him? Mrs. Huang-Chao will be ashamed of herself for her entire life, and Ch'eng will grieve deeply till his old age. But the correct relations between grandparents and grandchildren can never be broken'. The case was decided accordingly".

(From Fu Liang's biography in *Nan-shih*)

CYKC ch. 4, page 45.|

Fu Lung (傅 隆 369-451 A.D.) was a great scholar, expert on the Book of Rites. Ca. 425 A.D. he was appointed Executive Censor, and thereafter served as Prefect. He ended his career as Director of Imperial Sacrifices. Cf. his biography in *Nan-shih*, ch. 15, appended to that of his younger brother Fu Liang 傅 亮, where a more elaborate version of this case is given.

The sentence 不 以 父 命 辭 王 父 命 paraphrased in the translation "one should never place one's father before one's grandfather" means literally: "One should not because of an order from one's father refuse to follow the order of one's grandfather". These lines are quoted from the *Kung-yang-chuan* 公 羊 傳, the 3d year of Duke Ai (493 B.C.); they refer to the fact that the ruler Ling-kung 靈 公 appointed as his successor his grandson instead of his son; when the question was asked whether the grandson could accept this against the will of his father, the quoted lines were given as answer.

Kao Yao 皐 陶 was a Minister of the mythical Emperor Shun, said to have been the first Chinese law-maker.

The following table may elucidate the complicated family relations that figure in this case:

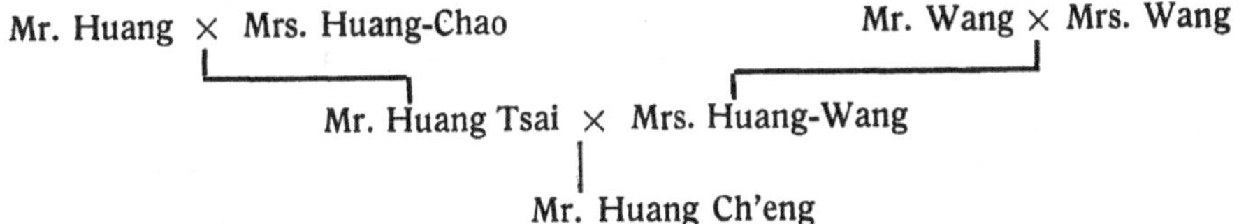

The basic fact is that Mrs. Huang-Chao killed her daughter-in-law, Mrs. Huang-Wang.

B.

"In the reign of the (Western) Han Emperor Ching (156-140 B.C.), the Commandant of Justice forwarded to the capital a prisoner called Fang Nien. Fang Nien's stepmother *née* Ch'en had killed Fang's father, whereupon Fang killed her. Since he had thus killed his mother, according to the law Fang Nien would have to be punished for a 'heinous crime'. The Emperor had doubts about this case. At that time the Crown Prince—the later Emperor Wu (140-87 B.C.)—was only twelve years old and happened to stand by his father's side. His father asked his opinion. The boy answered: 'A stepmother resembles a real mother, but she is clearly not the same. The only reason why she can be compared to a mother is her relation with the son's father. Now the stepmother committed an atrocious crime. She killed the son's father with her own hands; and at that moment the filial duties her step-son owed her ceased to exist. His deed must be judged as manslaughter, and not as the heinous crime (of matricide)''.

(From *T'ung-tien*, where the original source is not indicated)

CYKC ch. 4, page 45; IYC ch. 5, no. 80; YCTI no. 4; YP no. 1.

The *T'ung-tien* 通 典 is a historical encyclopedia in 200 ch., compiled by the T'ang scholar Tu Yu (杜 佑 735-812 A.D.).

Ta-ni 大 逆 "heinous crime"; these crimes are classified under the same category as *pu-tao* 不 道 ; cf. Hulsewé, page 156.

This case is also related in H. H. Dubs, *The History of the Former Han Dynasty*, vol. I (Baltimore 1938), page 323, in the footnote.

62. *Tai Chou contests unequal punishment; Hsü Yu-kung on degrees of implication*

A.

"In the T'ang Dynasty, when Tai Chou was Vice-President of the High Court, Ch'ang-sun Wu-chi was summoned by the Emperor and entered the Palace by the Eastern Gate, without taking off his sword. The Ministerial Right Executive Feng Te-i reasoned that the officer on guard at the gate who failed to notice (that Ch'ang-sun Wu-chi was still carrying his sword) deserved the death penalty, whereas Ch'ang-sun Wu-chi himself should be allowed to pay a fine instead. (The Emperor approved but) Tai Chou observed: 'Both the officer and Ch'ang-sun Wu-chi should receive the same punishment. Neither statesmen versus their ruler, nor children versus their father can ever adduce inadvertency as an excuse for a mistake. The law prescribes the death penalty also for mistakes consisting of improper handling of the Emperor's medicines, food, drink, or boats (i.e. mistakes which might also endanger the Imperial safety). Your Majesty might pardon Ch'ang-sun Wu-chi, on the strength of his meritorious service; but if Ch'ang-sun Wu-chi is fined, and the officer on guard executed, then this can not be called a correct punishment'. The

Emperor said: 'The law applies to the same extent to all under Heaven, how could We make an exception for Our relatives?' He ordered a second examination. Feng Te-i kept steadily to his original opinion and the Emperor was about to decide accordingly, when Tai Chou again opposed it saying: 'The guard's guilt originated in Ch'ang-sun Wu-chi's oversight; according to the law the guard's punishment should be lighter (than that of Ch'ang-sun Wu-chi). Since both are guilty of an oversight, it is not right that only one should be sentenced to death'. Thereupon the Emperor acquitted both the officer of the guard and Ch'ang-sun Wu-chi".

(From his biography)

CYKC ch. 4, page 48; IYC ch. 5, no. 84; YP no. 3.

This case, famous in Chinese legal literature, occurred in 626 A.D. It is quoted i.a. in the *T'ang-hui-yao*, and has been translated by Bünger, op. cit. pp. 188-189; for further comment the reader is referred to that source.

Here it may be added only that Ch'ang-sun Wu-chi 長 孫 無 忌 was the brother-in-law of the Emperor T'ai-tsung; he was a learned scholar who in 627 was charged to revise the Code, together with the great scholar Fang Hsüan-ling (房 玄 齡 578-648 A.D.). After the Emperor's death he became involved in political trouble and ultimately committed suicide.

Tai Chou 戴 冑 's biography is found in *Chiu-t'ang-shu* ch. 70, and *Hsin-t'ang-shu* ch. 99; both record this case in detail.

B.

"In the T'ang Dynasty, when Hsü Yu-kung was Assistant Secretary in the Ministry of Justice, Han Ch'un-hsiao accepted an unauthorized official appointment from (the rebel) Hsü Ching-yeh, but died before he could actually take up that office. The Investigating Judge of the High Court Ku Chung-yen memorialized the Throne to the effect that Han Ch'un-hsiao's entire family should be considered as implicated; the Emperor decided accordingly that all would be made Government slaves and that their possessions would be confiscated. But Hsü Yu-kung counselled saying: 'According to the law a man who plans revolt must be executed; but a dead man can not be executed any more. If the circumstances of the case make it difficult to forego decapitation, there can be issued an Imperial order to cut off the head of the dead body. This is the only way for obtaining a sound basis for reasoning. Now the implication (of the guilty man's family) is based on his being executed (for high treason). If he is not executed, how could there be any implication? Since the man who could implicate them is dead, the punishment of those he would have implicated should be lightened; lightening in this case means banishment for a limited period. But in such cases the implicated persons were often pardoned as a special favour. I do not know upon what article of the Code the present decision to make them slaves and to confiscate their property is based'. The Emperor ordered to decide the case as counselled by Hsü Yu-kung. Thus the order to make them slaves and to confiscate all the property was rescinded and several hundred families saved".

CYKC ch. 4, page 49; YCTI no. 7.

Hsü Yu-kung 徐有功 was a courageous official who on several occasions opposed the judgements by Lai Chün-ch'en and other cruel judges; cf. the note to Case 17-B above, and also Bünger, page 118. This case is recorded in his biography in *Hsin-t'ang-shu* ch. 113, but omitted in his biography in *Chiu-t'ang-shu* ch. 85.

For the meaning of the term *chi-mo* 籍沒 cf. Balazs, page 174.

63. *An officer of the tribunal argues about property;*
A Vice-Minister saves a person from banishment

A.

"The Han-lin Academician Shen K'uo says: 'In Ching-chou a robber murdered an entire family; the man and wife died immediately, their only son died the next day. The prefectural authorities allotted the entire property of the family to the married daughter, according to the rules applying in a case of a broken male lineage. An officer of the tribunal opposed this decision; he said: 'At the time when the father and mother died the son was still alive; therefore the property belongs to the son. The married daughter and her married sisters are not entitled to a share".

CYKC ch. 4, page 54.

With a few insignificant changes identical with the text in MHPT ch. 11; cf. the note to Case 59-A above.

B.

"Under the (Former) Sung Emperor Wen (424-453 A.D.) the law prescribed compulsory military service for all the relatives of a violent robber whose degree of relationship involved one full year of mourning.

When in Yü-hang a man called Po Tao-chi had committed a robbery with violence, he had two paternal first cousins called Tai-kung and Tao-sheng who would have to mourn for him only nine months. (When their implication in Po Tao-chi's punishment was being considered) someone observed that Tai-kung's and Tao-sheng's mother was still alive; since she was a relative bound to mourn a full year, therefore her two sons should follow her into military service. The Vice-Minister Ho Ch'eng-t'ien counselled: 'A woman has three stages of dependence; (when a girl she is dependent on her father, when married on her husband and) when her husband has died she is dependent on her son. Now Po Tao-chi has committed a robbery, and his father's younger brother has died; therefore his two paternal first cousins Tai-kung and Tao-sheng are not to be punished. If these two men were ordered to follow their mother into military service because she is a relative of the class that mourns one full year, this would· be contrary to the ruling that relatives of the class that mourns nine months are exempt. Moreover, it would be contrary to the principle of the three dependences of a woman'. It was decided that both the mother and her sons should be pardoned".

(From his biography in the *Nan-shih*)

CYKC ch. 4, page 54.

Ho Ch'eng-t'ien (何 承 天 370-447 A.D.) was a learned official who under the Chin Dynasty was Inspector of the Army of the Commander-in-chief Liu Yü (劉 裕 BD no. 1375). When Liu Yü had murdered the last Chin ruler and established himself as first Emperor of the Sung Dynasty, Ho Ch'eng-t'ien was promoted and in 439 A.D. he was appointed Executive Censor. The Emperor Wen used to discuss with him all important judicial cases. Cf. his biography in *Nan-shih* ch. 33, where this case is recorded.

For another case of Ho Ch'eng-t'ien see Case 72-A here under.

64. *An officer discovers a wrapped-up head;*
    Chang examines a criminal's forehead

A.

"In recent years there was a man who went on a journey to trade. When he came back he found that his wife had been murdered by an unknown person, and that her (severed) head was missing. His wife's family apprehended their son-in-law, and wrongly accusing him of having murdered their daughter, brought him to the tribunal.

The official in charge questioned him under torture, and he wrongly confessed. When the case was completed, the Prefect entrusted it to one of his assistants. This officer suspected the confession and asked that the case be adjourned. Then he ordered all the coroners in that district to state for how many families they recently had arranged a burial, making them personally report to him family by family. One coroner said: 'When recently I arranged a burial in the house of a wealthy man, they only said that a wet-nurse had died. When in (the beginning of) the fifth night watch we carried the coffin outside, it was as light as if there were nothing inside. The coffin was buried in such-and-such a place'. When that coffin was dug up, it contained only the severed head of a woman. Before having it added to the (headless) body (of the merchant's wife), the husband was asked to identify it. He said: 'That is not my wife'. Then the wealthy man was arrested and interrogated. It transpired that he had killed the wet-nurse, and wrapped up and buried her head. The headless body had been placed in the merchant's house, and the wife had been taken by the wealthy man as a secret paramour. He was publicly executed".

(From the *Yü-t'ang-hsien-hua*)

CYKC ch. 2, page 14; IYC ch. 2, no. 34; YP no. 18.

The *Yü-t'ang-hsien-hua* 玉 堂 閑 話 is a small work in 1 ch., by Ho Meng who wrote the sequel to IYC; the version reprinted in SF does not contain this story. The editor of CYKC says in a note that is occurred in the Ch'ien-yu era (948-950 A.D.) of the Later Han Dynasty, and that it was told to Ho Meng by his friend Wang Jen-yü 王 仁 裕 ; the latter's biography in *Chiu-wu-tai-shih* ch. 128 and *Hsin-wu-tai-shih* ch. 57 does not refer to this occurence.

Cheng K'o relates in CYKC a similar case (also given in the Appendix of IYC, the last case) which is worth quoting: "I heard recently that in T'ai-p'ing-chou a married woman went out together with her husband's younger brother. It started to rain and they took shelter in an abandoned temple, where they found a group of people who had arrived there before them. (Those people offered them wine and) the younger brother became drunk and fell asleep. He woke up when night had already fallen. All people had gone but his sister-in-law had been murdered, he found her headless body. Crying out loudly in fright and consternation he was arrested and taken to the tribunal. Since he could not bear the torture he wrongly confessed that he had wanted to violate his sister-in-law, and that he had killed her when she resisted; that he had thrown her severed head and the knife into the river. He was thereupon sentenced to death. Thereafter the woman's husband visited Lu-ling, and recognized his wife among the actors on a stage (where a traveling theatrical company was performing). The actors all fled, but they were overtaken and interrogated in the tribunal. It then transpired that the headless body (found in the temple) was in reality that of a woman belonging to the group that had taken shelter there. An actor had cut off her head and clad the body in the clothes of the married woman; the latter they had taken along with them. The wrong suffered by the younger brother was like this".

頃聞太平州有一婦人。與小郎偕出。遇雨入古廟避之。見數人先在其中。小郎被酒困睡。至晚方醒。人皆去矣。娒已被殺。而尸無首。驚駭號呼。被執送官。不勝拷掠。誣服强姦娒。不從而殺之。棄其首與刀於江中。遂坐死。後其夫至廬陵。於優戲場認得其妻。諸伶悉竄。捕獲伏法。蓋向者無首之尸。乃先在廟中之人也。伶人斷其首。易此婦人衣。而携去。小郎之寃如此。

It is difficult to decide on the basis of the meagre information supplied in how far the married women in these two cases were implicated in the murders. One feels inclined to assume that in the former case the merchant's wife had during her husband's absence willingly begun a love affair with the wealthy man, and that the two together concocted the scheme of the headless body; in that way they hoped that no inquiries would be made regarding the absconding woman, and that the husband would be effectively eliminated by execution. Perhaps the wealthy man had also bribed the wife's family to accuse the husband of the murder.

In the second case one might assume that the married woman and one of the actors fell in love in the temple at first sight; that the actor killed his own paramour because of this new love, and that the body was clad in the married woman's clothes in order to stop further inquiries and to implicate the young brother, a potential witness.

But perhaps we wrong both women. The former could have been taken away by the rich man against her will, and so could the latter. Neither a secret concubine in a large mansion, nor a woman attached to a group of traveling actors, if duly cowed by threats and harsh treatment, would have much inclination to denounce her abductors. Both cases leave a wide field for speculation.

B.

"When the President of the Ministry (of Works) Chang (Yung) was Prefect of Chiang-ning, a Buddhist monk (who for some unspecified reason had been brought before the tribunal) submitted his monk's certificate as proof (that he was a genuine monk). Chang Yung leaned forward over the bench and scrutinized him for a long time. Then he decided that he should be sent to the Police Inspectorate to be tried for murder. The officers of the prefecture did not understand the reason (for Chang's decision). Chang Yung then summoned the monk again and asked him: 'How many years ago were you ordained as a monk?' The monk replied: 'Seven years'. Then Chang said: 'Why then are there still on your forehead the marks of a head cloth?' The monk then confessed. He had travelled together with a monk, and murdered him on the way. (He had appropriated his victim's monk's certificate issued by) the Ministry of Rites, shaved his head and posed as a Buddhist monk himself".

(From the Record of Chung-ting's Words and Works, written by Li T'ien).

CYKC ch. 7, page 116; SF no. 10; IYC ch. 4, no. 69; YP no. 29.

Chang Yung (張 詠 lit. name Kuai-ai 乖 崖 946-1015 A.D.) was a scholar-official famous for his perspicacity as a judge; in his own life time already collections with his judicial decisions circulated widely among officials. He served as Prefect in several places, and occupied various high functions in the capital, including that of Censor. He received the posthumous title of Chung-ting-kung 忠 定 公 . Cf. his biography in *Sung-shih* ch. 293 where several cases solved by him are recorded, but not the present one.

Chang Yung was also noted for his extreme severity. BD no. 136 quotes the story that he once had an officer beheaded when he saw him leaving the treasury with a single cash sticking in his hair.

Li T'ien 李 畋 was among a group of deserving officials recommended by Chang Yung; TYPS-II notes that he served in the Bureau of Forestry, *Yü-pu* 虞 部 .

65. *Su has a tomb opened ;*

   Tung scolds a donkey thief

A.

"The Empress Wu (684-704 A.D.) of the T'ang Dynasty presented to the Princess T'ai-p'ing a set of golden hair-ornaments and other treasures; after a year they were stolen. When the Empress heard about this she was angry, and the Chief Administrator of Lo-yang and his subordinates were most anxious to catch the thief. The constables searched everywhere but failed to discover any clue. On the road they encountered Su Wu-ming, the Vice Governor of Hu-chou (who was traveling incognito, and arrested him as a suspect character). He asked to be taken to the tribunal. There they reported to the Sheriff: 'We have arrested a robber'. When the Sheriff asked Su Wu-ming who he was he said: 'I am the Vice Governor of Hu-chou'. The Sheriff said: 'How dare the constables thus insult you?' Su Wu-ming said: 'Do not be angry with them. On the various posts which I have occupied I have acquired some fame while arresting criminals and finding out secret plots. When your men perceived me they charged me wrongly with being a criminal trying to break through the cordon'. Thereupon he asked for an interview with the Chief Administrator and had him report to the Throne that he hoped to arrest the thief within about ten days. The Empress granted Su's request (to be assigned to the case). Thereupon Su Wu-ming warned the constables to watch out near the N.W. City gate for about ten Turks dressed in mourning clothes who would pass by there on their way to the mountains north of the city; they were to follow them and report (their doings). The constables indeed saw the group of Turks. They went to a new grave-mound and arranged their offerings; they were weeping but did not display real grief. When the offerings were finished, they went to the side of the grave mound, looked at each other and laughed. (When this was reported to Su Wu-ming) he had the Turks arrested and the grave mound opened. When the coffin was broken open and its contents inspected, it proved to contain the missing treasures. The Empress asked Su how he had located the thieves. He answered: 'On the day your servant came to the capital, I happened to see those Turks going out to bury the coffin. I then recognized them as thieves, but I did not know where they would bury (the loot). Since to-day is the Ch'ing-ming festival when people go to sweep the graves, I surmised that they would come out of the city; by following them we might obtain the loot. Because they wept without grief, I knew that they were not burying a dead body; because they went around the grave laughing, I knew that they had verified that their loot was still intact'. The Empress praised Su Wu-ming and promoted him to the second Court rank".

CYKC ch. 7, page 107; IYC ch. 3, no. 55. Source unknown.

About Su Wu-ming 蘇 無 名 I could find no further details.

Lai 來 in the second column of page 23 b is a mistake for *i* 衣.

B.

"In the T'ang Dynasty Tung Hsing-ch'eng of Ho-nei district in Huai-chou was an expert in the art of tracing criminals. A man coming from Ch'ang-tien in Ho-yang stole from a traveller a donkey and his sack with clothes. Early in the morning the thief arrived in Huai-chou, and Tung Hsing-ch'eng saw him on the market place. He shouted at him: "You are a thief!' The man was arrested and he confessed. Someone asked Tung how he had recognized the man as a thief. He said: 'That donkey ran fast and was covered with sweat; thereby I knew that the man had not come from afar. When he saw people he steered the donkey away from them; thereby I knew that he was afraid. Thus I knew that the man must be a thief'. Soon after the thief had been put in prison the owner came after him. Then it was proved that Tung had been perfectly right".

CYKC ch. 7, page 108; IYC ch. 3, no. 50.

About Tung Hsing-ch'eng 董 行 成 I could find no further details.

66. *Wang Tseng examines tax-records;*
   The Master of Works studies a document

A.

"When the Ministerial Vice-President Wang Tseng was still young he once paid a visit to the officers of a prefecture. Then there were two parties who had a dispute about a piece of land; since the boundary marks had all disappeared and since the deed of sale was lost, they could not decide this case. Wang Tseng said: 'If you examine the tax records relating to that piece of land, you will be able to decide who is wrong and who is right'. The officers in charge of the case followed this advice, and the party who was in the wrong confessed".

(From the "Record of the Words and Works of I-kung".)

CYKC ch. 6, page 97

Wang Tseng (王 曾 978-1038 A.D.) was a gifted scholar and poet. After having served as Vice-Administrator of Chi-chou 濟 州 , with the advent of Jen-tsung (1023-1063 A.D.) he was appointed Executive Secretary of the Chancellery, and ennobled as I-kung 沂 公 , Duke of I. As a Vice-President he fell in disfavour, and ended his career as a Prefect in the provinces. Cf. his biography in *Sung-shih*, ch. 310, where this case is not recorded.

TYPS-III, second column, 8th character: *tz'u* 次 should be *chüeh* 決 .

B.

"In the Western Han Dynasty (206 B.C.-24 A.D.) there lived in the Pei Commanderie a man whose property amounted to more than 200.

000 strings of cash. He had one son whose mother died when he was only three years old; he also had a (married) daughter who was a wicked woman. When the man fell ill he assembled the members of his clan and made a testament leaving all the property to his daughter. (To his son) he bequeathed only a sword, saying: 'When my son shall have reached the age of fifteen, this sword must be given to him'. After (the old man's death, however,) the daughter did not even give that sword to her brother; he went to complain to the Grand Administrator. The Grand Master of Works Ho Wu examined the testament, then turned to his assistants and remarked: 'The woman is violent and domineering, her husband is greedy and low-minded. Therefore the old man feared that they would harm his son (if he should leave all the property to him), and he let it be taken by his daughter. But in reality he only deposited the property with her temporarily; for the sword would be the means whereby a final decision would be reached. He surmised that after his son would have become fifteen, his intelligence would have sufficiently developed for enabling him to take independent action and if he reported to the authorities (sooner or later some magistrate would interpret correctly the old man's real intention and) justice would be done. So far ahead (the old man) planned!' Thereupon he returned all the property to the son".

(From the *Feng-su-t'ung*)

CYKC ch. 8, page 123; IYC ch. 2, no. 38; YP no. 56.

Ho Wu 何 武 served as Prefect of Yang-chou 揚 州 and later rose to Grand Master of Works. In the time of the Emperor Ai (6 B.C.-1 A.D.) he was calumniated by Wang Mang (王 莽 33 B.C.-23 A.D.; BD no. 2203) and committed suicide. Cf. his biography in *Han-shu* ch. 86, where this case is not related.

TYPS-III, fifth column, fourth character: *chü* 具 is a copyist's mistake for *ch'i* 其 .

This case is recorded in the fragments of the *Feng-su-t'ung* preserved in other sources; cf. the edition mentioned in the note to Case 4-B, page 106.

The motif of a man planning a just division of his property to be effected long after his death by some clever scheme has been often utilized by later Chinese writers of crime stories. The best known example is tale no. 3 of the collection *Chin-ku-ch'i-kuan* 今 古 奇 觀 , entitled *Teng-ta-yin-kuei-tuan-chia-szu* 滕 大 尹 鬼 斷 家 私 "Prefect Teng cleverly solves a case of inheritance" translated i.a. by Stanislas Julien as an addition to his *L'Orphelin de la Chine* (Paris 1834).

I myself used this interesting motif as the main theme when writing my Chinese crime novel *Ti-jen-chieh-ch'i-an* 狄仁傑奇案 (publ. Singapore 1953 by the Nan-yang Press); a Japanese translation was published previously in Tokyo (1951) under the title *Meiro-no-satsujin* 迷路の殺人.

67. *Wei Kao investigates sudden wealth;*
Chao Ho and the mortgaged property

A.

"In the T'ang Dynasty, when Wei Kao was Garrison Commander in Chien-nan, a wealthy merchant stayed overnight in an inn. He fell ill, and (the innkeeper) poisoned him, appropriating the money he had with him. (Since thus the innkeeper became suddenly rich,) Wei Kao heard about it. Then there was a merchant from the North called Su Yen who came to Szuchuan to do business; he fell ill and died (in the same inn). When this was reported to Wei Kao, he had the books of the dead man examined; but the innkeeper had in the meantime already falsified the entries (so as to conceal his having stolen his victim's funds). Wei Kao then instituted a thorough inquiry into this affair, and secretly questioned the people of that quarter; he found that there were many discrepancies in their testimony. Thereupon he investigated the people in the inn, and soon learned all the hidden deceit. He found that several thousand strings of cash had been distributed (by the innkeeper) among more than twenty small officers as bribes. He ordered that all be executed. Thereafter there were in Chien-nan no more cases of travellers being murdered".

CYKC ch. 6, page 82; IYC ch. 2, no. 45; YP no. 73.

Wei Kao (韋皋 746-806) was a famous general, who i.a. defeated the Tibetans in 801 A.D.; his exploits are related in Franke, vol. II pp. 481-483. He was appointed Regional Commander of Chien-nan in 785 A.D. Cf. his biography in *Chiu-t'ang-shu* ch. 140 and *Hsin-t'ang-shu* ch. 158; neither of these records the case related here.

TYPS-III, fourth column, sixth character from the bottom: *k'o* 客 is a copyist's mistake for *mi* 密.

B.

"In the T'ang Dynasty, in the beginning of the Hsien-t'ung era (860-873 A.D.), when Chao Ho was magistrate of Chiang-yin, in the

Huai-yin district of Ch'u there were two farmers whose lands bordered upon each other. The farmer on the east side (hereafter called A.; Transl.) mortgaged the title deeds to his land to the farmer on the west side (hereafter called B.; Transl.) for one million cash. After the lapse of one year (when there had been a good crop) A. first repaid B. 8000 strings of cash, planning to pay the following day the remainder, and thus redeem the title deeds. A. trusted the oral agreement and did not ask for a written contract. The next day he went to B. to hand him the remaining strings of cash, but B. did not acknowledge that there had been any such agreement (i.e. he kept both the 8000 strings of cash and the title deeds). There was no proof and no written document, thus when A. brought this case before the authorities no one could redress his wrong. Thereupon A. crossed the river (between Huai-yin and Chiang-yin) to the South and put his case before (Chao Ho, the magistrate of) Chiang-yin. Chao Ho said: 'My administration is very inferior, and moreover you are from outside my district; how could I plan to redress your wrong?' A. said weeping: 'If my case is not dealt with here, then there is no means left for me to have my wrong redressed!' Chao Ho then thought of a stratagem. One day he summoned a number of his constables and sent them with an official letter to the magistrate of Huai-yin saying that there had occurred a case of piracy on the river; that the investigation had been completed and that the arrested men had said that they had accomplices in such-and-such a place, mentioning names and details that pointed to B.; and requesting that B. be sent in chains to his tribunal. Now the regulations defining the mutual duties of the administrators of neighbouring districts state that in the case of armed pirates obstructing the river traffic, they shall not be kept hidden (but must be extradited on a magistrate's request). When B. was brought before him Chao Ho reprimanded him saying: 'Why did you commit piracy on the river?' B. said weeping: 'I am a farmer who has never even touched an oar!' Chao Ho said: 'All that stolen gold and valuables and silk and brocade ought not to be found in a farmer's house. Give an inventory of all your possessions so that I can investigate this'. B. saw a ray of hope and enumerated: 'So many pecks of grain, so many farm hands, so many bolts of silk woven on my own looms, and so many strings of cash that I received from A. for his mortgaged land'. Then Chao Ho said: 'I see now that you are not a pirate; but why do you keep the 8000 cash that A. paid you for redeeming his title deeds?' Then Chao summoned A. and confronted B. with his testimony. Thereupon B. was sent back in chains to his own district, the agreement was investigated and in the end he met his just punishment".

CYKC ch. 7, page 102; IYC ch. 3, no. 49; YCTI no. 14.

About Chao Ho 趙 和 I could find no further details.

IYC gives a more detailed version, where more realistic amounts of money are quoted: A. mortgaged his land for 1000 strings of cash, and as the first instalment paid back 800 strings.

68. *Liu Ch'ing has a placard put up;*
   Ch'en Piao wines and dines a prisoner

A.

"In the (Northern) Chou Dynasty (557-585 A.D.) when Liu Ch'ing, styled Keng-hsing, (was Vice-Governor of Yung-chou), a Turk was robbed with violence. The local authorities initiated an investigation, but no one knew where to look for the criminal; they therefore arrested several of the victim's neighbours. Liu Ch'ing, however, said that he could entice the real criminal by deceit. He drew up an anonymous letter and had it put up on all the gates of the official buildings. It read: 'I and some others have together robbed the Turk. Since many persons are concerned in this I fear that in the end the truth will come out. Now I desire to give myself up, but I fear that I shall not escape the death penalty. If the punishment of him who gives himself up first should be commuted, I shall come forward and report'. Thereafter Liu Ch'ing had again a notice put up promising a pardon. After two days a slave of Hsin, Prince of Kuang-ling, having covered his face, stood himself by the placard and gave himself up. Thereupon his entire band consisting of a great many persons was arrested".

CYKC ch. 7, page 120; IYC ch. 5, no. 94; YP no. 66.

Liu Ch'ing 柳 慶 was a just official, also known as a great wine bibber. He was a favourite of the Wei Emperor Wen, whose proclamations were mostly drafted by him. He served also under the N. Chou Emperor Ming (557-560 A.D.) occupying various posts as Prefect and distinguishing himself by his acumen in judicial matters. Cf. his biography in *Pei-shih* ch. 64 where some interesting cases solved by him are placed on record, including the present one.

TYPS-III, sixth column, third character from the top: *shih* 使 is a copyist's mistake for *pien* 便 .

B.

"In the (Eastern) Wu Dynasty (220-280 A.D.), when Ch'en Piao, styled Wen-ao, because his father had died fighting against the enemy, had been appointed military commander on his request, there were a number of people who stole government property, but only one man called Shih Ming was arrested. When questioned under torture he (being a very brave man) rather waited for his death than saying one word. The Commandant of Justice conceived doubts and reported the case to Sun Ch'üan. Since Ch'en Piao was very popular with the soldiers, Sun Ch'üan ordered to transfer Shih Ming to him. Ch'en Piao had the chains taken off the prisoner, gave him food and drink and had him take a bath, so as to bring him in a happy mood. Then Shih Ming confessed and denounced all his accomplices. Sun Ch'üan was pleased. In order to further enhance his fame he specially released Shih Ming, but had the accomplices executed. Shih Ming mended his ways and later became a general".

CYKC ch. 3, page 40; IYC ch. no. 32.

Ch'en Piao 陳 表 and his elder brother Ch'en Wu (陳 武 di ed 229 A.D.) were able military officers serving under Sun Ch'üan (cf. the note to Case 35-B above). Ch'en Piao was especially popular with the rank and file because of his genuine interest in their welfare. His biography in *Wu-chih* ch. 10 says that when he died at the early age of 34, his wife and children were left destitute because he had used all his funds for the training and upkeep of his soldiers. That source records the present case in full detail.

Chih 志 in the first line is superfluous.

69. *Chu Shou-ch'ang examines a bribed man;*
K'ung Hsün investigates scapegoats

A.

"When the Chung-san(-ta-fu) Chu Shou-ch'ang was Prefect of Ken-chou, a member of a prominent clan called Yung Tzu-liang killed someone. He then bribed a man from his village and made him give himself up to the authorities. When the case had been completed, Chu Shou-ch'ang had doubts. He took the prisoner apart and questioned him, but the man stuck to his confession. Then Chu said to him: 'I have heard that Yung Tzu-liang gave you hundred thousand cash and promised to have his son marry your daughter and to give his daughter in marriage to your son. Is this not true?' The prisoner showed emotion. Chu Shou-ch'ang continued: 'When you are dead, Yung Tzu-liang shall draw up a deed that makes your daughter his slave, and stating that the hundred thousand cash was the amount he purchased her for; his own daughter he shall give in marriage to some one else. What can you do then?' The prisoner burst out in tears, and then for the first time told the complete truth. Yung Tzu-liang was executed".

(From his tomb inscription composed by Tseng Kung)

CYKC ch. 6, page 84; IYC ch. 8, no. 160; YP no. 32.

Chu Shou-ch'ang (朱 壽 昌 1031-1103 A.D.) started his career by serving as magistrate in various places, distinguishing himself by his kindness to the people and his administrative abilities. After having served as Prefect of Ken-chou he was appointed at Court as Junior Lord of Agricultural Supervision, and received the honorary rank of *Chung-san-ta-fu* 中 散 大 夫 (first class of the 5th degree). Cf. his biography in *Sung-shih* ch. 456, where this case is recorded. He was especially famous as a paragon of filial piety; cf. BD no. 468.

For Tseng Kung see the note to Case 10-A above.

B.

"In the Later T'ang Dynasty (923-936 A.D.) when K'ung Hsün was temporarily charged with the affairs of the military administration of I-men (near K'ai-feng), there were in the Ch'ang-yüan district four great robbers who had amassed considerable wealth. When (at last) their plans miscarried, they implicated four poor men (who were to serve as scapegoats). The second in command of the Central Army called Han (he was a son-in-law of General Kuo Ch'ung-t'ao) fabricated in collusion with the court and the prison officers a confession; the four accused were not interrogated, but their alleged confession was forwarded to the higher authorities. It was decided that the four poor men would be executed in public. K'ung Hsün personally reviewed this case, (but when questioning the accused) they did not say one word in their defense. When being led away to be executed they repeatedly turned their heads round. K'ung Hsün conceived doubts because of this curious behaviour. He had them called back and questioned them again. Then they stated that they were being wrongly accused, adding that (during the previous questioning) a gaoler had raised the side of the cangue round their neck and thus prevented them from speaking. K'ung Hsün had the case immediately transferred to the Prefecture so that the Registrar could investigate it. It then proved that Han and scores of others had accepted bribes (from the robbers) to the amount of 7000 strings of cash. All were executed".

CYKC ch. 2, page 13; IYC ch. 2, no. 39; YP no. 31.

K'ung Hsün 孔循 was an official of obscure origin who gained the favour of T'ai-tsu (907-914 A.D.) of the Later Liang Dynasty; he changed his name several times and often changed his allegiance. His biography in *Hsin-wu-tai-shih* ch. 43 states that under Chuang-tsung (923-925 A.D.) of the Later T'ang Dynasty he served as temporary Prefect of K'ai-feng, but the rank *pang-chi-erh-shih* 邦 計 貳 職 is not mentioned there; *chi-pu* 計 部 was in the later T'ang Dynasty another term for *hsing-pu* 刑 部 Ministry of Justice,| but I suspect that the text is corrupt, and omit those four characters in the translation.

His biography adds that K'ung served under the Emperor Ming (926- 933 A.D.) as Commissioner of Military Affairs, and that he ended his career as Regional Commander; the present case is not related there.

For *chung-chün-tu-yü-hou* 中 軍 都 虞 候 "Second in Command of the Central Army" cf. des Rotours, page 647, note 1.

70. *Liu Ch'ung-kuei has a knife recognized;*
    Szu-ma Yüeh investigates a scabbard

A.

"In the T'ang Dynasty when Liu Ch'ung-kuei was Garrison Commander in Nan-hai (i.e. Kuangtung), there was a son of a wealthy merchant, a young and handsome man. When the boat (on which he was travelling) was moored on the river bank, he saw a beautiful girl standing in the gate of a large mansion, and who did not mind people noticing her. The young man started a frivolous conversation with her and (in the end) said: 'At dusk I shall come to see you!' The girl did not seem to object. That night she indeed left her door open and waited for him. Before the young man had arrived a robber entered the house. Seeing a room without a candle he wanted to steal there. The girl did not realize (in the dark that it was a robber) and went towards him full of joy. The robber thought that someone was trying to catch him and he killed her with a thrust of his knife; then he fled, leaving his knife behind. Soon thereafter the young man came. Stepping in her blood he slipped and fell on the floor. Groping with his hands he found the dead body. He rushed out, cut his boat adrift and went away. The following morning the girl's family traced (his bloody footsteps) to the bank of the river. The people living there all said that the passenger-boat of so-and-so had left that spot in the night. The authorities then sent officers who went after the boat (and brought the young man back). When he was questioned under torture he told everything and denied having committed the murder. Liu Ch'ung-kuei examined the knife left on the scene of the crime and saw that it was a butcher's knife. He therefore issued an order saying: 'On such-and-such a day there will be a great test. All the butchers of this region must assemble on the football ground, there to await (the test in) slaughtering'. After they had assembled he said to them: 'Since the hour is late you can go home and leave your knives in the kitchen. Come back tomorrow'. Then he took all the knives and replaced one by that of the murderer. The following morning all the butchers came for their knives. At last there was only one left who could not find his knife. When interrogated he said: 'That is the knife of so-and-so!' Liu Ch'ung-kuei ordered to arrest that man but he had already fled. Thereupon Liu had in the night a sentenced criminal put to death on the market, announcing that it was the wealthy merchant's son. When the absconding criminal heard that the young man had been executed, he came back to his house after a few days. He was arrested and executed. The merchant's son was given a whipping, being guilty of having entered a strange house in the night''.

CYKC ch. 1, page 11; IYC ch. 3, no. 54; YP no. 21.

Liu Ch'ung-kuei 劉崇龜 became *chin-shih* in 867 A.D. and served as Secretary in the Ministries of Rites and War, later as Censor. In 883 he became Academician of the Chi-hsien-yüan 集賢院, thereafter Prefect of Kuang-chou and Regional Commander of Ch'ing-hai 青海. These details are recorded in his biography in *Chiu-t'ang-shu* ch. 179. His biography in *Hsin-t'ang-shu* ch. 90 is mainly devoted to an abbreviated version of the present case—in a much less romantic form; there it is stated that the "handsome young man" was an ordinary merchant, and the woman a prostitute.

TYPS-II and CYKC read in the 7th column of page 28-b *ta-she* 大設 instead of *ta-chiao* 大教.

Ch'iu-ch'ang 毬場 "football ground". Football was popular in China already in early times. Originally it was called *ts'u-chü* 蹴踘 and played by a group of people standing close together and trying to keep a light ball from touching the ground while kicking it to and fro. In this form the game was introduced into Japan where it is called *ke-mari* 蹴 鞠 ; it was extremely popular in Court circles in the Heian period. In China the game was later developed in a manner curiously resembling our modern Western football; it was played on a spacious ground by two teams, each guarding a goal consisting of two high poles. This form of the game is referred to as *ts'u-ch'iu-hsi* 蹴 毬 戲 . Cf. the *Ts'u-chü-t'u-pu* 蹴 踘 圖 譜 by the Ming scholar Wang Yün-ch'eng (汪 雲 程 , ca. 1620 A.D.), in ch. 101 of the *Shuo-fu*.

B.

"In the Later Wei Dynasty (386-534 A.D.) when Szu-ma Yüeh was Prefect of Yü-chou, a man called Tung Mao-nu, from Shang-ts'ai, was murdered on the road when travelling with five thousand cash on him. Someone suspected a man called Chang Ti of having committed the crime. When in Chang's house five thousand cash were found, he being afraid of the torture wrongly confessed that he had murdered Tung. Szu-ma Yüeh suspected that this was not true. He summoned Tung's elder brother and said: 'Murdering a man and stealing his money, the criminal must at that moment have been in great fear, and most probably forgot something. Was there found anything (on the scene of the crime)?' The brother answered: 'We found the scabbard of the knife'. Szu-ma Yüeh examined it and said: 'This scabbard is not of the kind they make in the local shops'. He summoned the knife-makers of the prefecture and showed them the scabbard. One of them who lived near the city gate said that the scabbard had been made by him and that one year previously he had sold it to a man of the suburbs called Tung Chi-tsu. Szu-ma Yüeh had that man arrested and interrogated and he confessed".

(From Szu-ma Ch'u's biography in the Pei-shih; Yüeh was his grandson)

CYKC ch. 1, page 6

The biography of Szu-ma Ch'u-chih 司 馬 楚 之 in ch. 29 of *Pei-shih* does not mention Szu-ma Yüeh 司 馬 悅 . A note on him is appended to Ch'u-chih's biography in *Wei-shu* 魏 書 , ch. 37. There it is stated that Szu-ma Yüeh's style was Ch'ing-tsung 慶 宗 ; he was a military official known for his prowess and his acumen in judicial matters. He became Prefect of Yü-chou ca. 450 A.D. The present case is related there in a more elaborate version.

71. *Chang Tsu searches out a saddle;*
    Yen has a basket hauled up

A.

"In the T'ang Dynasty when Chang Tsu, styled Wen-ch'eng, was Sheriff of Ho-yang, the bridle with which a traveller on a donkey (had fastened it during the night) broke and the donkey together with its saddle were stolen. When an intensive search was instituted the thief became afraid and set the donkey free in the night; but he kept the saddle. Chang Tsu then gave orders not to feed the donkey, and to let it loose in the night. The donkey wandered off to the place where it had been fed the previous day. Chang Tsu had that homestead searched, and the saddle was found hidden under a heap of straw. People admired Chang's wisdom".

CYKC ch. 7, page 112; IYC ch. 3, no. 52; YP no. 67.
  For details about Chang Tsu see Case 45-A above.

B.

"In the T'ang Dynasty, when Yen Chi-mei was Garrison Commander in Chiang-nan, a boatman contracted to transport a travelling trader and his wares. The trader had hidden among his wares ten ingots of siver; the boatman had secretly observed this. He stole the silver and sunk it in the river on the place where the boat was moored. The boat left at night. When they had arrived at the military post, and the goods were inspected, the trader missed the silver. He had the boatman arrested and accused him before the Commander. Yen Chi-mei said: 'Boatmen who rent their ships all follow the same method for hiding stolen goods'. He asked the trader: 'Where did you stay yesterday night?' The man answered: 'Hundred *li* from here, at the watershed'. Yen Chi-mei ordered some soldiers to go there together with the trader, and drag the river with a hook. They indeed hauled up a basket with the silver ingots inside; the seal had not even been broken. The boatman then confessed".

CYKC ch. 7, page 109; IYC ch. 2, no. 37; YP no. 68.
  Yen Chi-mei 閻濟美 served in the end of the Chen-yüan era (785-804) as Regional Commander in Fukien, and thereafter in the same function in Chekiang. He ended his career as President of the Ministry of Works. His biography is briefly sketched in *Chiu-t'ang-shu* ch. 185 and *Hsin-t'ang-shu* ch. 159; neither of these records this case.

72. *Ho Ch'eng-t'ien discusses a shooting;*
A judge investigates a case of poaching

A.

"In the (Former) Sung Dynasty (420-479 A.D.) when Liu I was Garrison Commander of Ku-shu, he once went out on an excursion. An officer of the district tribunal of Yen-ling called Ch'en Man was hunting birds, and one of his arrows accidentally hit the General. Although the latter did not get wounded, Ch'en was to be publicly executed. Ho Ch'eng-t'ien said in counsel: 'Criminal cases should be decided according to the circumstances, and in cases of doubt one should be lenient. In the Han Dynasty a man frightened the horses of the chariot wherein the Emperor Wen (179-157 B.C.) was riding, and Chang Shih-chih had him judged for having offended against the rules for clearing the Emperor's way. He had to pay only a fine because it was clear that he had unintentionally frightened the horses. Thus the fact that such an exalted person was riding in the chariot did not cause heavier punishment. Now Ch'en Man was all intent on shooting the bird, he did not expressly hit a man. The law prescribes three years penal servitude for accidentally wounding some one; what then if he does not even wound him? A fine will meet the case".

(Formerly included in Ho's biography in the *Nan-shih*)

CYKC ch. 4, page 48; IYC ch. 2, no. 29.

For details about Ho Ch'eng-t'ien see the note to Case 63-B above; his biography in *Nan-shih* ch. 33 records this case.

Liu I 劉 毅 was a General who first fought together with Liu Yü (cf. the note to Case 63-B above) but later turned against him and was defeated.

Chang Shih-chih 張 釋 之 was a virtuous official who rose to high office under Emperor Wen; cf. BD no. 105.

B.

"In the (Former) Wei Dynasty (220-265 A.D.) when Kao Jou was Commandant of Justice, the laws on hunting were extremely severe. Liu Kuei, Inspector of Agriculture of I-yang, poaching on the Imperial Domain shot a hare. The Personnel Adviser Chang Ching went to the Inspector and reported it. The Emperor did not divulge Chang Ching's name but had Liu Kuei arrested and his case arraigned. Kao Jou then memoria-

lized the Throne asking for the name of the informer. The Emperor
flew in a rage and said: 'Liu Kuei must die. Why do you ask the name
of the accuser?' Kao Jou said: 'The Commandant of Justice is charged
with the preservation of the peace in the Empire, how could he
trample on the law just because of the joy or anger of the Sovereign?'
Thereupon he again memorialized the Throne. The Emperor then
realized that he had been wrong; he divulged Chang Ching's name
and sent him back for examination. Then both (Liu Kuei and Chang
Ching) received adequate punishment".

(From Kao Jou's biography in the *Wei-shih*)

CYKC ch. 4, page 47.

For details about Kao Jou see Case 32-B above; this case is recorded in his
biography in *Wei-chih* ch. 24.

TYPS, first column: *yü* "prison" is a mistake for *lieh* "hunting".

Hsiao-shih 校事 , here translated "Inspector", indicated in the Wei Dynasty
a kind of superior Government spy; also called *hsiao-kuan* 校官 .

TYPS-I and III add a comment by Cheng K'o saying that a man who proffers
a false accusation must receive the same punishment as would have been allotted
to the accused; but I do not see why Chang's accusation was false, since Liu indeed
shot the hare.

Kuei Wan-jung's Postface

"In the seventh moon of the year 1234 I, in my quality of Ministerial Secretary of the Right, was granted the favour of addressing the
Throne. First I respectfully spoke about the Emperor preserving the
unity of purpose of all officials [1] who (in their turn), by their dilligence
keep in order the basic principles of government. Thereafter I respectfully discoursed on the Throne's curbing the avidity of the small
officers, thereby strengthening the foundations of the State.

"Notwithstanding the wide gulf that separates the Throne from my
person, the Emperor deigned to confer praise, and the Precious Voice
said: 'We have seen the book *T'ang-yin-pi-shih* formerly written by
you and thereby We know that you have ability in the solving of
judicial cases'. I then respectfully submitted: 'When Your Majesty's
servant had been designated Prefectural Police Inspector of Chien-
k'ang, my provisional appointment lasted a long time. Thus I utilized

---

[1] The term *i-hsin* 一 心 refers to the phrase in the section *T'ai-che* 泰誓
in the Book of Documents reading "I have three thousand officials but they are
all one in their purpose" 予有臣三千惟一心 .

that period (of waiting) for compiling this book, in order to broaden my knowledge. How could I have hoped that the Throne, lavish in its favours, would deem this undeserving book [1] worthy of one glance?' The Emperor granted me to withdraw from the audience hall, I respectfully accepted my dismissal and left the Palace.

"Then there were some persons who insisted upon having this book. I therefore took the first edition printed in far-away Hsing-chiang [2] and had it reprinted for wider circulation, hoping that perhaps above it may make known the Emperor's virtue of love for all living beings, and below increase among those in office their tendency to sympathize with those they rule.

"Respectfully written on fullmoon's day of the 10th moon by the Ch'ao-san-ta-fu Kuei Wan-jung, newly appointed Academician of the Pao-chang Pavilion, Prefect of Ch'ang-te".

Chang Fu's Colophon

"Judicial cases are grave matters, and cases where there is ground for doubt are matters still more grave; the Superior Man should give these his wholehearted attention. But can those at present charged with that office really give their wholehearted attention to it?

"My brother-in-law Kuei, styled Meng-hsieh, is a great reader, but he does not read the Penal Code. Yet the innocently persecuted always fill him with pity. When his term of office as Sheriff had expired, he returned to his native place, being provisionally assigned to the post of Prefectural Police Inspector. When people asked him (why he had been content with the humble office of Sheriff) he replied: 'It accorded with my disposition'. And when (people asked him) why he acquiesced in five years of provisional designation, he replied: 'That is exactly what I wanted'. It is then that he selected from old books material concerning the solving of judicial cases, displaying therein a more subtle judgement and greater familiarity with the subject than Ho Duke of Lu in writing his *I-yü-chi* and Mr. Cheng K'o in compiling his *Che-yü-kuei-chien*. Parallel cases suddenly showed their affinity, and the rhymes of the title-phrases suddenly

---

[1] *Wu* 誤 or *miu* 謬 are often used as polite expressions meaning that the person conferring the favour did so "wrongly", because the recipient was unworthy of it.

[2] *Hsiang-chiang* 星 江 refers to Nan-k'ang; cf. my remarks on page 8 above.

became pairs; thus he assembled altogether seventy-two articles. They prove that if (a judge) is careful in his approach, he can hope never to be in need of repenting his decisions afterwards.

"I have respectfully read this book and I consider that it supplies the officials of our present time with the most important methods for searching out hidden evil [1], thereby broadening their knowledge. Those who have mastered its content will find all the many other simllar books superfluous. As soon as this book is in circulation there will probably be left no one in our Empire who is suffering under a wrong. Furthermore, thinking over its content, I venture to state that the whipping of silk to make iron filings come forth (cf. Case 26-A), the flogging of a lamb skin to verify the presence of salt (cf. Case 26-B), the opening of a tomb to find robbers (cf. Case 65-A), and having gold modelled in order to prove a false accusation (cf. Case 57-B) —all such stratagems were not employed in the days of glorious antiquity, they occur only in later ages. Is this not because the customs of old were still pure so that there was no need for the methods of investigating criminals? But the people of later times were like devils and goblins [2]; thus, if judges did not employ those methods, they would never discover the truth.

"When I meditate on the words of our Master Confucius [3] that '(the Superior Man) discusses criminal cases in order to remit death sentences', I find that this is based solely on the explanation of 'Complete Trust' [4]; only those in the Empire who are of the utmost sincerity can move people (to tell the truth) and understand all situations, they will uncover even what is protected by bronze or stone, and influence even ghosts and spirits.

"Now developing my argument farther, if one 'searches the feelings of the accused by listening to his speech', and 'ascertains and veri-

---

[1] I take *kou-yüan* 鉤元 (*hsüan* 玄) to be an equivalent of the term *kou-t'e* 鉤慝, a standard term in legal literature.

[2] *Yü* 蛓 are a particularly malicious kind of goblins who lie hidden in the sand at the bottom of a river; if the shadow of a human being appears on the water, they kill him.

[3] TYPS-III has *t'ien-tzu* 天子 instead of *fu-tzu* 夫子.

[4] *Chung-fu* 中孚 is the name of the 61st hexagram of the *I-ching*; the term *chih-ch'eng* 至誠 is also borrowed from the explanation of this hexagram.

fies his guilt on the basis of the five pleadings' [1], without bending or flinching, then the atmosphere in the tribunal will be bright and clear, the Imperial prestige shall be respected, broadly supporting all those in office [2]. That in such circumstances human feelings can not be detected, this I refuse to believe. In any case, my brother-in-law exerted himself [3] to attain to this.

"When I was posted in East Chekiang [4], in charge of the maintenance of the peace, my brother-in-law came (to Shao-hsing) and showed me the manuscript of his book. Soon thereafter he had to proceed to Nanking to take up office, and again passed Shao-hsing. I then returned the manuscript to him, adding this colophon in lieu of a parting present".

"Written on fullmoon's day of the 10th moon of the year 1211, by Chang Fu".

Chang Yüan-chi's editorial note

"In the Sung Dynasty Kuei Wan-jung of Szu-ming compiled this book by selecting judicial cases from the *I-yü-chi* by Mr. Ho and his son, adding material from Cheng K'o's *Che-yü-kuei-chien*. He arranged 72 parallels according to the rhymes of the title-phrases, altogether 144 cases, and published it first in 1211 [5], thereafter in 1234. In the Ching-t'ai era (1450-1456) of the Ming Dynasty, Wu No from Hai-yü abbreviated the book to 80 cases, added a sequel of 50 cases selected by himself, and published the text in this new form [6]. The item inclu-

---

[1] Quoted from the chapter *Lü-hsing* of the Book of Documents; see page 49 above.

[2] *Yang-yang tsai-shang* 洋洋在上 ; I take this to mean that if the Imperial prestige is firmly established by the right administration of justice, this prestige will in its turn act as support of the entire administration.

[3] TYPS-III has *chih-chih* 知之 instead of *mien-chih* 勉之.

[4] In the S. Sung Dynasty Chekiang was divided into two halves, roughly North and South of the Ch'ien-tang River; the S. half was called *Che-chiang-tung-lu* 浙江東路 , abbreviated to *Che-tung*.

[5] As shown on page 8 above, this statement is incorrect; the first edition of the TYPS was printed ca. 1220 A.D.

[6] Chang Yüan-chi should have added that Wu No published his version of the TYPS as part of his *Hsiang-hsing-yao-lan* (cf. page 23 above), so as to amplify his statement made further on that Wu No's version was not published as a separate work.

ded in the Imperial Catalogue refers to this version. At that time Kuei Wan-jung's original edition had not come to light, hence the officials in charge (of compiling the Catalogue) had many doubts about the additions made by Wu No. I have seen the version incorporated in the *Hsüeh-hai-lei-pien*, it has not yet been published separately. In 1849 Chu Hsü-tseng from Shang-yüan published a reprint of the Sung edition emanating from the collection of Huang (P'ei-lieh, lit. name) Jao-pu, but this reprint is now extremely scarce. The present text is a manuscript from the Chih-pu-tsu-chai, corrected all through by Pao (T'ing-po, styled) I-wen with his own hand, and with added textual notes. Although this famous document is not the Sung impression, it may yet be considered as second-best".

Chang Yüan-chi from Hai-yen.

INDEX

Other titles by R. H. van Gulik, available from Orchid Press:

Mi Fu on Ink-stones

Scrapbook for Chinese Collectors: A Chinese Treatise on
    Scrolls and Forgers

Hayagriva: Horse Cult in Asia

The Lore of the Chinese Lute: An Essay in the Ideology of the
    Ch'in

R. H. van Gulik biography available from Orchid Press:

Dutch Mandarin: The Life and Work of R. H. van Gulik

www.ingramcontent.com/pod-product-compliance
Lightning Source LLC
Chambersburg PA
CBHW081359130726
47998CB00011B/3011